ANCIENT INDIA

Books by Upinder Singh

Political Violence in Ancient India (2017)

Portraits of Power (2017)

The Idea of Ancient India: Essays on Religion, Politics, and Archaeology (2016)

*A History of Ancient and Early Medieval India:
From the Stone Age to the 12th Century* (2008)

*The Discovery of Ancient India:
Early Archaeologists and the Beginnings of Archaeology* (2004)

Mysteries of the Past: Archaeological Sites in India (for children, 2002)

Ancient Delhi (1999)

*Kings, Brāhmaṇas, and Temples in Orissa:
An Epigraphic Study (AD 300–1147)* (1994)

Books edited by Upinder Singh

*The World of India's First Archaeologist:
Letters from Alexander Cunningham to J. D. M. Beglar* (2021)

Buddhism in Asia: Revival and Reinvention (2016)

Asian Encounters: Exploring Connected Histories (2014)

Rethinking Early Medieval India: A Reader (2011)

Ancient India: New Research (2009)

Delhi: Ancient History (2006)

ANCIENT INDIA

CULTURE OF CONTRADICTIONS

UPINDER SINGH

ALEPH

ALEPH BOOK COMPANY
An independent publishing firm
promoted by *Rupa Publications India*

First published in India in 2021
by Aleph Book Company
7/16 Ansari Road, Daryaganj
New Delhi 110 002

Copyright © Upinder Singh 2021
Photo credits on pp. 236–41 are an extension of the copyright page

All rights reserved.

The author has asserted her moral rights.

The views and opinions expressed in this book are those of the author and the facts are as reported by her, which have been verified to the extent possible, and the publisher is not in any way liable for the same.

The publisher has used its best endeavours to ensure that URLs for external websites referred to in this book are correct and active at the time of going to press. However, the publisher has no responsibility for the websites and can make no guarantee that a site will remain live or that the content is or will remain appropriate.

No part of this publication may be reproduced, transmitted, or stored in a retrieval system, in any form or by any means, without permission in writing from Aleph Book Company.

ISBN: 978-93-90652-61-7

5 7 9 10 8 6 4

Printed in India

This book is sold subject to the condition that it shall not, by way of trade or otherwise, be lent, resold, hired out, or otherwise circulated without the publisher's prior consent in any form of binding or cover other than that in which it is published.

For Raghav, Madhav, and Rini

CONTENTS

Introduction		ix
1.	Inequality and Salvation	1
2.	Desire and Detachment	40
3.	Goddesses and Misogyny	83
4.	Violence and Non-violence	131
5.	Debate and Conflict	178
Epilogue		228
Acknowledgements		235
Photo Credits		236
Bibliography		242
Index		252

INTRODUCTION

The existential question, 'Who am I?' is as fundamental as the social question, 'Who are we?' The first demands personal introspection and philosophical reflection. The second leads us to genetics and history. Scientific evidence shows that the world's entire population is ultimately descended from African ancestors who moved into Asia thousands of years ago and gradually spread across the earth.[1] In recent years, a burgeoning personal genome industry urges us to locate our more recent ancestry, for a price. Laboratory tests now track biological lineages across generations. But cultural lineages are much more complex. No DNA test can explain them.

This book was conceived in the BC (Before Covid) era, while I was designing a course on 'Indian Civilizations' in Ashoka University. The prospect was daunting. How could I approach such a grand theme without being atrociously superficial, selective, and simplistic? Was it possible to convey anything meaningful about something so momentous within the span of a mere thirteen weeks? Was my course not doomed to failure even before it began? Instead of despairing, I decided to be upfront about the difficulties and to structure the course around key contradictions in ideas and attitudes in early Indian history (my own area of expertise), many of which are still discernible in India today. This book developed out of that initial impulse and was written during the ongoing Covid-19 crisis. There is nothing like a global pandemic to remind us of our mortality, to provide an incentive to complete

---

[1]For an excellent explanation of how ancient DNA offers an exciting window into the story of early humans, see David Reich, *Who We Are and How We Got Here*, Oxford: Oxford University Press, 2018. For a lucid discussion of the role of genetics and archaeology in understanding early cultures in the Indian subcontinent, see Tony Joseph, *Early Indians: The Story of Our Ancestors and Where We Came From*, New Delhi: Juggernaut Books, 2018.

unfinished business, and to underscore the oneness of humanity. Unfortunately, the continuing conflict and strife in India, and indeed across the world, shows that even a pandemic is not enough to replace the divides between countries and communities with the realization that we are all humans, alike not only in our susceptibility to microorganisms, but in more profound ways as well.

The great deal of popular interest in ancient India these days and the fact that the subject is both a political mine and minefield, make it more urgent than ever before to move discussions out of universities and academic journals into the wider world. Opinions are not the same as history. The discipline of history requires a careful examination of primary sources, the use of reason, rigorous analysis, and a conscious attempt at objectivity. For far too long, most Indian historians have chosen to magisterially speak from the pulpit, usually to other historians, rarely to ordinary people. The misconceptions and misinformation circulating at the popular level about history are a reflection of historians' refusal (or inability) to communicate with a larger audience. Now, with the realization that this is a problem that must be addressed, there is a sudden spurt in books written by historians for 'normal people'.

But old habits die hard. Indian historians have routinely framed their debates in terms of 'left' versus 'right', both sides selectively citing evidence to fit their predetermined positions. For several decades, left historians ruled Indian academia and had the last word, one that could be contradicted or questioned only at one's peril. Today, the pendulum has swung to the other extreme, with the right stirring the communal cauldron and producing its hyper-nationalist brand of history. The flagrant politicization of history seems to have reinforced already-held beliefs and has done little to promote open-minded enquiry. It has also led to popular suspicion about the credentials and agendas of the discipline of history itself. The feelings of belonging and alienation that history can arouse make it highly susceptible to manipulation; this susceptibility makes it all the more necessary to explain historical methods to non-historians.

Many misperceptions about ancient India arise from a lack of understanding of the primary sources which historians use to write their histories. These varied sources are the filter through which the past reveals itself; they include texts, archaeological remains, inscriptions, and coins, all of which need to be carefully contextualized and analysed. Ancient Indian texts were written in languages such as Sanskrit, Pali, Prakrit, Apabhramsha, Tamil, Kannada, and Telugu. Many were composed by multiple authors over long periods of time. The dates of many texts, including the Rig Veda, Ramayana, Mahabharata, Tipitaka, Jaina canonical texts, and *Arthashastra* have been debated for decades, but it is clear that their composition stretched across several centuries. For instance, the Mahabharata was composed between c. 400 BCE and 400 CE.[2] The very idea of a text evolving, growing, and changing over eight centuries is mind-boggling. Scholars have tried to reconstruct the original content of such texts by comparing their manuscripts to create critical editions, which are believed to represent their original core.

Because many texts contain several chronological layers, they may speak in different voices and represent different points of view. The authors are often anonymous, but their social background and perspective can be ascertained from the content of their work. So, instead of simplistically and selectively plucking out statements, texts have to be read carefully, keeping in mind their compositional history, historical context, genre, authorial perspective, and intended audience. Many works are normative or prescriptive—that is they lay down the ideal situation according to their authors' point of view. Many contain inconsistent and contradictory statements. No text is a simple reflection of the realities of its time; it is a complex representation of those realities.

Throughout history, in all cultures, in all parts of the world, subordinated and marginalized social groups have been deliberately deprived of opportunities to participate in the production and dissemination of knowledge. Hence, ancient texts largely reflect the perspectives and ideas of political, social, or religious elites. Almost all of them were written by upper-class men for other upper-class men. Some,

---

[2]These days, historians use BCE (Before Common Era) instead of BC (Before Christ) and CE (Common Era) instead of AD (Anno Domini). The 'c.' in front of dates stands for 'circa,' which means 'approximately'.

for instance, the Puranas, Mahabharata, Ramayana, and the hagiographies of the Buddha, Mahavira, and religious saints, reflect a historical consciousness—that is a sense of the past and an attempt to preserve certain aspects of the past that were considered valuable. These traditional histories are, of course, different from modern historical research. It is possible to tease out hidden meanings from texts by reading them against the grain and supplementing their testimony with other sources.

People often think that archaeology provides hard, objective evidence. However, only a small fraction of the total material remains of the past survive and that which does can be interpreted in different ways, even when scientific techniques are used. For instance, pollen analysis from lakes in Rajasthan has been cited to support a theory that the Harappan civilization declined due to a decrease in rainfall as well as for a theory that there was no significant climate change during that period. Further, while archaeology is well-equipped to give detailed data on material culture, technology, and trade, it is not as eloquent on social and political life, customs, and attitudes. Because it is geared towards revealing slow-moving processes rather than specific events, there are many questions that archaeology cannot answer.

The fact is that the written word and the material artefact do not capture the entire range of human experience. They offer partial, refracted images of the past, which get more and more diffused and faint as we go further back in time. Many important aspects of everyday life—such as the oral, personal, emotional—get left out or are very dimly discernible. As we move back centuries or millennia, the quantum and type of data available for more recent history is simply not there; the stories of specific individuals and events are difficult to locate and are replaced by broad brush strokes of historical processes. So, although we have to make the best of the available sources, many aspects of the lives and experiences of our remote ancestors will always remain elusive and beyond our grasp.

Modern nation state boundaries are irrelevant for ancient history. So 'India' in this book's title should be taken as a shorthand for the Indian subcontinent, or South Asia, which includes the areas today covered by India, Pakistan, Bangladesh, Nepal, Bhutan, and Sri Lanka. This is an enormous expanse and naturally, there were great differences in the textures and pace of historical developments across regions. For instance, at the time when the urban Harappan civilization was flourishing in the north and north-west, other parts of the subcontinent were inhabited by villagers, pastoralists, and hunter–gatherers, some still in the Stone Age. In north and central India, the second urbanization and formation of states occurred in the sixth century BCE, but these developments took place several centuries later in the far south. Not only are there differences in patterns and timings, the information from various regions is also uneven, in large part due to historians' neglect or indifference.

As a historian of ancient India, the question I am most often asked is: How ancient is ancient India? If the question is about the earliest evidence of hominin presence in the subcontinent, the answer is: at least 2 million years old.[3] Homo sapiens are believed to have evolved about 200,000 years ago, so the earliest remains of culture belong to archaic hominin species. Stone tools found in the Shivalik mountains are approximately 2 million years old. Recent excavations at Attirampakkam in Tamil Nadu have given evidence of stone tools dating from around 1.07 to 1.7 million years ago.[4] New discoveries in archaeology and genetics will no doubt continue to provide more and more information that illuminates our understanding of early humans, their movements, and their achievements.

In view of the early dates for the beginning of prehistoric cultures in the subcontinent, a university course on ancient Indian history could stretch from 2 million years ago to 800 CE, 1000 CE, or 1200 CE, blending into the early medieval period at the later end.[5] A course on medieval India could stretch from any of these points up to the eighteenth century,

---

[3]Hominin is a broad category that includes modern humans (Homo sapiens), extinct human species, and all our immediate ancestors including members of the genera Homo, Australopithecus, Paranthropus, and Ardipithecus.

[4]See Shanti Pappu, Yanni Gunnell, Kumar Akhilesh, Régis Braucher, Maurice Taieb, François Demory, and Nicholas Thouveny, 'Early Pleistocene presence of Acheulian hominins in South India', *Science*, vol. 331, issue 6024, 25 March 2011, pp. 596–99.

[5]'Early medieval' is a term used by historians to refer to the history of India between the sixth and the twelfth/thirteenth centuries.

that is the early modern period. Histories of modern India usually focus on the eighteenth to the twentieth centuries—just three centuries, compared to the eight to ten centuries for the medieval period and the 2 million years or so for the ancient period! This book's main focus is on c. 600 BCE–1000 CE, but it sometimes moves beyond this.

It is worth remembering that the changes revealed in a 'centuries view' of early history actually took place very gradually and were not palpable or visible to the people who lived through them.

The fact that history is (or ought to be) interesting should be good enough reason to read it. But there is another point to it. This is not because (as many people think) history repeats itself or that it teaches us to avoid mistakes made in the past. The lessons of history are often not of an earth-shattering kind, nor do they necessarily form a guide to everyday living. A person can aspire to a reasonably happy and successful life without reading history books. The connections between the past and the present are often subtle and difficult to discern and are pierced through by rupture and change. In one sense, the past is irretrievably dead and gone. And yet, while we concentrate on living in the here and now, it helps to have a sense of who we are in relation to the spaces we inhabit and the historical processes of which we are a part.

This book does not offer a detailed chronological history of ancient India, or rather, South Asia. For that, you are invited to read my *History of Ancient and Early Medieval India*.[6] Instead, I have chosen a few themes that are central to understanding ancient Indian history, culture, and thought by focusing on the coexistence of certain radical tensions and oppositions—between social inequality and salvation, desire and detachment, goddesses and misogyny, violence and non-violence, and debate and conflict.

The level of detail in this book is to enable readers to understand and appreciate the complexities of the evidence, while quotations from ancient texts give a flavour of some of the exciting original sources. I have tried to keep footnotes to the minimum, but there are citations

---

[6]Upinder Singh, *A History of Ancient and Early Medieval India: From the Stone Age to the 12th Century*, New Delhi: Pearson, 2008.

of good English translations of ancient texts for those interested and further references to secondary readings for those who want more details on specific issues.[7] The visuals in this book are extremely important for several reasons. Visual sources are evocative windows into the past and often convey much more than words. In fact, it is impossible to understand ancient Indian history and culture without understanding ancient Indian art. While this book contains many images of ancient sculpture, it also contains images of medieval paintings and more recent popular, folk, and high art. Collectively, they bring home the point that ancient India has not only produced a great abundance and variety of exquisite art, but that the ancient past has formed a rich source of inspiration for a remarkable range of creative expression right down to the present, and will continue to do so in the future.

Many terms that are grammatically singular and seemingly static must be understood conceptually as plural and dynamic. 'Ancient India' does not represent a single, homogeneous, unchanging culture. It refers to the long and incredibly complex story of the human presence in the subcontinent, marked by an enormous amount of diversity and change. 'Indian culture' (or 'Indian civilization') can be compared to the images seen in a kaleidoscope—always moving, changing, creating new patterns. It does not only include India's ancient past; it includes the medieval Islamicate heritage,[8] the period of colonial rule, the decades after Independence, right up to the present. This book explores the early part of that very long and exciting story.

The past can be beautiful, uplifting, and inspiring; it can also be ugly, unsettling, and disturbing. This book invites readers to abandon simplistic stereotypes and to try to grasp some of its complexities, instead of sitting in judgement. The powerful contradictions discussed in this book are not part of a dead, fossilized past. They exist even today in refracted memories of that past and in the lived realities of the present.

---

[7]Many of the articles cited in this book are available at https://jstor.org and/or https://www.academia.edu.

[8]Islamicate refers to the various features of regions influenced by Islam; it is a broader term than 'Islamic', which refers to only the religion.

1

INEQUALITY AND SALVATION

On 17 January 2016, Rohith Vemula, a Dalit student in the University of Hyderabad killed himself, leaving behind a searing critique of caste discrimination in his suicide note, describing his birth as his fatal accident. This event produced an enormous outpouring of emotion—anger, sorrow, guilt—across the country, inside and outside university campuses, making it difficult for even the most insulated, indifferent, or hard-hearted to ignore the continuing reality and cruelty of caste discrimination in India. The Indian Constitution declares untouchability to be abolished; its practice in any form is considered a criminal offence punishable by law. And yet, over seven decades after Independence, living in a free country, governed by a Constitution that promises equality to all citizens, inequality continues to exist.

Of course, inequality is not just an Indian phenomenon; it is woven into the fabric of all societies. Some of its forms, such as those based on class, income, and status, are found across cultures. If caste is a culturally specific manifestation of inequality in India, in the Western world, its counterpart is race. In fact, in 2001, certain Dalit groups used the platform of the United Nations World Conference against Racism in Durban to argue that caste discrimination can be equated with racial discrimination. The most obvious difference between the two is the fact that racial differences are ostensibly based on visually identifiable physical characteristics, especially skin colour, while caste differences are not. But theories of race and caste both consider certain groups as intrinsically superior to others on the basis of inherited traits. Both are the basis of deep and continuing social inequality. So, while race and caste are not identical, they are comparable.

In Western political thought, the ideas of natural equality, rights, and freedom were subjects of lively debate from the seventeenth century onwards. Ironically, this was the very time when European colonizers were busy subjugating the people of Africa and Asia for commercial profit. Political theorists who wrote about equality and liberty did not usually consider the colonized (or women, for that matter) as part of the community of equals or as entitled to liberty. In fact, this was also the very time when the proponents of race theory used pseudo-scientific data to argue that the white race was naturally superior to all others. So the idea of natural inequality is not just an Indian, or an Asian, or an Eastern phenomenon.[1] It is deep-rooted and global, but it has also been challenged from time to time.

In the twenty-first century, political structures that claim to promote equality of one kind or another range from totalitarian regimes to democratic ones (though the dividing line between them is getting increasingly blurred). Democracy does not entail economic equality. Communism promises but does not create equality and comes at the cost of liberty. Today, there are (hopefully) fewer people across the world who would stand up and say that they believe in inequality compared to those who would assert their belief in equality, even if the degree of sincerity will vary. But what exactly does it mean when we say that all men and women are equal? Is it an assertion or an aspiration for equality—of economic opportunity, quality of life, social status, participation in political processes, legal rights, or all of these?

Looking at inequality historically involves asking many more questions such as: What are the types and degrees of inequality across time? In which institutions was inequality embedded? How was it rationalized and ingrained among different social groups? How was it perpetuated? Who were its guardians, beneficiaries, and victims? How did its forms change over time? Where and when did the challenges to inequality appear and to what extent were they successful? The search

---

[1]The sociologist Louis Dumont argued that Western societies are structured around the principle of equality and Eastern ones around the principle of hierarchy. For a critique of Dumont's idea, see André Béteille, 'The idea of natural inequality', in André Béteille, *The Idea of Natural Inequality and Other Essays*, New Delhi: Oxford University Press, [1983], 2003, pp. 7–34.

for answers to these questions takes us to the very heart of societies and cultures, to their ideas about human worth and purpose.

Class inequality, based on unequal access to productive resources, is part of Indian history from the sixth century BCE onwards. The first part of this chapter focuses on the early history of four other bases of inequality—slavery, varna, caste, and untouchability. (Gender inequality will be discussed in Chapter 3). The history of these institutions and practices and the experiences of subordinated and marginalized groups has to be reconstructed on the basis of sources that give a partial, biased, and from-the-top view representing the interests and ideas of upper classes and religious elites. It is only in more recent times that Dalit writing, especially autobiography, has revealed graphically how caste inequality and oppression is experienced by those who are relegated to a place beyond the margins.[2] The views expressed in ancient texts are often disturbing, even upsetting, but the aim here is to try to understand ideas, even if we find them unacceptable. The second part of the chapter explores the questioning of inequality, which mainly took place at the religious and soteriological levels.[3]

Dasas and dasis

In the late fourth century BCE, a Greek named Megasthenes arrived in the city of Pataliputra, capital of the kingdom of Magadha in eastern India. As an envoy of the Hellenistic ruler Seleucus Nicator or of Sibyrtius, the Macedonian satrap of Arachosia, to the court of the Maurya king Chandragupta, Megasthenes probably spent most of his time in Pataliputra, with little exposure to what was going on in other

---

[2]For B. R. Ambedkar's moving autobiographical writings, see 'Waiting for a Visa' in *Dr. Babasaheb Ambedkar: Writings and Speeches*, vol. 12, compiled by Vasant Moon, New Delhi: Dr. Ambedkar Foundation, 2004, pp. 661–69 (also available online). Other important writings that should be read by all thinking Indians include Kancha Ilaiah Shepherd, *Why I am Not a Hindu: A Sudra Critique of Hindutva Philosophy, Culture and Political Economy*, New Delhi: SAGE, [1996], 2019; Suraj Yengde, *Caste Matters*, Gurgaon: Penguin Viking, 2019; Anand Teltumbde, *Dalits: Past, Present and Future*, Oxford and New York: Routledge, [2017], 2020.
[3]'Soteriological' refers to religious doctrines of salvation or liberation.

parts of the country. Not knowing the local languages must have been a big hurdle. Megasthenes wrote a book called the *Indica* about the land and people of India. The book is lost, which means that the text has not survived; but some of its contents are cited in the works of later Greek and Roman writers. Megasthenes did not want to convey dry factual details about India to his Greek audience; he wanted to entertain them. He got some things right and many things wrong. For instance, he was wrong in his notion that Indian society was divided into seven classes. He was also wrong in thinking that slavery did not exist in India. In Greece, slaves routinely worked in households, manufacturing, mines, and quarries (in fact, in all except the political and military spheres).[4] In India, they must have been much less visible. But slaves definitely existed in fourth century BCE India. In fact, the idea of freedom in both ancient Greece and ancient India emerged as a response to slavery. To be free meant to not be a slave.

There were slaves in other parts of the ancient world too—among the Egyptians, Sumerians, Chinese, Romans, and many others. In fact, the history of this extreme form of inequality stretches into recent times. Colonial empires were sustained by slaves from Africa and the Caribbean. The formal abolition of slavery occurred at different points of time—in 1833 in some parts of the British empire; in 1861 in India; in 1865 in the United States of America; and as recently as 1981 in Mauritania in northwest Africa. Although slavery now stands abolished worldwide, there are still people who live in slave-like conditions, for instance, bonded labour and the victims of human trafficking.

Generally speaking, a slave was considered socially and legally the property of the master. For women slaves (as well as some male ones), in addition to exploitation of their labour, enslavement usually involved sexual exploitation. There were different kinds of slaves and

---

[4]M. I. Finley describes slavery as 'a basic element in Greek civilization' that was never challenged by the intelligentsia. Capture in war was a major source of slave supply and the majority of slaves were foreigners. Finley estimates that the ratio of slaves to free people in ancient Greece was probably 1:4; of slaves to citizens less than 1:1. M. I. Finley, *Economy and Society in Ancient Greece*, Brent Shaw and Richard Saller (eds.), New York: Viking, 1982, pp. 103–04, 111, 123.

slavery sometimes blended with other forms of social subordination. There must have been kind masters and cruel masters, but the basic structure of the institution of slavery was one of extreme inequality and exploitation.

As the script of the Harappan civilization (c. 2600–1900 BCE) has not been deciphered, the details of its social organization are difficult to reconstruct. The Harappans did not produce anything comparable to the temple towers of ancient Mesopotamia or the royal tombs of the Egyptian pharaohs, but theirs was not a society of equals. The planning and amenities of cities like Mohenjodaro, Harappa, Dholavira, and Rakhigarhi are impressive, but then as now, urban life was sustained by countless workers who built the structures, cleaned the drains and sewers, and provided labour and services to keep the cities going. It is not clear whether slavery existed.

The earliest clear references to slaves occur in the Rig Veda Samhita, a text composed during c. 1500–1000 BCE in the valleys of the Indus, its tributaries and the Ghaggar–Hakra, covering the present-day North West Frontier and Punjab provinces of Pakistan and the Punjab and Haryana states of India. There are two theories about the composers of this text. One is that they were the original inhabitants of India. The other, for which there is convincing evidence, is that they were immigrants from the north-west.

The Rig Veda Samhita, comprising ten mandalas or books, was composed by members of a priestly elite for members of the priestly elite. Books 2–7 are considered the oldest and are known as the 'family books' because they are supposed to have been composed by families of certain rishis or sages. Later parts of the Vedic corpus include the later books of the Rig Veda Samhita; the Sama Veda, Yajur Veda, and Atharva Veda; Brahmanas (texts on yajnas or sacrificial rituals); Aranyakas (which interpret the yajnas in symbolic or philosophical ways); and the Upanishads (philosophical works that deal with many concepts, especially atman and brahman). All these texts were composed between c. 1000 and 500 BCE, in the areas of present-day Punjab, Haryana, and western Uttar Pradesh.

Scholars use the linguistic–cultural term 'Indo-Aryan' for the people to whom these texts belonged. The composers of the Rig Veda describe themselves as arya, a Sanskrit word which meant cultured, civilized people. Rig Vedic society was a tribal society, with differences based on rank, wealth, and gender. It included male and female slaves. In most places in the Rig Veda, dasa refers to certain tribes or people who were enemies of the aryas. One view is that the dasas and dasyus were the indigenous inhabitants of India. Another view is that they refer to previous waves of Indo–Aryan immigrants with whom the Vedic Aryans had cultural differences and bitter enmity.[5] In several places in the Rig Veda, the word dasa, along with its feminine counterpart dasi, clearly refers to slaves. The fact that dasa is used both for enemies and slaves suggests that wars were a major source of slaves. Male and female slaves were used in households and do not seem to have been involved to any significant extent in activities related to economic production.[6]

Vedic texts refer to gifts of cows, horses, land, dasas, and dasis. For instance, the *Aitareya Brahmana* talks of a gift of 10,000 dasis and 10,000 elephants made by a king to his purohita or royal priest on the occasion of the royal consecration ceremony. Children born of slave women could rise in the world. For instance, the Rig Veda mentions the sage Kakshivan, who was the son of sage Dirghatamas by a woman slave. Kavasha Ailusha, author of a Vedic hymn, is also said to have been the son of a woman slave. But these must have been exceptional success stories.

---

[5]Dasas and dasyus are described as not obeying the orders of the gods and not performing yajnas (sacrifices). Their speech is said to be unclear or uncouth. In three places in the Rig Veda, the dasyus are said to be dark-skinned. In one passage, the dasas are described as flat-nosed or mouthless (perhaps meaning people whose speech was incomprehensible). While differences in physical appearance cannot be ruled out, most of the references point to the dasas and dasyus being different from the Vedic people with respect to their religious practice, mode of speech, language, or dialect.

[6]For an overview of slavery in early Sanskrit texts, see P. V. Kane, *History of Dharmaśāstra* (*Ancient and Mediaeval Religious and Civil Law*), vol. 2, part 1, 3rd edn., Pune: Bhandarkar Oriental Research Institute, [1941], 1997, Chap. 5; and Dev Raj Chanana, *Slavery in Ancient India*, New Delhi: People's Publishing House, [1960], 1990. For a longer-term historical view, see Indrani Chatterjee and Richard M. Eaton (eds.), *Slavery and South Asian History*, Bloomington: Indiana University Press, 2006.

Slavery continued to exist in later centuries. The Mahabharata frequently mentions dasas and dasis. The most famous event connected with enslavement in the epic occurs in the Sabha Parva, when Yudhishthira foolishly gambles away all he owns in a dicing game against the crafty Shakuni, with the nobles and elders looking on. After staking and losing his wealth and his kingdom, goaded on by his adversary, Yudhishthira stakes and loses his brothers, himself, and his wife, Draupadi, into slavery to the Kauravas. Duhshasana (one of the Kaurava brothers) rushes into Draupadi's inner apartments. He violently drags her out to the assembly hall by the hair and tells her that there is no point crying, because she has been won in the game, and one can lech at a slave as he wishes.

Duryodhana laughs loudly and calls Draupati 'dasi', while Karna and other members of the Kaurava gang cheer and applaud. Although anguished and distraught in the face of the insults and humiliation, Draupadi shows tremendous spirit and presence of mind. She asks the men in the assembly whether they consider what is happening to be in accordance with dharma. She also asks a technical question: Did Yudhishthira stake her before or after he had staked himself? If he had done so afterwards, then as a slave, he had no right to stake his wife.

Then, as now, political life was marked by sycophancy and duplicity. When Draupadi demands answers to her questions, there is silence. Even the elderly Dhritarashtra and Bhishma refuse to take a stand. Only Vidura (the wise uncle of the Pandavas and Kauravas) and Vikarna (the one righteous Kaurava brother) have the courage to speak up and voice their disapproval, but they are a minority of two. Karna taunts Draupadi, ordering her to come and serve the Kauravas:

> There are three who own no property,
> A student, a slave, a dependent woman:
> The wife of a slave, you are *his* [Duryodhana's] now, my dear:
> A masterless slave wench, you are now slave wealth![7]

---

[7]Mahabharata 2.63.1. J. A. B. van Buitenen (trans. and ed.), *The Mahabharata, Book 2: The Book of the Assembly Hall and Book 3: The Book of the Forest*, Chicago: University

Duhshasana proceeds to disrobe Draupadi in front of all the men in the assembly, but the god Krishna intervenes, and the cloth pulled off her body becomes a never-ending ream. Suddenly, a bad omen—a jackal's cry—brings Dhritarashtra to his senses. He abruptly announces an end to the proceedings and offers Draupadi a boon. The boon she asks for is that her husband Yudhishthira be unenslaved, for it would be unbearable if their son Prativindhya was taunted and died of shame when he learnt that he was the son of a slave. For Draupadi—and for the composers of the Mahabharata—enslavement was the lowest position to which a man or woman could be reduced, the worst possible humiliation. It was equivalent to, possibly worse than, death.

Theoretical treatises on dharma known as Dharmashastra, composed from the third century BCE onwards by Brahmana dharma scholars, describe their vision of an ideal society. The *Manava Dharmashastra*—known as the *Manu Smriti* for short—is the most famous text of this corpus and was composed in the second and third centuries CE.[8] In the twentieth century, it came to symbolize Brahmanical oppression and the evils of caste and untouchability. On 25 December 1927, in a powerful act, B. R. Ambedkar publicly burnt a copy of the *Manu Smriti*. In his essay, 'The Annihilation of Caste' (1936), he explained why. 'There is no code of laws more infamous regarding social rights than the Laws of Manu. Any instance from anywhere of social injustice must pale before it.'[9]

The *Manu Smriti* does not only justify untouchability, it also justifies slavery. It lists seven types of slaves—one captured in war; who becomes a slave for food (in time of food scarcity); born in a house (offspring

---

of Chicago Press, 1975, p. 150. The ongoing Chicago University Press translations are authoritative translations of the Mahabharata Critical Edition. For a good abridged translation of the text, see John D. Smith, *The Mahābhārata: An Abridged Translation*, New Delhi: Penguin Books, 2009.

[8] For the text and translation, see Patrick Olivelle, *Manu's Code of Law: A Critical Edition and Translation of the Mānava-Dharmaśāstra*, New Delhi: Oxford University Press, [2005], 2006.

[9] B. R. Ambedkar, 'The Annihilation of Caste', in Valerian Rodrigues (ed.), *The Essential Writings of B. R. Ambedkar*, New Delhi: Oxford University Press, [2002], 2004, p. 283.

of a household female slave); bought; given (for instance by kinfolk); inherited; enslaved due to judicial decree or in order to pay off a fine. The later *Narada Smriti* (composed in the fourth/fifth century) lists fifteen types of slaves. It also describes a manumission ceremony through which a slave could be freed: the master takes from the slave's shoulder a jar filled with water and smashes it to the ground. He then sprinkles a mixture of water, rice grains, and flowers on his head, says, 'You are not a slave' three times, and then sends him off, facing east.

Kautilya's *Arthashastra* is a brilliant treatise on statecraft which discusses how a king can acquire, maintain, and enhance his power. At one time, it was thought to belong to the Maurya period, but recent research suggests a later period of composition, between c. 50 and 300 CE.[10] Kautilya's classification of slaves is similar to the one in the *Manu Smriti*. In the section on slaves and workers, most of the discussion is about debt-pledges and slaves. In several places, Kautilya uses arya and dasa as opposites. But he also seems to suggest that an arya who is enslaved does not fully lose his arya status. He singles out the enslavement of minor aryas for special censure. In the *Arthashastra*, slaves (especially minor slaves) have some rights. They can have property that is inherited by their paternal relatives, and in their absence, by their owner. Certain norms of treatment apply to pledges and slaves. Kautilya recommends punishment for someone selling or pledging a pregnant female slave without providing for her support. A child fathered by a slave owner on his dasi was to become adasa, a non-slave, along with his mother.

The well-off protagonists of Sanskrit plays often have servants and slaves. For instance, in Shudraka's *Mrichchhakatika* (probably composed in the fourth/fifth century), Vasantasena has a slave woman named Madanika who eventually manages to purchase her freedom. Terms of abuse in ancient Sanskrit drama are similar to modern ones, in that most of them involve casting aspersions on the mother and paternity. So there are terms like kanelimata (bastard) and kulataputra or veshyaputra (son of a whore). Dasiputra (son of a slave) and garbhadasi-putra (son

---

[10]Patrick Olivelle, *Kingship, Governance, and Law in Ancient India: Kauṭilya's Arthaśāstra*, New Delhi: Oxford University Press, 2013, pp. 25–31.

of a born slave woman) too are also used for abuse.

As we shall see in Chapter 2, the only time when enslavement is emptied of its lowly, negative connotations is in the context of love, where it becomes a metaphor for complete commitment and surrender to the beloved, even more so when the beloved is a god.

The theory of the four varnas

There is a popular view that for centuries on end, ancient Indian society was divided into four varnas or hereditary social classes—Brahmanas (priests), Kshatriyas (warriors and kings), Vaishyas (herdsmen, farmers, and businessmen), and Shudras (servile labour). It is believed that men lived their lives according to the ashrama system, moving sequentially from the stage of brahmacharya (celibate studenthood) to grihastha (the householder stage), vanaprastha (partial renunciation), and sannyasa (total renunciation). This idea about the lives of ancient Indians is false.

A fully developed idea of a society divided into four varnas or social classes appears in later parts of the Rig Veda and in later Vedic texts.[11] A Rig Vedic hymn, often referred to as the 'Purusha-sukta', expresses one of several ideas about the origins of the world in the text. It describes a great sacrifice supposed to have been performed long ago by the gods, demigods, and sages, in which Purusha—a primaeval giant with a thousand heads, eyes and feet—was the sacrificial offering. Many things were born from this sacrifice—the moon was born from Purusha's mind; the gods Indra and Agni from his mouth; the wind from his vital breath; the middle realm of space from his navel; the sky from his head; the earth from his feet; and the quarters of the sky from his ear. Further: 'His [Purusha's] mouth became the Brahmana, his arms were made into the Rajanya [Kshatriya], his thighs the Vaishya, and the Shudra was born from his feet.'[12]

---

[11]For a recent translation of the Rig Veda see Stephanie W. Jamison and Joel P. Brereton (trans.), *The Rigveda: The Earliest Religious Poetry of India*, 3 vols., New York: Oxford University Press, 2014, (South Asia Research series), available at https://www.academia.edu.

[12]Rig Veda 10.90.

The body symbolism indicates that the four varnas were visualized as interrelated parts of an organic whole, but also as a hierarchy, with the Brahmana at the top and the Shudra at the bottom. It is no accident that the Brahmana emerges from the mouth of Purusha and the Shudra from the feet, and not the other way around.[13] The fact that the varnas are described as created at the same time as the earth, sky, sun, and moon indicates that they were considered part of the natural and immutable order of the world.

Varna was not simply a description of a society divided into four strata. It was an ideology that justified social differences and defined social status, roles, boundaries, and ritual purity. From whose point of view? Obviously from the point of view of its Brahmana composers. Varna was based on birth. Members of the four varnas were supposed to have different innate characteristics that made them naturally suited to certain occupations and gave them a certain social rank. Varna remained an important part of Brahmanical social discourse for many centuries. As will be discussed later in this chapter, it was accepted, although in a significantly modified form, by the Jainas and Buddhists as well.

In course of time, the idea of varna got connected with the idea of dharma. Dharma is a word that occurs in Vedic texts but is unimportant and has a narrow meaning there.[14] It became important in Buddhist and Jaina works and in Dharmashastra. It is likely that it was Buddhism that injected it with ethical content and gave it a new meaning, referring to the ideal, good life. In Dharmashastra, dharma refers to the duties of a person as part of society, and society is visualized as organized along the two axes of varna and ashrama.

The Dharmashastra texts lay down the duties and appropriate functions and occupations of the four varnas. The ideal activities of the Brahmana are studying and teaching the Veda, performing sacrifices for himself and others, and giving and receiving gifts. Those of the

---

[13]Later texts, such as the *Manu Smriti*, describe the four varnas as emerging from different parts of the body of the god Brahma.
[14]See Patrick Olivelle (ed.), *Dharma: Studies in its Semantic, Cultural and Religious History*, Delhi: Motilal Banarsidass, 2009.

Kshatriya are studying, performing sacrifices for himself, bestowing gifts, and more especially, protecting people through soldiering and ruling. The Vaishya shares the first three activities, but his specific occupations are agriculture, cattle-rearing, trade, and moneylending. The Shudra is supposed to obtain his livelihood by serving the higher varnas. The first three varnas are known as dvija, literally 'twice-born', i.e., those entitled to the performance of the upanayana or sacred thread ritual that was considered to be a second birth.

In early Dharmashastra, the four ashramas—brahmacharya, grihastha, vanaprastha, and sannyasa are considered alternative ways of life that a man belonging to the upper three varnas could choose after the completion of his Vedic study. The Smritis introduced a significant change—instead of seeing the ashramas as *alternative* ways of life, they present them as four *consecutive* stages.[15] The householder stage is considered the most important (probably in response to the life-long renunciation promoted by Buddhism and Jainism) while sannyasa was not considered obligatory. This does not mean that all Brahmana, Kshatriya, and Vaishya men divided their lives into four parts according to the ashrama system. Life expectancy and lifestyles must have varied a great deal. Along with varna, the ashrama scheme was part of a *theoretical* Brahmanical model of an ideal society.

There were some caveats and flexibility in the varna model. Apart from shruti (literally, 'that which has been heard', the Veda) and smriti ('the remembered tradition', which includes Vedanga texts, Dharmashastra, the Mahabharata, Ramayana, Puranas, and Nitishastra, i.e., works on politics), the dharma experts include custom (sadachara or shishtachara) as a source of dharma. They also put forward the idea of dharma in times of emergency (apad-dharma). According to this, in times of extreme difficulty or distress, it was all right for a person to follow occupations that would normally be considered inappropriate for a member of his varna. However, lower varnas could not follow the dharma of the higher varnas under any circumstances.

---

[15]Patrick Olivelle, *The Āśrama System: The History and Hermeneutics of a Religious Institution*, New York, Oxford: Oxford University Press, 1993.

The varnas were ideally, but not necessarily, endogamous—that is, people did not have to marry into their own varna. Certain types of inter-varna marriages—those between a man of a higher varna and a woman of a lower varna—were referred to as anuloma marriages and were accepted. On the other hand, marriages between a woman of a higher varna and a man of a lower varna were referred to as pratiloma unions and were not approved of. According to the Brahmana dharma experts, the mixture of varnas though pratiloma marriages would lead to social chaos and ruin.

The Mahabharata has many discussions on the subtlety of dharma but emphasizes that a person must follow the dharma of the varna he is born into, regardless of how difficult or unpleasant it may be and how much unhappiness it may bring. But it also frequently talks about another dharma called moksha-dharma. This is the dharma that leads to liberation from samsara (the cycle of rebirth), which requires true knowledge, control of the senses, and complete detachment. The Bhagavad Gita (Song of the Lord), is part of the Bhishma Parva, the sixth book of the Mahabharata and was composed between c. 200 BCE and 200 CE. The Gita weaves together strands from the philosophies of Samkhya, Yoga, and Vedanta with the ideas of duty and religious devotion (bhakti) and brings dharma and moksha together. It emphasizes the eternal nature of the atman (self) and the importance of following the dharma of one's varna. According to the Gita, true renunciation is not the renunciation of action but of the fruits of action. This means that a householder can simultaneously be a renouncer.

Varna is very important in other ancient texts such as the *Arthashastra*. For Kautilya, the life, property, and value of a person depended on the varna to which he or she belonged. The punishments recommended by Kautilya for various crimes vary according to the varna of the persons involved. Brahmanas, especially learned scholars of the Vedas, are given special legal privileges. For instance, Kautilya suggests that if a Shudra strikes a Brahmana, his hand should be cut off, but such a severe punishment is not suggested if the roles are reversed. If a Kshatriya has sexual relations with an unguarded Brahmana woman, Kautilya recommends a high fine; for a Vaishya, confiscation of his entire property; a Shudra who does this should be burnt in a fire of straw. Of course, the *Arthashastra* is a theoretical work on statecraft. To what extent its recommendations were actually put into practice is anyone's guess.

Apart from the dharma of the varnas and moksha-dharma, there were various other dharmas. These include kula-dharma (the duties of lineages) and desha-dharma (the duties of different lands). There is a dharma for women (stri-dharma). There is also a dharma that applies to everyone, known as samanya dharma or sadharana dharma. This includes controlling anger, truthfulness, sharing, forbearance, begetting children on one's wife, cleanliness, freedom from malice, rectitude, supporting one's dependents, honouring guests, and performing the shraddha ceremonies for the ancestors. It can also include self-knowledge, non-violence (ahimsa), and non-cruelty (anrishamsya). But in the Brahmanical tradition, this 'dharma for all' was not as important as the dharma of the varnas and ashramas.

While varna was a powerful social ideology whose beginnings can be traced to around 1000 BCE, people in ancient India did not live their lives according to this system. Take the Brahmanas, for instance. Over the centuries, Brahmanas are known to have followed different occupations. Some were scholars of the Vedas and devoted themselves to performing sacrifices. Epic characters include martial Brahmanas such as Dronacharya and Parashurama. The Jataka stories feature Brahmana caravan-guards, farmers, animal-herders, hawkers, carpenters, snake charmers, carriage drivers, and wheelmakers. There were dynasties of Brahmana rulers such as the Shungas, Mitras, Kanvas, Satavahanas, Kadambas, Vakatakas, and Pallavas. There were Brahmana administrative and military officers, bards, astrologers, philosophers, poets, dramatists, and landowners. 'Brahmana' remained an important social category based on birth, associated with high social status (though not necessarily with wealth or political influence), whose members followed different occupations. 'Kshatriya' started out as a status based on birth, but it soon became a status claimed by lineages that became politically powerful. Vaishya and Shudra seem to be more nebulous categories when it was a matter of how people in society identified themselves. At least from the sixth century BCE, as far as social identity and social interaction are concerned, leaving aside Brahmana status (which remained important across the centuries), what really counted was lineage, family, class, and jati.

What was going on in the land known as Tamilakam in the far South? The early Tamil poems of the Sangam corpus were composed between the second/first centuries BCE and second/third centuries CE. They belong to the time when the Chola, Chera, and Pandya kings ruled their kingdoms in the midst of many chieftaincies. Cities hummed with commercial activities and supported a vibrant, sophisticated literary culture. Sangam poems mention Brahmanas but the four-fold varna system does not seem to have made any deep impression. The social milieu of the Tamil poems is very different from that reflected in northern Sanskrit texts. It was based on clans and lineage-based descent groups known as kutis.

The early history of caste

The English word 'caste' comes from the Portuguese castas, which refers to animal and plant species or breeds, as well as to tribes, clans, races, or lineages. Castas was first used by Portuguese traders to describe Indian society on the western coast in the sixteenth and seventeenth centuries. The Indian word that best corresponds to caste is jati. Like castas, it has a broad range of meanings, including birth and type. The characteristics of the Indian caste system include hierarchy, endogamy (marriage within the group), commensality (rules about inter-dining and the giving and accepting of food and drink), and hereditary occupation.

People often confuse varna and jati. This is not surprising, considering that both are hierarchical, hereditary social classifications and the fact that ancient texts sometimes use these words interchangeably and also connect them. But there are several differences. There are four varnas but the jatis (including castes and sub-castes) are so numerous that they cannot be counted. The ranking among the four varnas is fixed, while there is some fluidity and ambiguity in the ranking of the jatis within certain ranges. The relative ranking of castes can vary across regions and localities and depends on a number of factors including control over land, wealth, and political power. Castes have often tried to 'upgrade' themselves (a process sociologists refer to as Sanskritization), and sometimes get 'downgraded'. Upgrading usually involves adopting practices associated with higher castes, e.g., vegetarianism, restrictions on women, and change in occupation. While social interaction and the acceptance of certain kinds of food by higher varnas from lower ones may have been discouraged, the rules of commensality are more clearly defined and established with reference to the jatis. The varnas are not endogamous units, since a number of inter-varna marriages (the anuloma ones) were considered permissible. The jatis, on the other hand, are generally supposed to be endogamous. The varnas are associated with a range of functions, while the jatis (at least initially) were associated with specific occupations. The jati system anchored itself to the varna system in order to give itself legitimacy. Members of a caste often claim to belong to a particular varna, but varna and jati are not the same thing.

Caste is not just a simple division of labour. It is a complex system involving control over material resources, value systems, and knowledge production. Ideas of purity and pollution help justify hierarchy, separation, and the position of the upper castes. Because endogamy is so important, the perpetuation of the caste system depends on controlling women's sexuality and reproduction. Sociologists and historians have interpreted caste in various ways—as a product of religious and cultural ideas related to purity and pollution; as a powerful ideological justification for economic inequalities; as a part of the process of agrarian expansion; and as a system that rationalized and camouflaged material inequalities through an idiom of purity and pollution. There is also a connection between caste and the political sphere, specifically with the emergence of kingship and proliferation of kingdoms.[16] Some historians have argued that caste was 'invented' by British colonial rulers. What

---

[16]For overviews of the various theories and aspects of caste, see Dipankar Gupta (ed.), *Interrogating Caste: Understanding Hierarchy and Difference in Indian Society*, New Delhi: Penguin Books, 2000; Declan Quigley, *Interpretation of Caste*, New Delhi: Oxford University Press, [1993], 1999; and Ishita Banerjee-Dube (ed.), *Caste in History* (Themes in Indian History series), New Delhi: Oxford University Press, 2010.

this means is that the nature of the caste system changed significantly during the colonial period. For instance, the censuses conducted by the British from 1871 onwards, where people were asked to state their caste, gave it a new kind of fixity. But when did something caste-like originate? And what did it look like in ancient times?

The answers should be sought in evidence of social units marked by hereditary occupation, endogamy, and commensality. These are usually traced to North India in the sixth/fifth centuries BCE, although there is uncertainty about the extent to which endogamy and commensality were firmly established at the time. In the early Buddhist canon, the Pali Tipitaka (supposedly written down in Sri Lanka in the first century BCE), the varna order is still an important reference point. However, while many people in the Tipitaka are identified as Brahmanas and Kshatriyas, very few are identified as Vaishyas or Shudras. Those who would theoretically have belonged to the latter two categories are generally described with reference to their specific occupation, which was in turn tied up with kula (family/lineage) and jati (caste). This suggests that by this time, the four-fold varna system was largely a theoretical construct tied to the upper classes and that an ordinary person's social identity was based on occupation, caste, and family.

The Dharmasutras (these are early Dharmashastra texts composed from the third century BCE onwards) explain the origins of jatis through the ingenious but fictitious theory of the mixture of varnas (varna-sankara). According to this, castes were the outcome of various kinds of inter-varna marriages. In this way, Dharmashastra was able to stand by the varna theory but acknowledge and explain the existence of jatis. In actual fact, the emergence of jatis may have been the result of a combination of several factors such as the hereditary nature of crafts and occupations, the assimilation of tribal groups into the Brahmanical fold, and a social system that attached importance to birth and a strict regulation of social hierarchy, separation, and interaction.

Social inequalities are not only visible in normative texts; they are vividly portrayed in literature. The main characters of Sanskrit drama are high-born men and women, but there is a supporting cast of servants, slaves, and lower class and lower caste people. Distinctions between high and low are reflected not only through content, but also through language. Sanskrit drama is actually bilingual—men and upper-class characters speak Sanskrit. Women (even queens) and lower-class characters speak Prakrit.

Varna and jati are not features of Sangam society, that is, the time when the Sangam poems were composed. Some historians trace the beginnings of caste in South India to lineage-based descent groups known as kutis. It is possible that when Brahmanas became landholders, the old kin-based system of agrarian organization broke down and a new kind of social order emerged, based, among other things, on caste. However, the early history of caste in South India remains imperfectly understood.

It becomes easier to track down the history of caste during the early medieval period (c. 600–1300 CE). During this period, caste spread along with the expansion of kingdoms and Brahmanical influence to many new areas, including those inhabited by tribal communities. An interesting fact is that although 'Brahmana' appears very often in inscriptions, references to other varnas and to jatis vary considerably from region to region. Inscriptions from Karnataka mention various terms that could be names of agricultural, artisanal, and trading castes. The inscriptions of Orissa, on the other hand, hardly mention any specific occupational groups that can be identified as caste groups. Neither do Andhra inscriptions. In fact, the Andhra inscriptions turn varna on its head—several inscriptions of the Kakatiya kings proudly claim that they were Shudras. This suggests that the spread of ideas and practices related to varna and jati were uneven and different across the regions of the subcontinent.

Large-scale deforestation in India took place during the colonial period, when the extension of the railways, increase in population, and the commercialization of agriculture led to a dramatic reduction in forest cover. Until then, large tracts of land were inhabited by forest people who had their own distinctive modes of subsistence, social structure, and cultural traditions. We do not get a picture of these communities from within; we only get glimpses from the outside, from extremely biased sources. The pejorative word 'mlechchha' appears in later Vedic texts and was used thereafter to refer to forest tribes and foreigners, who were considered as culturally inferior barbarians. One of the accounts of the origins of kingship in the Shanti Parva of the Mahabharata mentions the Nishada (a forest tribal) as unfit to rule; but the fact that he is mentioned at all is an acknowledgement of the political importance of the forest tribes in ancient times. The gradual expansion of the caste system over the centuries involved, among other things, the incorporation of tribal communities into its fold, by giving them a place on the lower rungs. The details of this process are not documented and are difficult to reconstruct, but it must have involved a great deal of conflict and violence.

The idea and practice of untouchability

A disclaimer and trigger warning are in order here: The word 'untouchable' is being used in this book only to convey what the ancient texts say and does not imply an acceptance or endorsement of their highly prejudiced views. In fact, these views are likely to strike sensible readers as extremely disturbing and shocking.

The earliest occurrence of the word 'asprishya' ('untouchable') occurs in the *Vishnu Smriti*, but the practice of untouchability, an extreme form of social subordination, marginalization, segregation, and oppression, existed from earlier times.[17] Texts mention many groups considered 'untouchable' by others, but the one mentioned most frequently is the Chandala.

In Vedic texts, groups such as the Chandalas were clearly looked on with contempt by the elites, but there is no clear evidence of the practice of untouchability. This appears in the Dharmasutras, which describe any kind of physical contact, even accidental, with a Chandala as polluting and to be remedied by expiation. According to the *Apastamba Dharmasutra*, if one touches a Chandala, one should immediately bathe; if one talks to a Chandala, one should immediately talk to a Brahmana; if one sees him, one should immediately look at luminous bodies in the

---

[17]For an overview of the early history of untouchability, see Vivekanand Jha, 'Caṇḍāla and the Origin of Untouchability', *Indian Historical Review*, 13, 1986–87; reprinted in Aloka Parasher-Sen (ed.), *Subordinate and Marginal Groups in Early India* (Themes in Indian History series), New Delhi: Oxford University Press, 2004, pp. 157–209.

heavens (the sun, moon, or stars). The *Manu Smriti* refers to Chandalas as hunters, butchers, executioners, and corpse carriers. In one place, it explains them as the offspring of Shudra men and Brahmana women. Elsewhere, it describes birth as a Chandala as the result of evil deeds in an earlier life. Chandalas are associated with pollution and any contact with them requires purification. Unless he is starving, a Brahmana must not eat food given by a Chandala, nor should he have sexual relations with a Chandala woman.

> Chandalas...must live outside the village.... Their property consists of dogs and donkeys. Their garments are the clothes of the dead; they eat in broken vessels; their ornaments are of iron; and they constantly roam about. A man who follows dharma should never seek any dealings with them. All their transactions shall be among themselves, and they must marry their own kind. They depend on others for their food, and it should be given in a broken vessel. They must not go about in villages and towns at night; they may go around during the day to perform some task at the command of the king, wearing distinguishing marks. They should carry away the corpses of those without relatives—that is the settled rule.[18]

Dharmashastra texts of later centuries (for instance the *Vishnu, Yajnavalkya,* and *Narada Smriti*s) indicate hardening attitudes towards 'untouchables'.

Kautilya refers to Chandalas having separate wells, and states that they live outside settlements near cremation grounds. In the *Arthashastra*, Chandalas are one of many categories of people (including women, the physically handicapped, and outcastes) who cannot bear witness for anyone other than members of their own group. They are given a role in public punishments, no doubt to emphasize the reprehensible nature of certain crimes. For instance, in the case of a woman talking with a man in a suspicious place, Kautilya suggests that a Chandala should give her five lashes between her shoulders, in the middle of the village. Kautilya also makes an 'untouchable's' touching a higher up person a criminal offence and recommends a hefty fine of 100 panas (these were

---

[18]*Manava Dharmashastra* 10.51-56. Patrick Olivelle (trans.), *Manu's Code of Law*, p. 210.

silver coins) for a Chandala who touches an arya woman. But he also suggests that Chandalas could be put to good use by the state—along with forest dwellers, tribals, trappers, and mountain-dwellers, they should be employed as guards in the areas between frontier forts.

In the Ramayana, there is the legend of Trishanku, a king of Ayodhya, who was cursed to become a Chandala due to a curse pronounced by the sons of the sage Vasishtha. He is described as ugly, dressed in rags, wearing wreaths from the cremation ground, and shunned by townsmen and officials. Brahmanas are horrified at being invited for a yajna by him. There is also the story of the sage Vishvamitra cursing Vasishtha's sons to be born as 'untouchables' known as Mushtikas for 700 births.[19]

Given these ideas of extreme prejudice, the Mahabharata story of the sage Vishvamitra and the Chandala may come as a surprise. During a terrible drought that had reduced people to acute desperation, a starving Vishvamitra lands up in a Chandala hamlet and is on the verge of stealing some dog meat from a Chandala's house. A debate ensues. The Chandala is horrified that a sage of Vishvamitra's stature should want to eat something so impure and begs him to refrain from doing so. But Vishvamitra convinces him that in acute crisis—and this was one because he was starving—no sin would be incurred by such an act. This is cited as an example of apad-dharma (dharma in time of emergency).[20]

As already mentioned, Sangam poems do not indicate the existence of a caste system in the far south in early historic times.[21] There were ideas of impurity, and of high and low social status, but these did not amount

---

[19] For an abridged translation of the Ramayana, see Arshia Sattar, *The Rāmāyaṇa: Vālmīki*, New Delhi: Penguin Books, 1996. For a complete translation of the Critical Edition, see Robert P. Goldman (gen. ed.), *The Rāmāyaṇa of Vālmīki: An Epic of Ancient India*, 6 vols., Delhi: Motilal Banarsidass, [1984], 2007; and Robert P. Goldman and Sally J. Goldman (trans.), *The Rāmāyaṇa of Vālmīki: An Epic of Ancient India*, vol. 7: Uttarakāṇḍa, Princeton: Princeton University Press, 2017.

[20] This story is narrated in Mahabharata 12.139.25-90. For an English translation, see James L. Fitzgerald edited and annotated, *Mahābhārata*, vol. 7: *11: The Book of Women and 12: The Book of Peace, Vol. II*, Chicago: University of Chicago Press, 2004, pp. 536–41.

[21] See K. R. Hanumanthan, 'Evolution of Untouchability in Tamil Nadu up to AD 1600', in Aloka Parasher Sen (ed.), *Subordinate and Marginalized Groups in Early India*, New Delhi: Oxford University Press, 2004, pp. 125–56.

to the practice of untouchability. Nor are taboos on intermarriage and inter-dining visible. In fact, some of the groups who were considered 'untouchable' in later times (e.g., the Paraiya, Panan, Tutiyan, and Katampan) have a fairly respectable status in Sangam poems. But caste and untouchability did take root in South India sometime between the third and sixth centuries. The earliest evidence comes from a post-Sangam work called the *Acharakkovai*. This states that glancing at a Pulaiya is polluting and that water that has been touched by him is polluted and unfit for drinking by others. The ideas of caste and untouchability are even more visible in South India during the Pallava period (sixth to ninth centuries). The hymns of the bhakti saints suggest that 'untouchables' were not allowed to enter temples. Pallava kings, who claimed to be Brahmanas of the Bharadvaja gotra, patronized Brahmanas by giving them land grants and announced themselves as upholders of the order of varnas and ashramas in their inscriptions. The spread of caste and untouchability in South India seems to be directly connected with royal patronage of Brahmanas. This not only led to an increasing Brahmana influence in royal courts but also to the emergence of Brahmanas as authoritative mediators of social and religious values and practices at the village level.

Jaina and Buddhist challenges

The Upanishads (composed during c. 1000–500 BCE) have sometimes been seen as anti-sacrifice and anti-Brahmana. However, they do not reject sacrifice; rather, they re-describe and reinterpret it symbolically and allegorically. The Upanishads deal with many issues but are especially concerned with the concepts of atman and brahman. Liberation (moksha, mukti) from samsara could not be achieved through ordinary intellectual exertion, nor through the performance of rituals; it could only be achieved through the realization of a profound knowledge. In several places in the Upanishads, this knowledge is associated with kings or Kshatriyas. Nevertheless, Brahmanas are still very much central figures, not as ritual experts but as thinkers and philosophers. So, it is an exaggeration to see these texts as reflecting a strong attack launched by Kshatriya philosophers against Brahmanas. After all, the Upanishads

Ancient India: Culture of Contradictions

were ultimately incorporated into the Vedic corpus.

Individually and collectively, the thinkers of the sixth/fifth centuries BCE represent the first major challenge to Brahmana claims to social superiority and spiritual knowledge and to their ideas about the ideal social order. Much was happening at the time—some tribal principalities (mainly in northern India) were mutating into states and the emergence of cities was eroding old social ties.[22] The fact that the intellectual ferment was most intense in the middle and lower Ganga valley was because these areas were not as brahmanized as the regions lying to the west.

The sixth/fifth centuries BCE are often known as the age of the Buddha and Mahavira but there were many other thinkers moving around at that time, giving their take on the meaning of human existence, making this one of the most exciting periods in the history of human thought. Many of these thinkers advocated giving up worldly life and were collectively known as shramanas (literally, 'one who strives'). [Fig. 1.1] They included men like Makkhali Gosala, Purana Kassapa, Ajita Keshakambalin, Pakudha Kachchayana, and Sanjaya Belatthaputta (more on them in Chapter 5). As their following died out and their texts (if there were any) have not survived, we know about them only through unflattering portrayals in Buddhist and Jaina texts. We will focus here on Jainism and Buddhism as they had the greatest impact in the long run. Whether or not men like Mahavira and the Buddha sought to establish 'religions' is immaterial—the fact is that they created new kinds of lay and monastic communities.

Jainism is older than Buddhism, perhaps by a couple of centuries, as Mahavira is the last in the line of twenty-four Jaina saints known as Tirthankaras or Jinas. Tirthankara means 'ford-builder'. He is one who builds fords that help people across the ocean of suffering. Jina means 'victor', a person who has attained infinite knowledge and teaches others how to attain moksha. 'Jaina' means follower of a Jina. Vardhamana (the future Mahavira) had an aristocratic Kshatriya background. His father,

---

[22]There is continuing debate over the date of the Buddha's death. While some historians place it in 544/543 BCE, others place this event between 486 and 477 BCE, between 400 and 350 BCE, or in 368 BCE. The Buddha's date has major implications for the dating of several other historical events and texts.

Fig. 1.1: Terracotta tile with impressed figures of emaciated ascetics and couples on balconies, Harwan, Kashmir, fifth–sixth century

Siddhartha, was chief of the Jnatri clan, his mother, Trishala, was a sister of the Videhan king Chetaka. According to Shvetambara tradition, Vardhamana was conceived by a Brahmana named Rishabhadatta in the womb of his wife Devananda, but the god Indra transferred the embryo to Trishala's womb, on the grounds that a Brahmana woman or one from a low family was not worthy of giving birth to the future Tirthankara.

Jaina texts assert the idea of the superiority of Kshatriyas over Brahmanas in other ways as well. They criticize Brahmanas, their sacrifices, lavish lifestyle, and arrogance. At the same time, they talk of the true or ideal Brahmana, giving the word new content, shifting the focus from birth to good conduct. Thus redefined, only a Jaina monk was worthy of being called a Brahmana. Chandalas are described as the result of a mixture of varnas and are connected with cremation grounds and corpses.

And yet, along with a certain level of acceptance of social inequality, there is also some critique of prevailing ideas of high and low. After Mahavira wandered for six months without consuming food or water, his fast is said to have been broken when he was offered some lentils by a slave girl named Chandana, who later became a leader of the Order of nuns. The Uttaradhyayana Sutra narrates the story of a monk named Harikeshiya who belonged to a Chandala family. Hungry and in search of food after concluding a long, arduous fast, he arrives at an enclosure where Brahmanas are performing a sacrifice. The arrogant Brahmanas abuse him and refuse to give him food. When Harikeshiya tries to reason with them, the Brahmanas attack him viciously, stopping only when a yaksha (demigod) intervenes. Realizing that they have erred, the Brahmanas ask Harikeshiya's pardon. He graciously forgives them and proceeds to lecture them on the uselessness of performing sacrifices; true sacrifice consists in practising the Jaina discipline.

The Tirthankaras offered two sets of interrelated but distinct teachings for monastics (monks and nuns) and lay followers. [Figs. 1.2, 1.3] The Jaina sangha (monastic Order) was open to all, regardless of social background. Yet all the chief disciples of Mahavira were Brahmanas. Many of the Jaina acharyas (heads of monastic Orders) were also Brahmanas. Among the laity, Jainism consistently attracted the allegiance and patronage of the affluent urban merchant class.

The Buddha has often been portrayed as a reformer, even a revolutionary, who spoke up against social discrimination and advocated equality for all. The tendency to equate Buddhism with social equality became especially pronounced after Ambedkar's mass conversion of members of the Scheduled Castes to Buddhism in 1959. But Ambedkar's was a new, highly idealized interpretation of Buddhism, appropriately called Navayana (the new vehicle). Like Jainism, ancient Buddhism was a religion that promised salvation, not social equality.

In Buddhism, all social relationships are a source of suffering. A person can attain nibbana (liberation from the cycle of birth and death) only by breaking free from them. Like Mahavira, the Buddha offered two sets of teaching—one for monks and nuns; the other for lay householders. [Figs. 1.4, 1.5] His doctrine was certainly more socially

Fig. 1.2: Jinas, sandstone, Uttar Pradesh, c. sixth century CE

Fig. 1.3: Meditating Tirthankara, marble, Gujarat or Rajasthan, eleventh century

Ancient India: Culture of Contradictions

Fig. 1.4: Buddha in protection-granting abhaya mudra, sandstone, Mathura, c. second century CE

Fig. 1.5: Meditating Siddhartha in dhyana mudra, schist, Gandhara, c. third century CE

inclusive than the Brahmanical varna–jati ideology, but it did not aim at overturning or abolishing social differences. In fact, in certain respects, it sought to maintain the status quo by not rocking the boat too much.

Early Buddhist texts contain many references to male and female slaves (dasas and dasis).[23] There are also dasa-kammakaras and dasa-kammakara-porisas, workers whose status was in between that of slaves, servants, and wage labourers. Slaves could be of many types—the offspring of a woman slave; a slave who is bought; one brought from another country and enslaved; and one who has himself accepted to be a slave. Women slaves included the kumbha-dasi, whose job was to fetch water for her master. Masters were exhorted to be kind and caring towards their slaves.

Slaves could only join the Order if they were freed by their masters, but once in, they were seen as having the potential to attain nibbana. The Therigatha (Songs of the Sisters) contains a rare expression of what it was like to be a slave woman, in the words of Punna, a slave who became a nun. This is how Punna taunts a Brahmana who is bathing in cold water to wash off his sins:

> I carried water,
> Even when it was cold
> I still went down into the water,
> Afraid of the sticks of my mistresses,
> Afraid of their words and their anger.
>
> But what are you afraid of, Brahmana
> when you go into the water,
> your body shivering
> as you feel the biting cold?[24]

Interestingly, the few references to rebellious slaves in ancient Indian texts come from early Buddhist texts. The Vinaya Pitaka refers to the dasa-kammakaras of the Shakyas attacking the womenfolk of their

---

[23] See Chanana, *Slavery in Ancient India*, pp. 64–86.
[24] Charles Hallisey (trans.), *Therigatha: Poems of the First Buddhist Women*, Murty Classical Library of India, Cambridge MA: Harvard University Press, 2015, p. 123.

masters in the woods as an act of vengeance. The Majjhima Nikaya tells the story of the dasi Kali and her mistress Vaidehi. Vaidehi had a reputation of being extremely gentle and even-tempered. Kali was submissive and hard-working and came to the conclusion that her mistress's cheerful nature was the result of her own exemplary conduct. She tested Vaidehi's patience by waking up late and not heeding her mistress's calls three days in a row. Vaidehi couldn't take it. She got increasingly angry and finally beat up Kali in fury. Kali was proved right.[25]

Apart from texts, evidence of slavery in ancient India comes from inscriptions as well. The Maurya emperor Ashoka (c. 268–232 BCE) was an ardent follower of the Buddha's teaching and is famous for his passionate propaganda of dhamma through inscriptions inscribed on rocks and stone pillars as well as through other means.[26] Dhamma is the Prakrit form of the Sanskrit dharma. Ashoka wanted to make people good and virtuous, to live their lives in a manner that would lead to their accumulating merit (punya) and attaining happiness in this life and the next. His inscriptions explain dhamma as including non-violence, gentleness, compassion, self-control, purity of thought, generosity, gratitude, firm devotion, truthfulness, and purity. It also included obedience to mother and father; respect for elders; courtesy and liberality towards Brahmanas and shramanas; courtesy to slaves and servants; generosity towards friends, acquaintances, and relatives; moderation in expenditure and possessions; and careful speech. Ashoka

---

[25]Chanana, *Slavery in Ancient India*, pp. 56–57.

[26]Ashoka's edicts have been classified into minor rock edicts, major rock edicts, separate rock edicts, major pillar edicts, minor pillar edicts, and cave inscriptions. Most of the inscriptions are in the Brahmi script and in dialects of Prakrit. Mansehra and Shahbazgarhi in Pakistan have sets of rock edicts in the Prakrit language and Kharoshthi script. The northwestern part of the empire (which included areas of modern Pakistan and Afghanistan) also yielded one Greek, four Aramaic, one Greek–Aramaic, and one Aramaic–Prakrit inscription. For the inscriptions, see E. Hultzsch, *Corpus Inscriptionum Indicarum*, vol. 1: *Inscriptions of Aśoka*, New Delhi, Archaeological Survey of India, [1924], 1991. On Ashoka, see Upinder Singh, *Political Violence in Ancient India*, Cambridge MA: Harvard University Press, 2017; Nayanjot Lahiri, *Ashoka in Ancient India*, Ranikhet, Permanent Black, in association with Ashoka University, 2015; Romila Thapar, *Aśoka and the Decline of the Mauryas*, 3rd edn., New Delhi, Oxford University Press, 2012.

recognized the existing status quo, the existence of high and low, rich and poor. He did not reject these distinctions, but what he said was radical for his time—that regardless of their social or economic standing, everyone could follow dhamma and attain heaven. Whether this included slaves is an open question.

As Buddhist monasteries grew, so did their needs for various kinds of labour and services. Monks did not themselves perform manual labour and must have employed workers and slaves. Inscriptions found in monasteries in India and Sri Lanka refer to aramikas, who may have been slaves or servants.

Buddhism accepted the idea of varna but unlike the Brahmanical tradition, considered it man-made. In the Agganna Sutta, the Buddha declares:

> For those who rely on clan, the Kshatriya is the best in this world; [but] the person endowed with wisdom and [good] conduct is the best in the whole universe.[27]

Like Jainism, Buddhism reversed the Brahmanical order of rank and placed the Kshatriya higher than the Brahmana. Like Jainism, it criticized Brahmanas for their lack of true knowledge, their performance of sacrifices, and their opulent lifestyle, but retained the idea of the true Brahmana—not someone born in a Brahmana family, but one who had true knowledge.

Pali texts refer to high and low jatis. The former include Brahmanas, Kshatriyas, and landowners known as gahapatis. The low jatis include the Chandalas, basket makers, hunters, charioteers, and sweepers. High occupations include farming, cattle-rearing, trade, banking, accounting, and writing; low ones include the professions of the leather-maker, reed-worker, potter, tailor, painter, weaver, and barber.[28]

Some of the most renowned early Buddhist monks were Brahmanas

---

[27]Steven Collins, *Aggañña Sutta: The Discourse on What is Primary (An Annotated Translation from Pali)*, Delhi: Sahitya Akademi, 2001, p. 49.
[28]Uma Chakravarti, *The Social Dimensions of Early Buddhism*, New Delhi: Oxford University Press, 1987; Narendra K. Wagle, *Society at the Time of the Buddha*, Bombay: Popular Prakashan, [1966], 1995.

or Kshatriyas. On the other hand, the distinguished monk Upali was originally a barber of the Shakyas. The fact that bhikkhus (monks) were supposed to accept food from everyone, regardless of class or caste, suggests a deliberate disregard for practices connected with ideas of purity and pollution. The Buddha himself did not observe any such restrictions. He not only enjoyed the hospitality of wealthy gahapatis and setthis (businessmen) but also dined with humble folk. His last meal is said to have been at the home of a blacksmith named Chunda.

Stories of the previous lives of the Buddha known as Jatakas indicate that Chandalas were considered a lowly group, but also question this attitude. Just as the Buddhist texts talk about men who are Brahmanas due to the excellence of their character, they also talk about men who are Chandalas due to their bad conduct and qualities. In fact, in the Anguttara Nikaya, there is mention of a Brahmana–Chandala—a Brahmana who leads a morally depraved life and is hence the equivalent of a Chandala. In several Jatakas, the bodhisattva (Buddha-to-be) is born as a Chandala. The Setaketu Jataka tells the story of an arrogant Brahmana named Setaketu, the pupil of a bodhisattva. One day, when returning from an out-of-town trip with other students, he saw a Chandala coming down the road from the opposite direction. He was afraid that the wind would strike the Chandala's body and then touch him, so he told him to move leeward. The Chandala was defiant and moved windward and then challenged Setaketu to answer a question, which he accepted. The question was: 'What are the quarters?' Setaketu answered that they were north and the rest. 'Wrong answer,' said the Chandala and pushed him to the ground between his feet. When Setaketu's fellow students told their teacher (who was actually a bodhisattva) about the incident, the latter advised Setaketu not to be angry: the Chandala was wise, and his question was about a different sort of quarter. At the end of the story, the Chandala is revealed to be none other than the famous Buddhist monk Sariputta in another birth.

Jainism and Buddhism appealed to the laity because they had a coherent teaching that offered solutions to the perennial problems of human existence, especially inner suffering; a new kind of ethical life that promised achievable rewards; and an acknowledgement of the status of upwardly mobile and affluent social groups. While these teachings—which eventually became the basis of highly organized religions—certainly shook things up and challenged Brahmanical privilege and authority, they did not aim at changing society. They created new communities of monastics and laity, bound together by the teaching of a great man (or men), and by shared doctrines and ethics. They did not advocate the abolition of caste or other social distinctions, but they did critique the idea that human worth was based on birth, and offered the possibility of salvation to all, regardless of caste, class, and gender. By our own standards, early Jainism and Buddhism's stand on social equality falls short. But by the standards of their own time, it was radical.

Communities of bhaktas

The Brahmanical tradition was not something fixed or static. It responded to challenges and social changes by gradually acknowledging and incorporating certain subordinated and marginalized groups into its social framework. Unlike the religion of the Vedas which was based on the performance of yajnas, the religiosity reflected in the Sanskrit Puranas was based on bhakti or devotion to deities who were worshipped in temples through puja (devotional practices). The Puranas recommend pious activities that were open to all, including Shudras and women. Merit could be acquired by performing vows (vratas), going on pilgrimage (tirtha), and charitable acts such as making gifts, setting up alms-houses, and digging wells.

The Sanskrit word bhakti comes from the root bhaj, which means to share or participate. The bhakta is one who shares or participates in the divine. The roots of bhakti (devotion to a god, saint, or teacher) go back to c. 200 BCE. The idea is found in the Bhagavad Gita as well as in remains of religious images in modest temple structures.[29] The Gita

---

[29] There are many good translations of the Bhagavad Gita. For a scholarly, authoritative one, see J. A. B. van Buitenen, *The Bhagavadgītā in the Mahābhārata: Text and Translation*, Chicago and London: University of Chicago Press, 1981. Also see Winthrop Sargeant (trans.), *The Bhagavad Gītā*, New Delhi: Aleph Book Company, 2016.

describes the relationship between devotee and god in the following manner:

> He who offers to Me with devotion and a pure heart a leaf, a flower, a fruit, or water, that offering of devotion I accept from him....
>
> I am the same (Self) in all beings; there is none disliked or dear to Me. But they who worship Me with devotion are in Me, and I am also in them....
>
> They who take refuge in Me, Arjuna, even if they are born of those whose wombs are evil (i.e., those of low origin) women, Vaishyas, even Shudras, also go to the highest goal.[30]

Over the subsequent centuries, bhakti gradually created communities bound by sentiment and devotional belief and practice. Within Hinduism, the most important foci of worship were Vishnu, Shiva, and Devi. The relationship between the Vaidika Brahmanas (Brahmanas who followed the path of the Vedic texts) and the devotional sects was neither simple nor straightforward. From the sixth century CE onwards, devotion to Vishnu (and his incarnations, especially Krishna) and Shiva received a new, powerful expression in the songs of the twelve Alvar and sixty-three Nayanmar (or Nayanar) saints. Their devotion was deeply rooted in the Tamil land, language, and ethos. Alvar means 'one who dives deep' or 'one who is absorbed in the divine'. In Vaishnava Alvar bhakti, the relationship between the devotee and Mayon or Mal (Krishna) is often expressed in terms of the relationship between the lover and beloved. For a devotee of the lord, the performance of sacrifices or other conventional acts of religious piety were meaningless. Nayanmar is an honorific. The Shaiva Nayanmar saints did not refer to themselves by this name; they described themselves as atiyar (servants) or tontar (slaves) of Shiva. The word used by the saints to express their love for god was anbu and the word used for the god's love for his devotee was arul. Alvar and Nayanmar songs reflect a devotion that is intimate, intense, and ecstatic. The saints were worshipped from the Chola period onwards and their songs are still sung in temples in South India.

---

[30]Bhagavad Gita 9.26,29,32, trans. Sargeant, *The Bhagavad Gītā*, pp. 139–41.

Many of the Alvar and Nayanmar saints were Brahmanas, but they also came from other backgrounds. Two saints—the Shaiva Nandanar and the Vaishnava Tiruppan Alvar—are described as 'untouchables'. Nandanar earned his living by killing animals for leather used to make drums and gut for stringed musical instruments. According to his hagiography (sacred biography), Shiva ordered the priests of the Chidambaram temple to light a fire in front of the temple, through which Nandanar passed unscathed. His desire to see his lord being fulfilled, he disappeared under the foot of the dancing Shiva. Tiruppan Alvar longed to see Lord Vishnu at Srirangam. The god is said to have appeared in a dream to one of the Brahmana temple priests and instructed him to carry Tiruppan on his shoulder into the inner sanctum. Having seen his lord, he sang his last song and merged into the image of Vishnu. The stories of Nandanar's and Tiruppan's lives can be read in two ways. On the one hand, they suggest that the path of bhakti was open to all. On the other hand, the entry of these saints into their god's sanctum was no easy task. It required divine intervention and resulted in death.

Social status was supposed to be irrelevant for bhaktas. In the words of the Vaishnava saint Appar:

> Whoever they be
> wherever they be
> if they bow to Shiva
> Shiva who carries
> Ganga in his locks
> to me they are as gods—
> they may be
> lepers foul
> with rotting flesh
> or outcastes
> of the lowest breed
> they may even skin the cow

and eat its flesh—
if they but love Shiva
to them I bow
to them
I offer worship.[31]

Other bhakti saints too critiqued the idea of caste and deemed it irrelevant. Avvaiyar (there are three women saints who share this name) is described in hagiographies as the daughter of a Brahmana man and an 'untouchable' woman. This is one of her songs:

There are no castes, but two if you want me to tell—
The good men who help the poor in distress
The other, that will not so help
These are the low born.[32]

The Virashaiva or Lingayat sect originated in Karnataka in about the twelfth century. It was anti-Brahmana and anti-caste; it rejected the Vedas, sacrifices, rituals, and ideas of pollution. Intense devotion towards Shiva was everything. The popularity of the sect had a great deal to do with Basavanna or Basava. Born in a Brahmana family, he rebelled at a young age from Brahmanical ritualism, refusing to don the sacred thread when he was eight years old. Although the leadership of the Virashaivas was largely Brahmana, its social base comprised artisans, traders, and farmers. This community of bhaktas too was open to all, regardless of caste or gender.

As early Buddhism and Jainism had done several centuries previously, bhakti created religious communities with the potential for cutting across social boundaries and hierarchies. Inequality could not be eradicated but it could be transcended at the religious level. The debate on what really made a person superior or inferior continued in later centuries as well. These were not attempts to change society,

---

[31] *Tirumurai* 6, hymn 95, verse 10; cited in Vidya Dehejia, *Slaves of the Lord: The Path of the Tamil Saints*, New Delhi: Munshiram Manoharlal, 1988, p. 38.
[32] C. Rajagopalachari, *Avvaiyar: A Great Tamil Poetess*, Bombay: Bharatiya Vidya Bhavan, 1971, p. 9.

but the questioning did have an impact. Medieval bhakti saints such as Kabir and Nanak extended the questioning beyond social distinctions to the religious differences between Hindus and Muslims.

Critique and satire

There were also non-religious critiques of social inequality. A text called the *Vajrasuchi*, attributed to Ashvaghosha (its date and authorship are uncertain), directly challenges the varna system and uses statements from brahmanical texts such as the Vedas, *Manu Smriti*, and Mahabharata to refute the idea that Brahmanas are inherently superior to others.[33] It poses the question: 'Who is a Brahmana?' and concludes that brahmanhood is not fixed, nor is it based on birth. One who is free from selfishness and desire and is non-violent, truthful, self-controlled, and compassionate is a true Brahmana.

> A man is not Brahmana by birth or by lineage, or by ceremonies. Even if a Chandala possessed good conduct, he is a Brahmana....
> Even if a Shudra possesses good conduct and merit, he becomes a Brahmana, and if a Brahmana is without good actions, he is inferior to a Shudra.[34]

Not only does the *Vajrasuchi* reject distinctions based on birth and varna, it asserts that there is in fact, only one varna, not four. The only true distinction between people is the one based on character.

The fourth century *Panchatantra* (The Five Books or The Five Topics), with its lively animal stories, describes itself as a treatise on statecraft but can just as easily be read as advice for everyday life. Dharma is of little consequence here and the stories emphasize cunning, quick thinking, and killing before being killed. The cat Dadhikarna, devoted to austerities, learned in the Dharmashastra and outwardly full of compassion, is actually a fraud. Brahmanas are laughed at for their foolishness, wandering ascetics for their hypocrisy, and monks meet

---

[33]Sujit Kumar Mukhopadhyaya, *The Vajrasuchi of Asvaghosa*, Santiniketan: Visva-Bharati, [1950], 1960.
[34]*Vajrasuchi* 40, 43; Mukhopadhyaya, *The Vajrasuchi of Asvaghosa*, pp. 21–22.

a bloody end. Political satire, social critique, and humour go hand in hand. While upholding certain ideas of real politik, the *Panchatantra* is a socially and politically subversive text.

The most irreverent—and entertaining—social critiques come from literature. Although most Sanskrit playwrights were upper-class Brahmanas patronized by kings (some were kings themselves), and although they generally upheld the Brahmanical social order, they also sometimes voiced cynicism, irony, and critique, especially through characters such as the vidushaka (the hero's sidekick) and vita (the pander). Shudraka's fourth/fifth century *Mrichchhakatika* can be taken as an example. Charudatta, the hero of the play is a poor, noble, kind, generous Brahmana merchant, married to a dutiful wife named Dhuta; the heroine is a wealthy ganika (courtesan) named Vasantasena. The major themes of the play include poverty, Brahmanahood, love, and the status of the courtesan. The cast of characters include Sharvalika, a Brahmana adventurer, who uses his sacred thread as a measuring tape while committing a robbery in order to get money to redeem his lover, and a woman slave named Madanika. The courtesan's palace has a caged parrot who recites Vedic hymns like a Brahmana whose belly is filled with curds and rice. Two Chandalas who accompany Charudatta to the venue of his public execution declare that although they have been born in a Chandala family, they should not be called Chandalas; the real Chandalas are those who persecute virtuous men. The villain Shakara's slave Sthavaraka defiantly refuses to obey his master's order to kill Vasantasena, telling him that he was born a slave due to fate, but would rather die than acquire more demerit by committing a sinful deed.[35] The vita, a witness to this spirited exchange, observes philosophically that character is more important than birth.

A much more trenchant social critique occurs in the works of Kshemendra, a brilliant intellectual and writer who lived in Kashmir during the tenth and eleventh centuries. Kshemendra came from an affluent, well-connected family, but does not seem to have been part

---

[35]M. R. Kale, *The Mrichchhakatika of Śūdraka*, Bombay: Booksellers' Publishing Co., [1924], 1962, pp. 281–83.

of the court circle. He studied literary theory with Abhinavagupta, in addition to Vaishnava and Buddhist philosophy. He wrote in Sanskrit and his extant works include abridged versions of the Mahabharata and Ramayana, and verse works on the Buddha's former lives and the ten incarnations of Vishnu. He also wrote several prose satirical texts. The *Samayamatrika* (Little Mother by Compact) describes the adventures of a prostitute named Kankali who becomes the 'mother by compact' of another prostitute named Kalavati. Kshemendra's other satires are the *Narmamala* (Garland of Mirth), *Kalavilasa* (A Dalliance with Deceptions), and *Deshopadesha* (Advice from the Countryside).[36]

The world that Kshemendra depicts in his satires is a far cry from the beautiful, sophisticated, cultured world of Sanskrit kavya. He rips off the polished veneer and reveals the grim and grimy underbelly of society. The list of people he makes fun of is long and includes administrative officials, ascetics, monks, nuns, doctors, astrologers, gurus, widows, surgeons, merchants, singers and other entertainers, goldsmiths, lawyers, relatives, outcastes, villains, misers, courtesans (he really has it in for them), procuresses, parasitic libertines, students, old men's wives, poets, alchemists, gamblers, fools, gurus, devotees, lute players, doctors, retirees, scholars, scribes, and ascetics. Even the gods are not spared. Kshemendra seems to take on everyone—everyone except kings. Kshemendra was no advocate of social equality but his ruthless description of the hypocrisy, mendacity, and exploitativeness of people of substance is a powerful counter-narrative to the picture of the upper classes in the works of other writers.

◆

How were the many forms of inequality in ancient times perpetuated? Was there docile acquiescence or was there resistance and revolt? The guardians and enforcers of inequality included rulers, the upper classes,

---

[36]See A. N. D. Haksar (trans.), *Kshemendra, The Courtesan's Keeper: Samaya Mātrikā*, Gurgaon: Penguin Random House, 2014; and A. N. D. Haksar (trans.), *Kshemendra, Three Satires from Ancient Kashmir*, Gurgaon: Penguin Random House, 2011.

and upper castes. Social and political ideologies made inequality seem natural and unquestionable and helped to maintain the status quo. Coercion, violence, and the threat of violence also played important roles. Events comparable to the peasant rebellions in China or the slave revolts in the Roman empire did not happen in ancient India, or if they did, are not documented. But political texts do express fears of social upheaval and rebellion.

The most influential questioning of inequality occurred at the religious level. This did not take the form of a clarion call for social equality but an assertion of the potential of all to attain spiritual goals. These ideas led to the creation of new kinds of religious communities, such as the monastic and lay communities of the Jainas and Buddhists, and those based on devotion to a supreme deity in the bhakti-oriented religions. Social inequality could not be abolished, but it was questioned, and one could opt out of it by giving up worldly life or focusing on higher religious or soteriological aspirations.

A great deal has changed over the centuries, but inequality is still a fact of life. Religion continues to offer a refuge, but there are many other institutions and instruments that seek to establish and affirm the principle of equality. Constitutional provisions, the enactment of progressive laws, and social and political activism and mobilization are some of the ways in which the problems and realities of social inequality have been addressed in more recent times. But inequalities and prejudices, including those based on caste, still exist in India. So does the idea of untouchability, even though its practice is banned by law. Although caste is closely associated with Hinduism, its imprint can also be seen on religions that ostensibly have a more egalitarian social outlook. Dalit converts to Sikhism, Christianity, Islam, and Buddhism do not suddenly find themselves treated as equals by their co-religionists. Every day, newspapers and news channels carry stories of brutal caste oppression and violence, and of honour killings where young people who dare to love across caste boundaries are killed, usually by their own close kin. All around us, we see all too vividly how violence is woven into structures of inequality and oppression. Can we really believe it was otherwise in times gone by?

2

DESIRE AND DETACHMENT

A visit to any historical monument in India is likely to reveal a great deal of lovers' graffiti and engraving. The epistles are usually short and unimaginatively repetitive, sometimes embellished with very basic artwork in the shape of a heart pierced through with an arrow. Most would dismiss them as crude vandalism. But if analysed dispassionately, many questions arise: What exactly does the word 'love' mean in this 'love graffiti'? Does it represent a one-sided crush or infatuation, a deep-seated longing, a commitment, a memory of a past or continuing affair, or a yearning for one? Why are such declarations inscribed in these spaces? Perhaps they represent a desire to make a 'public' announcement of innermost feelings in a place where lovers can meet freely, without attracting social or parental censure, under the cloak of near anonymity.

In India, the oldest love engraving is found in the Jogimara cave, located in the midst of dense jungle on Ramgarh hill in the Surguja district of Chhattisgarh. Here is a five-line inscription in a Prakrit dialect engraved in Brahmi letters of the third or second century BCE. Translated, it reads:

> Sutanuka by name, a *devadasi*; the excellent among young men, Devadinna by name, the *rupadaksha*, loved her (*kamayitha*).[1]

Who was Sutanuka? In later times, the word devadasi referred to a temple woman, but this meaning is unlikely in such an early inscription. Who was Devadinna? Rupadaksha could mean a skilled sculptor, or a scribe, or an officer connected with coinage. But there are paintings on the cave roof, so maybe it means a painter or an artist. I used to

---

[1]H. Lüders, 'A List of Brāhmī Inscriptions from the Earliest Times to About A. D. 400', *Epigraphia Indica*, vol. 10, 1909–10, Appendix, No. 921, p. 93.

imagine the artist Devadinna sitting desolately in this cave, inscribing his love for his beloved. Sutanuka literally means 'one who has a slender or beautiful body' and I imagined that she lived up to her name. Now I wonder whether this inscription (written in the third person) could have been inscribed not by Devadinna, but by someone else—perhaps by a person who knew one or both the lovers, or had heard of their love. It could have been inscribed by Sutanuka herself, although a woman knowing how to write would have been unusual for that time. What sort of love was Devadinna and Sutanuka's? Was it infatuation? Had they been lovers? The inscription's past tense lends it a melancholy tone and hints at separation—was it due to falling out of love, family pressure, or death? So many romantic stories can be woven around this inscription but perhaps it is best to leave it alone, because the more it is analysed, the more its beauty and mystery are destroyed. This brief foray into dissecting this short inscription alerts us to the fact that it is not easy to decode ancient love.

Fast forward to the twenty-first century. Thanks to globalization and consumerism, Valentine's Day, a Western festival of uncertain origins, has become popular among India's urban youth. On 14 February, in the metropolitan cities, lovers indulge in public displays of affection, inviting a backlash by the moral police who argue that this sort of celebration of love is against Indian culture. But—and this is what we are in fact trying to understand in this book—what is 'Indian culture'? And what, indeed, is love? Can it be defined? Is it an emotion, a combination of emotions, or an experience that gives rise to many kinds of emotions? What exactly does it mean when lovers in different cultures, in different times say 'I love you' in different languages?

Love is not easily defined, yet it is one of the deepest and most profound emotions experienced by humans and other animal species. Neuroscience and biochemistry have not succeeded in completely explaining love nor in dispelling the aura of mystery around it. Sexual desire, often tied to romantic love, is a powerful source of pleasure which drives the propagation of life. Ideas and practices related to love and sex are not fixed or static; they vary enormously across cultures and time. It is not easy to understand the most intimate feelings and experiences of people who lived and loved centuries ago. We have to be satisfied with some tantalizing glimpses.

Desire and love feature in the oldest Indian texts. In a profound Rig Vedic hymn (often called the Nasadiya), kama (desire) and heat are part of the process of creation. Love is part of the plot in the ancient epics—recall the deep love between Rama and Sita in Valmiki's Ramayana, and the numerous romantic liaisons in the Mahabharata. But at the turn of the millennium, a new kind of expression made its appearance in Tamil, Prakrit, and Sanskrit literature, which gave an especially detailed treatment and celebration of love. Ancient poets wrote beautifully about the ecstasy of union and the despair of separation, but the best love poetry is about the latter.

In ancient Greece, eros meant love associated with sexual attraction, which could either be heterosexual or homosexual. Sappho, a poetess who lived in the seventh/sixth century BCE on the island of Lesbos, describes her intense jealousy as she watches a man talking intimately with the woman she loves:

> Chill sweat slides down my body,
> I shake, I turn greener than grass.
> I am neither living nor dead and cry from the narrow between.
>
> But endure, even this grief of love.[2]

As we shall see, many ancient Indian texts, too, speak frankly of erotic love. Some move beyond sexual and gender binaries. For instance, the theoretical works on pleasure recognize the 'third nature' and same-sex love. Ancient Indian mythology contains several episodes that involve androgyny, gender ambiguity, and sex change.[3] And yet, all the surviving literature written across the centuries deals with heterosexual love.

---

[2]Guy Davenport (trans.), *Archilochus, Sappho, Alkman: Three Lyric Poets of the Late Greek Bronze Age*, Berkeley: University of California Press, 1980, p. 85.

[3]See Robert P. Goldman, 'Transsexualism, Gender and Anxiety in Traditional India', *Journal of the American Oriental Society*, vol. 113, no. 3, July–September 1993, pp. 374–401.

Literature and art are the most eloquent windows into ideas of love in ancient India and fortunately for us, both are available in abundance. Exploring these expressions of love and longing requires sensitivity to their idiom and conventions. A great deal of flavour and nuance is lost while reading ancient love poetry in translation and reader reactions are bound to vary considerably. Some poems, such as those in the Sangam corpus, seem to connect with our modern sensibility in spite of the passage of centuries. The ornate Sanskrit verses on love may appear beautiful to some and contrived to others. The voluptuous yakshi sculptures that adorn many Buddhist sites may strike some as beautiful and sensuous and others as vulgar and inappropriate. The best approach is to immerse ourselves in the world of ancient words and images and to try to understand them in the context of their time, rather than ours.

Along with fine love poetry, sensuous art, and scholarly works on pleasure, ancient India also produced a strong tradition that emphasized the control and elimination of desire. One strand of this was directed towards the containment of women's sexuality and procreative potential within the framework of the patriarchal family. The second strand, which emphasized the elimination of desire, had philosophical and religious roots, and took the form of a powerful tradition of renunciation. In this tradition, the body, desires, and emotions were seen as sources and symptoms of bondage and suffering that had to be transcended in order to attain liberation from the cycle of life and death. This chapter discusses the many different attitudes towards love and sex in ancient India within the larger social and historical context.

Love and landscape in early Tamil poetry

The oldest Indian love poems are to be found in two anthologies of Tamil poems known as the *Ettutokai* (The Eight Collections) and *Pattupattu* (The Ten Songs) which are part of the Sangam corpus.[4] The poems have two broad themes—akam (pronounced 'aham', meaning

---

[4]As mentioned in Chapter 1, these poems were composed in the far south in the land known as Tamilakam, between the second/first centuries BCE and third/fourth centuries CE and were compiled much later.

inner) and puram (outer), referring respectively to love and war. Although modelled on old bardic songs, they are not folk songs. This is sophisticated poetry, following distinctive literary conventions. The anthologies include a total of 2,381 poems ascribed to 473 poets, 30 of whom were women. The poets came from cities and villages and had varied social and professional backgrounds. Their expressions of love and longing are remarkably beautiful and moving even after the passage of so many centuries, even in translation.[5] The poet does not speak through his or her own personal voice, but through the voice of characters such as the heroine, her friend, her foster mother, or the hero. The words used for love include kamam, inpam, and anpu.

A striking aspect of Tamil poetic theory is the idea of the five tinai or poetic settings, each named after a flower and associated with a specific situation and mood of love. The kurinchi or mountain landscape is the setting for poems about the union of lovers; palai, the desert or arid terrain, for separation; mullai, the pastoral or forest region, for patient waiting; neytal, the seashore, for pining and lamenting; and marutam, the riverine tracts, for jealousy, sulking, and quarrelling. In following tinai conventions, the Sangam poets did not merely create an evocative backdrop for their poems; they fused love with landscape.

The poems are often short and rely on understatement and suggestion to convey deep emotion. Some speak of the consternation caused by love. A man muses over how he is agitated by a young girl, as a jungle elephant is troubled by a little white snake with beautiful stripes on its body.[6] Another contrasts the joy of union with the grief of separation:

When my lover is by my side
I am happy
as a city
in the rapture of a carnival,

---

[5] For translations, see A. K. Ramanujan (trans.), *The Interior Landscape: Love Poems from a Classical Tamil Anthology*, Bloomingdale and London: Indiana University Press, 1975; George L. Hart, *Poets of the Tamil Anthologies: Ancient Poems of Love and War*, Princeton: Princeton University Press, 1979.

[6] Catti Natanar, Kuruntokai 119; Ramanujan, *The Interior Landscape*, p. 54.

and when he is gone
I grieve like a deserted house
in a little hamlet
of the wastelands

where the squirrel plays
in the front yard.⁷

The poets describe encounters between young girls and handsome men from the mountains. Sometimes only looks are exchanged; sometimes there is sex; sometimes we do not know exactly what transpired. Many poems speak of passion. This one speaks of the fear of love's waning:

Even if desire should cease,
man from where a great midnight rain beats down
with thunder and lightening
and makes a waterfall resound through a cave,
will the bond wear away
that links me to you?⁸

The *Gatha Sattasai*

If Tamil Sangam poems conjure images of tender love, those in the *Gatha Sattasai* (700 Verses in the Gatha Form) composed in Maharashtri Prakrit, express frank eroticism.⁹ The *Gatha* anthology is divided into seven sections, each consisting of about 100 couplets.¹⁰ The poems were mostly composed during the first four centuries of the Common Era. Although many have rural settings and characters, this is not folk poetry.

---

⁷Anilatu Munrilar, Kuruntokai 41; Ramanujan, *The Interior Landscape*, p. 38.
⁸Kapilar, Kuruntokai 42; Hart, *Poets of the Tamil Anthologies*, p. 56.
⁹These days, scholars usually prefer to use the term 'Middle Indic' rather than 'Prakrit'. I have retained the term that is likely to be more familiar to readers.
¹⁰For translations, see Arvind Krishna Mehrotra, *The Absent Traveller: Prākrit Love Poetry from the Gāthāsaptaśatī of Sātavāhana Hāla*, Delhi: Ravi Dayal, 1991, and other sources cited further on. For select translations and an excellent discussion, see Martha Ann Selby, *Grow Long, Blessed Night: Love Poems from Classical India*, New York: Oxford University Press, 2000.

It is poetry created by city poets for an audience of urban connoisseurs, including the royal court circle. The first and last poems in the *Gatha* are in praise of Shiva, but the rest are, by and large, non-religious.

References to the Vindhya mountains and the Tapi, Reva, and Godavari rivers indicate that the *Gatha* poets lived in western India. A Satavahana king name Hala is supposed to have composed some of the poems and compiled the anthology. One commentary lists 262 poets, including six or seven women. The poems circulated widely all over the subcontinent. Experts on Sanskrit poetics knew them well and considered them models of refined lyric poetry. Some of the Sanskrit poems of the seventh-century *Amaru-shataka* were directly based on them.

The themes include kings and nature, but most of the poems—especially the most memorable ones—are about lovers eager to get to their rendezvous. As in the Sangam poems, the natural landscape—riverbank, rice fields, village pond—plays a prominent role. The wide cast of characters includes young girls, wives, mature women, prostitutes, farmers, hunters, monks, and travellers. As in the Sangam poems, the poets speak through characters such as the lover, beloved, female messenger, and the beloved's friend. Most speak through a woman's voice. The poems talk of awkward young love, experienced mature love, and the love shared by old couples. They deal with the anticipation of union as well as the pain of separation. The women of these poems are sexually charged beings, eager to engage in passionate, often adulterous, love. Words for love and desire include kama, pemma (prema), and rao (raga).

The poems seem simple but are anything but that. The poets used a variety of poetic devices such as similes, metaphors, and double entendre. But their favourite device was something that the later Sanskrit experts on poetics called dhvani—suggestion or implied meaning. Martha Ann Selby has referred to the unique ambiguity of the *Gatha* poems as the 'poetics of anteriority'—that is, the meaning of the poem lies outside the words.[11] The meaning is often not immediately apparent; it has to be prised out. Sometimes it is elusive and opaque; sometimes a poem can

---

[11]Selby, *Grow Long, Blessed Night*, p. 84.

be interpreted in many different ways. Later commentaries can help, but their explanations are sometimes rather contrived. The *Gatha* poems are unlike any others. They are like puzzles that invite readers to decipher them by giving free rein to the imagination.

Consider the following poem. It is short and simple, erotic in its extreme understatement, creating the image of an intense encounter unfolding as it were in slow motion: two lovers, frozen, mesmerized, gazing into each other's eyes, prolonging their seemingly chance encounter:

> As the traveler, eyes raised,
> > Cupped hands filled with water, spreads
>
> His fingers and lets it run through,
> > She pouring it reduces the trickle.[12]

Many poems describe the joy and excitement of passionate lovemaking:

> Braids scattered,
> earrings and necklaces tossing about,
> a half-flying
> half-divine creature
> she mounts her
> beloved.[13]

There are poems of separation and longing.

> Fortunate are those women
> who see their beloved ones in dreams.
> But I get no sleep without him.
> Who then will dream a dream?[14]

Some poems talk frankly about adulterous liaisons. A woman tells her lover:

---

[12]*Gatha Sattasai* 161, Mehrotra, *The Absent Traveller*, p. 13.
[13]Andrew Schelling (trans. and selected), *The Cane Groves of Narmada River: Erotic Poems from Old India*, New Delhi: Aleph Book Company, [1998], 2017, p. 26.
[14]*Gatha Sattasai* 4.97; adapted from Radhagovinda Basak, trans. *The Prākrit Gāthā-Saptaśatī Compiled by Sātavāhana King Hāla*, Calcutta: Asiatic Society, 1971, p. 87.

It's spring in the hills
of Malaya
and Mother-in-law
bars me from leaving the house
She must know
the fragrant *ankota* tree
luring me out
to the one
death worth dying.[15]

Very different from poems of suppressed electric passion is the one that describes the weathered and withered love of a married couple who have been together for many long years:

Friends
have gone on before us
twisted stumps
stand alone in the desolate grove
Who would have thought youth could vanish?
or love
Have its roots cut?[16]

While these poems are easy enough to understand, others are more challenging. Take, for example, one of the most famous poems in the *Gatha* anthology:

Look,
    a still, quiet crane
    shines on a lotus leaf
    like a conch shell lying
    on a flawless emerald plate.[17]

---

[15] *Gatha Sattasai* 5.97; Schelling, *The Cane Groves of Narmada River*, p. 23.
[16] *Gatha Sattasai* 3.32; Schelling, *The Cane Groves of Narmada River*, p. 18.
[17] *Gatha Sattasai* 1.4; Selby, *Grow Long, Blessed Night*, p. 94. According to Mammata's commentary, the context of this poem is a woman and a lover walking along a riverbank. The woman suggests a deserted spot as a good place for a rendezvous. Or perhaps she is chiding her lover for lying and not showing up for an earlier meeting. Alternatively,

Love imagined in Sanskrit kavya

The Mahabharata and Ramayana, written in Sanskrit verse, talk of love and desire, including within the context of different marriage models—polyandry, polygyny, and monogamy.[18] Even though Rama ultimately chooses duty and reputation over love, he does love Sita. His father Dasharatha had four wives, he has only one. After Sita is abandoned in the forest, he does not remarry, and has a golden effigy of his wife by his side while performing sacrifices. The Mahabharata abounds in stories of romantic and sexual liaisons, some of which have a major impact on the story line. Shantanu, grandfather of Dhritarashtra and Pandu, first falls madly in love with Ganga and then with a fisherman's daughter Satyavati, due to which Bhishma takes a vow of life-long celibacy. Satyavati's son Vichitravirya dies sonless, so she asks the sage Vyasa (her son through a previous liaison) to father sons on Vichitravirya's wives Ambika and Ambalika. This was in accordance with the practice of niyoga (levirate), where a man's sexual rights over his wife could be delegated to a man of equal or superior status, for the sole purpose of producing heirs, to prevent the lineage from dying out.[19] Pandu and Dhritarashtra are the product of niyoga. Kunti's curiosity to try out a boon given by the sage Durvasa (that she could call on any god to impregnate her), leads to her bearing a child (Karna) out of wedlock. Kunti's subsequent unions with various gods enable Pandu to have sons—Yudhishthira, Arjuna, and Bhima. Pandu has been cursed that he will die if he has sex. One day he makes love to his wife Madri and this leads to his death.

---

going by the commentator Gangadharabhatta, the woman is telling him to fix his mind on a crane so that their lovemaking can be prolonged (Martha Ann Selby, 'Desire for Meaning: Providing Contexts for Prākrit Gāthās', *Journal of Asian Studies*, vol. 55, no. 1, February 1996, p. 90).

[18]Polygamy refers to marriage where a spouse has multiple partners. There are two types—polygyny is when a man has many wives, polyandry is when a woman has many husbands.

[19]On niyoga, see Kane, *History of Dharmaśāstra*, vol. 2, part 1, pp. 599–607. Niyoga was the subject of heated debate in Dharmashastra across the centuries. While *Manu Smriti* 9.57–70 discusses the practice, it does not approve of it and describes it as pashu-dharma (the dharma of beasts).

Mutual love is part of the relationship between Draupadi and her five Pandava husbands. Arjuna falls in love with Subhadra and kidnaps her with Krishna's approval. In the Mahabharata, sexual abstinence is not a necessary condition for asceticism or divinity. There are many stories of sages and gods whose austerities were disturbed by desire.

But the full flowering of literary expressions of love in Sanskrit occurred in poems and plays written from the early centuries CE onwards. Kavya means literature and includes poetry, prose, and drama.[20] Kings were major patrons, but literary connoisseurs and audiences included merchants, courtesans, and other urban groups. As for the Tamil and Prakrit poets, love was a favourite theme for the Sanskrit kavis (litterateurs) too. Sanskrit kavya, especially the mahakavya (long poems) and nataka (drama) made possible a more detailed treatment of love, expanding on the narrative element and the description of emotions. As tragedy is practically absent in Sanskrit kavya,[21] all love stories have a happy ending. Sanskrit allows enormous possibilities in the sequence of word arrangement, long and complicated compounds, synonyms, and puns. The beauty of all these, as well as the sounds, metre, rhythm, and alliteration are lost in translation. In fact, the artistry and skill of the Sanskrit poets may come across as awkward and stilted in English translations. The many Sanskrit words for love and passion include kama, prema, priti, anuraga, and sneha, all of which have different nuances.[22]

Almost all the surviving kavya works are by men. The only complete surviving kavya that seems to have been written by a woman is the *Kaumudimahotsava*, attributed to Vijjika, a Chalukya queen. Later works on poetics mention poetesses and cite some of their verses. A verse by the

---

[20] For good overviews of kavya, see Siegfried Lienhard, *A History of Classical Poetry: Sanskrit–Pali–Prakrit*, Wiesbaden: Otto Harrassowitz, 1984, Jan Gonda (gen. ed.), *A History of Indian Literature*, vol. 3, fasc. 1; A. K. Warder, *History of Indian Literature*, 8 vols., Delhi: Motilal Banarsidass, 1972–2011.

[21] The exception are two of Bhasa's plays, *Karnabhara* and *Urubhanga*.

[22] For an interesting discussion of the Sanskrit vocabulary of love, see Minoru Hara, 'Words for Love in Sanskrit', *Rivista degli studi orientali*, Nuova Serie, vol. 80, fasc. 1/4, Atti Del Convegno: 'Passioni ed Emozioni in India e in Tibet', Sapienza–Universita di Roma, 2007, pp. 81–106.

poetesss Shilabhattarika, talks regretfully about the waning of passion:

> He who was the stealer of my virginity is my husband now; those very same nights in the month of Chaitra have arrived; the same breezes fragrant with the smell of the *malati* flower are blowing through the *kadamba* tree; I am also the same old self. Still my heart is longing for stolen amorous sport under the cave creepers on the bank of the river Reva.[23]

The writing of poetry, prose, and drama was accompanied by works on poetics and dramaturgy, of which the *Natyashastra* is the earliest. Two important concepts that were important for the theoreticians as well as the kavis were rasa and bhava. The rasa theory was part of an aesthetic shared by literature, music, dance, and art. Rasa is the 'flavour', aesthetic experience of the audience, listener, or reader.[24] In plays, bhavas are the emotions simulated and portrayed by the actors. One of the eight rasas was the sensitive shringara rasa and its corresponding bhava was rati (love). Shringara rasa is of two types—sambhoga (of union) and vipralambha (separation).

The kavis usually celebrated the love affairs of high-born elites, especially kings.[25] The king was expected to be a lover par excellence, the most fitting subject for the experience and expression of love. It is only when his sexual indulgence became excessive and detrimental to his performing royal duties that it was considered a vice. The four royal vices (vyasanas) mentioned in political treatises and elsewhere

---

[23] After J. B. Chaudhari, *Sanskrit Poetesses: Contributions of Women to Sanskrit Literature*, vol. 2, Part A, Calcutta: self-published, 1941, verse 82. On Sanskrit poetesses, also see Shalini Shah, *Love, Eroticism and Female Sexuality in Classical Sanskrit Literature: Seventh-Thirteenth Century*, New Delhi: Manohar, 2009, pp. 166–75.

[24] The eight rasas are the sensitive shringara rasa associated with love; the comic hasya rasa associated with humour; the compassionate karuna rasa associated with grief; the furious raudra rasa associated with anger; the heroic vira rasa associated with energy; the apprehensive bhayanaka rasa associated with fear; the horrific bibhatsa rasa associated with disgust; and the marvellous adbhuta rasa associated with astonishment.

[25] See Daud Ali, *Courtly Culture and Political Life in Early Medieval India*, Cambridge: Cambridge University Press, 2004.

are drinking, hunting, gambling, and womanizing, all of which were considered legitimate in moderate doses, but destructive in excess.

It is impossible to give a comprehensive treatment of love in Sanskrit kavya, so we will focus here on Kalidasa, one of the greatest Sanskrit poets. Kalidasa lived in the fourth/fifth century and was probably patronized by one of the Gupta kings. He was one of the foremost exponents of the western Indian Vaidarbha literary style, noted for its clarity and mellifluous flow. His works include three plays (*Abhijnanashakuntala*, *Vikramorvashiya*, and *Malavikagnimitra*) and three long poems (*Raghuvamsha*, *Meghaduta*, and *Kumarasambhava*).[26] Kalidasa is known for his masterly descriptions of love and nature and his ability to combine the two. Although the two works where kings are shown as besotted with a love interest are *Malavikagnimitra* and *Vikramorvashiya*, we will look at three other works in which love features in more interesting and profound ways—*Abhijnanashakuntala*, *Meghaduta*, and *Kumarasambhava*.

The *Abhijnanashakuntala* (The Recognition of Shakuntala) is a seven-act play that tells the story of Shakuntala and King Dushyanta of the Puru lineage. Shakuntala is the daughter of the nymph Menaka and sage Vishvamitra, but is adopted by the sage Kanva and grows up in his hermitage in the forest.[27] The play focuses on the conflict between love and duty, and between the values of the court and the forest hermitage. Dushyanta arrives on the outskirts of Kanva's ashrama while hunting. He and Shakuntala see each other and are smitten. There is much that we will recognize in Kalidasa's description of their state of being 'in love'— intense feelings of pain, inflamed and feverish bodies, becoming thin and wasting away, pining, feeling that one will die, obsessive thoughts about the beloved, sleeplessness, and yearning for a glimpse of the beloved.

Although there are some similarities between Dushyanta and Shakuntala's state, there are also differences. Dushyanta is a worldly man, experienced in love. Shakuntala is a young, innocent girl, brought

---

[26] According to some scholars, the *Ritusamhara* was not written by Kalidasa.
[27] For the text and translation of the *Abhijñānaśākuntala*, see C. R. Devadhar, *Works of Kālidāsa*, vol. 1, Delhi: Motilal Banarsidass, [1966], 2005.

Fig. 2.1: 'Shakuntala writing love letter to Dushyanta', late nineteenth century oleograph by Raja Ravi Varma

up among the trees and deer in Kanva's hermitage. Dushyanta spends a great deal of time musing about Shakuntala's physical beauty, feature by feature, limb by limb. But she focuses on her own feelings, which she does not quite understand, because this is the first time she is in love. She shyly scratches a simple love letter to Dushyanta on a leaf with her nails. [Fig. 2.1] He declares his love boldly, inviting her to marry him through the gandharva rite of a mutual declaration of love. She does not want to overstep the bounds of modesty and hesitates to reciprocate without her father's permission. Shakuntala's friends Priyamvada and Anasuya too are worried that Shakuntala may end up being one more plaything in the king's harem, but he vows that this will not happen. When the lovers are left alone, Dushyanta lifts Shakuntala's face to kiss her lips, but they are interrupted by an offstage call. Dushyanta is left despondent:

> Why didn't I kiss her face
> as it bent near my shoulder,
> her fingers shielding lips
> that stammered lovely warning?[28]

[28] *Abhijnanashakuntala* 3.24; Barbara Stoler Miller (trans.), *Theatre of Memory: Plays of*

As in the Hindi films of the 1960s and 1970s, kissing—let alone anything more explicit—was not to be shown in Sanskrit drama.

Dushyanta and Shakuntala are married by the gandharva rite and the king goes off to the city, leaving her his ring as a token of his love. But she is cursed by a bad-tempered visiting sage that the one she is thinking of will not remember her. On her way to the city to meet her husband, the ring floats away in a river as she is washing her hands. When Shakuntala arrives in court (pregnant to boot), the king does not remember her and spurns her. She goes off to the abode of the apsaras (celestial nymphs), where she gives birth to a son, the great king Bharata. (This is the Bharata after whom the land of Bharatavarsha is named.) The royal ring is swallowed by a fish that is caught by a fisherman and ultimately reaches the royal court. On seeing it, the king remembers everything, and he is eventually united with his wife and son.

The *Meghaduta* (Cloud Messenger) is a poem consisting of a little over 100 verses. A yaksha is banished from his lord Kubera's court for a year due to dereliction of duty and is separated for the first time from his beloved wife. He is exiled in Ramagiri (somewhere in the south) and she lives in Alaka (somewhere in the north). As the rainy season sets in, the yaksha cannot bear the pain of separation, and seeing a cloud in the sky, he begs for help. He asks the cloud to carry his message of love to his beloved, to describe his state (hot, emaciated, miserable, tormented) and his intense love and yearning, and to bring back the yakshi's reply, along with a token of her love. The poem contains a beautiful, detailed description of the route the cloud should follow. It also contains stirring descriptions of the yaksha's lovelorn state and how he imagines his beloved to be similarly suffering. When the cloud reaches the window of his house, the yaksha suggests:

> At that time, O cloud, if my beloved should be asleep,
> be patient for a watch, attending on her without thundering;

Kālidāsa, Delhi: Motilal Banarsidass [1984], 1999, p. 119. There are several good parallel text editions of Kalidasa's works which give the Sanskrit text and English translation of Kalidasa's works. These include those by M. R. Kale and C. R. Devadhar, as well as the more recent publications in the Clay and Murthy library series.

When with difficulty she may have found me, her lover, in a dream,
let not her close embrace suddenly have the knot of its creeper-like
arms fall from my neck.[29]

The *Meghaduta* set off a fashion of messenger love poems. Many other poets tried their hand at them, but it was difficult to surpass the superb literary quality of Kalidasa's work.

Kumarasambhava (Birth of Kumara) was probably Kalidasa's last work. This long poem, consisting of eight cantos, has exquisite descriptions of the seasons, nature, the gods, and above all, the love between Shiva and Parvati. The demon Taraka is tormenting the gods and Brahma informs them that he can only be defeated by the son of Shiva and Parvati. The great sage Narada has prophesied that Parvati, daughter of Himalaya, will marry Shiva. She has gone to his abode on Mount Kailasa, accompanied by two friends, in order to serve him. But Shiva is in mourning due to the recent death of his wife Sati. He is practising fierce asceticism and shows no interest whatsoever in Parvati. How will they produce a son? The gods rope in Kamadeva, the god of love, but just as he is about to shoot his arrow at the meditating Shiva, the latter opens his fiery third eye which reduces Kamadeva to smouldering ashes. The plan has flopped. [Fig. 2.2] Parvati goes off to the forest and devotes herself to incredibly difficult ascetic practices in order to attain powers that she hopes will one day help her win Shiva.

Parvati is Kalidasa's strongest heroine. She is shy and inexperienced, but strong and determined. She has decided that Shiva is the one for her; she will have no other. Shiva visits her, disguised as a Brahmana ascetic; he is impressed and pleased by the rigour of her asceticism. He proposes marriage. She tells him to ask her parents, Himalaya and Mena, who accept the proposal. As with his other heroines, Kalidasa describes Parvati's physical beauty in great detail, feature by feature: her beautiful legs, thighs, hips, navel, waist, breasts, arms, hands, neck, face, smile, voice, glance, eyebrows. But he also humanizes the gods by describing their emotions. Shiva passes the three days leading up to the marriage

---

[29] A. K. Warder (trans.), *Indian Kāvya Literature*, vol. 3, Delhi: Motilal Banarsidass, [1977], 1990, p. 147.

Fig. 2.2: Shiva enraged by Parvati's interruption of his meditation, Guler, Himachal Pradesh, early nineteenth century

in great restlessness, longing for union with Parvati. Kalidasa describes the groom's marriage procession, the bride's friends joking with the shy bride. He describes how on the wedding night, Shiva tries to make his bride feel at ease by making small talk. Parvati's friends have given her some tips, but in her consternation, she has forgotten them all.

> In their kissing, she wouldn't let
> her lower lip be drunk.
> In his merciless embraces
> her hands hung at her side.
> Though love was painful for her
> and she was lacking in response,
> making love to his wife
> was dear to her Lord.[30]

After a month, Shiva and Parvati return to Mount Kailasa. A hundred or more seasons passed in mutual ecstasy.

Kalidasa's description of the lovemaking of Shiva and Parvati became the subject of a long-standing debate. While the Kashmiri rhetorician Mammata Bhatta considered it highly inappropriate to describe the lovemaking of deities in such a graphic manner, the brilliant aesthetician Anandavardhana (also of Kashmir) asserted that any impropriety was cancelled out by Kalidasa's poetic genius.

The art of pleasure

Apart from literature, there was also serious scholarship on sex and pleasure. Sexual organs and bodily fluids were discussed in medical treatises. In ancient Ayurveda, conception was seen as the result of the union between male semen and the remnants of female menstrual discharge. According to this medical theory, natural urges, including sexual ones, should not be suppressed because suppression could lead to disease.

Sanskrit texts list three purusharthas (goals of human life)—dharma (social duty), artha (material gain), and kama (sensual pleasure). Later, a fourth one—moksha—was added. Just as there were experts who wrote treatises on dharma and artha, there was a long tradition of the study of sensual pleasure. Vatsyayana's *Kamasutra*, written in a prose sutra

---

[30]*Kumarasambhava* 8.8; David Smith (trans.), *The Birth of Kumāra by Kālidāsa*, (Clay Sanskrit Library, 2005), p. 301.

(aphoristic) style, with some verses, is the oldest book on the subject in India.[31] Its frank and matter-of-fact discussion of sex has given it an international reputation. This text is famous for its description of various sexual positions (some requiring extraordinary bodily contortions), but there is actually much more to it.

Vatsyayana must have lived somewhere in North India in the third or fourth century CE. His *Kamasutra* is held up by some as proof that ancient Indians were not puritanical; that they were full-blooded folk who practised sex with uninhibited, lusty abandon combined with acrobatic skill. Actually, the *Kamasutra* does not describe the sex life of ancient Indians. It reflects neither popular ideas nor those of the intelligentsia at large. It contains the ideas of a very specific type of intellectual—an expert on pleasure.

The *Kamasutra* is about kama (sensual pleasure), in which samprayoga (sex) has a central place. Vatsyayana talks about the sixty-four kalas (arts) that should be studied along with the *Kamasutra*; these include singing, playing musical instruments, dancing, painting, flower arrangement, preparing wines, telling jokes and riddles, poetic improvisation, dicing, etiquette, cultivation of athletic skills, cooking, needlework, weaving, reading aloud, staging plays, and dialogue.

The *Kamasutra* describes itself as part of an older tradition of writing on the subject. It refers to many points of scholarly debate—for instance, on when it was permissible for a man to seduce other men's wives, techniques of lovemaking, whether virgins should make sexual advances, and whether or not women experience sexual climax. Vatsyayana mentions various experts on such issues, cites their views, and agrees or disagrees with them.

Vatsyayana piously acknowledges the importance of dharma and artha, and says that a man should study the *Kamasutra* as long as it does not interfere with the time he devotes to dharma and artha. Perhaps he was paying lip service to convention in order to assert the respectability

---

[31]For an English translation, see Sudhir Kakar and Wendy Doniger, *Kamasutra: A New Complete Translation of the Sanskrit Text with Excerpts from the Sanskrit Jayamangala Commentary of Yashodhara Indrapada, the Hindi Jaya Commentary of Devadatta Shastri, and Explanatory Notes*, Oxford: Oxford University Press, 2002.

of his work. But he also gives a spirited defence of kama and refutes those intellectuals who disapproved of pleasure. Although he adds a caveat about the dangers of overindulgence in pleasures, he justifies them, stating that like dharma and artha, they are a means of sustaining the body. Vatsyayana observes that unlike sex in the animal world, sex among men and women requires a method. The need for a method is the raison d'être of the *Kamasutra*.

According to Vatsyayana, one can learn about pleasure by reading the *Kamasutra* and by associating with the nagaraka. The nagaraka is a man about town, an urbane sophisticated connoisseur. His family or social background are not mentioned; he has no job or occupation except the pursuit of pleasure. From his lifestyle, he seems to be upper class, educated, and financially well-off. The nagaraka's female counterpart is the ganika, who figures in Sanskrit kavya as a sophisticated courtesan, learned in the various arts; she is different from the veshya, the ordinary prostitute.

Although much of the *Kamasutra* is addressed to men, Vatsyayana recognizes the possibility of women reading, in fact, studying his work. Rebutting those experts who held that it was pointless teaching women about the subject because they were too stupid to grasp anything, Vatsyayana points out that women understood the practice of kama. He refers to ganikas and the daughters of kings and ministers, whose understanding had been sharpened by the text. He recommends that a woman could study the *Kamasutra* before she reached the prime of youth, and could continue to do so even after she was married, if her husband so wished. Book 3 of the *Kamasutra* gives advice to virgins trying to get husbands, Book 4 offers instructions to wives, and Book 6 is said to have been commissioned by the courtesans of Pataliputra, supposedly for their own use. So, women are part of Vatsyayana's audience.

Many statements about virtuous wives in the *Kamasutra* sound as though they are right out of the *Manu Smriti*. For instance, Vatsyayana urges a wife to treat her husband like a god, to wash his feet when welcoming him home, to seek his permission for everything, and to offer him complete obedience. In the morning, she should wake up before him; at night, she should lie down after him; she should never wake him from sleep. She should take good care of the household, supervise servants, maintain accounts, and serve her in-laws. She should make herself attractive to her husband for sex and should not chide him too much for his infidelities. When her husband was away, she should stay at home and fast.

And yet, there is a world of difference in the overall perspectives of Dharmashastra and Kamashastra (the study of pleasure). In Dharmashastra, sex is primarily for the sake of procreation within marriage, especially for the production of sons, who are considered necessary for the continuation of the family line. Men can have many wives, but a woman should have only one husband and must remain faithful to him even after his death. Adultery is a crime and there is a very close monitoring and restriction of women's sexual activity. Vatsyayana has very different views on life, love, and sex. Pleasure, not marriage, is centre stage. He describes the gandharva marriage—one based on mutual love—as the best. He warns the nagaraka that it is dangerous to enter the king's harem, but if he cannot resist, tells him how to go about doing so. He suggests techniques of seducing married women. Much in the *Kamasutra* that would have been considered routine by the kama experts would have been considered highly inappropriate and transgressive by the experts on dharma and politics. But a shastra on pleasure was obliged to give importance to pleasure, just as Dharmashastra and Arthashastra were obliged to give primacy to dharma and artha respectively.

Like other ancient Indian intellectuals, Vatsyayana was fond of classification. In the *Kamasutra*, men and women are sometimes spoken of in generic terms but they are also classified according to the size of their sexual organs and their different styles of lovemaking. There are three types of men—hare, bull, and stallion; and three types of women—doe, mare, and elephant cow. Vatsyayana discusses various lovemaking techniques and sexual positions. Although he refers without disapproval to times when a woman gets on top in the throes of passion, the normal position according to him is where the man is on top. He discusses aphrodisiacs, sex tools, orgies, ways of increasing the size of the sexual organ, and the use of spells and magic to rekindle or prolong passion.

Some aspects of the *Kamasutra* may strike the modern reader as quite progressive. Vatsyayana considers women as active agents with sexual desires and needs which must be understood by men in order to enjoy mutual pleasure. After marriage, he advises a husband not to approach his wife sexually for three nights and to use this time to understand her feelings, win her trust, arouse her love, and obtain her consent. He urges men to be gentle in their lovemaking and alerts them to the importance of reading a woman's signals accurately. He gives arguments to prove that there is no difference between men and women in their ability to orgasm, and urges men to ensure that their partners orgasm before they do. In this respect, Vatsyayana anticipated the discoveries of modern sexologists by many centuries. Ancient Chinese sex manuals also urge men to ensure that their female partner achieves orgasm; but the reason had nothing to do with giving primacy to a woman's pleasure. It had to do with a belief that men and women had a ching or refined essence which was contained in concentrated form in their sexual fluids emitted at the time of orgasm. The man was advised not to ejaculate, at least not completely, in order to retain his ching, but to help his female partner orgasm in order to absorb hers.[32]

Vatsyayana explains women's point of view. He quotes them using direct speech on various points (unlike in Sanskrit drama, here they speak Sanskrit). He discusses the reasons why women are unfaithful, explains to a male seducer why a woman he desires may not want to commit adultery (she may be devoted to her husband!). He warns that if a man uses force with a woman, she will leave him and hate men and sex for the rest of her life. At the same time, there are aspects of the *Kamasutra* that would, by today's standards, be considered as sexual assault, violence, and exploitation. These will be discussed in Chapter 4.

Although the *Kamasutra*'s main focus is on heterosexual sex, it does discuss transgenderism and homosexuality. Apart from men and women, Vatsyayana refers to the tritiya prakriti (third nature). He talks of two types of the third nature—one in the form of a woman, the other in

---

[32]See Paul Rakita Goldin, *The Culture of Sex in Ancient China*, Honolulu: University of Hawai'i Press, 2002, pp. 6–7.

the form of a man. The former type imitates a woman's attire, manners, deportment, feelings, speech, and delicacy. The latter type earns her living as a masseur and conceals her feelings when she desires a man.

Both of these are men who desire men and Vatsyayana uses the feminine pronoun 'she' for them. He gives a long description of male oral sex in the context of men who care for and pleasure each other. But he disapproves of lesbianism and describes women performing oral sex on one each other as a practice mainly of women living in distant lands.

Although the *Kamasutra* contains a great deal of advice on pleasure, Vatsyayana is aware of the limits of his teaching.

> The territory of the texts extends
> only so far as men have dull appetites;
> but when the wheel of sexual ecstasy is in full motion,
> there is no textbook at all, and no order.[33]

Vatsyayana states at the end of the *Kamasutra* that he had composed this text in chastity and in the highest meditation, for the sake of worldly life, not for the sake of passion. In the Indian tradition, control over the senses is considered an important means of attaining all kinds of goals. So it is not surprising that Vatsyayana tells us that there is a method to sensual pleasure, and that enjoying it does not mean giving free rein to hedonistic impulses. The *Kamasutra* is the best-known Sanskrit text on pleasure, but it is not the only one. There were others such as the *Nagarasarvasva* (written sometime between the tenth and fourteenth centuries), *Ratirahasya* (dated to before the thirteenth century), *Panchasayika* (fourteenth century), and *Anangaranga* (sixteenth century). These later texts resemble sex manuals.

Some of the issues discussed by the pleasure experts were the subject of debates in a wider arena. For instance, in the Anushasana Parva of the Mahabharata, Yudhishthira asks Bhishma who enjoys sex more—men or women? In response, Bhishma narrates the story of King Bhangashvana who was turned into a woman due to Indra's anger. Later, when Indra offers to turn her back into a man, she refuses.

---

[33]*Kamasutra* 2.2.31; Doniger and Kakar, *Kamasutra*, p. 42.

Ancient India: Culture of Contradictions

The reason? She tells him that she had experienced greater sexual pleasure as a woman than she ever had as a man. This is reminiscent of the Greek legend of Tiresias, who was turned into a woman due to Goddess Hera's curse. Summoned to give testimony in a debate between Zeus and Hera on whether men or women experience greater sexual pleasure, he stated that it was women. Hera was so annoyed by this that she struck Tiresias blind. Zeus, on the other hand, rewarded him with the gifts of prophecy and long life. The comparison between male and female sexual pleasure was clearly a topic of considerable interest across cultures, across time.

The conquest of desire

We have already noted the importance of the 'renunciatory turn' of the sixth/fifth century BCE. The life stories of the Buddha and Mahavira describe them as initially leading a life of pleasure and comfort, as well as familial affection. They marry and enter a householder's life. At some point, after experiencing an existential crisis, they give all this up and move from home to homelessness in search of truth. The conquest of desire was central to their quest and to the solution they offered.[34]

In biographies of the Buddha, the evil god Mara launches a full-fledged attack on the meditating Siddhartha as he sits under the Bodhi tree, on the verge of enlightenment. Mara is accompanied by an army of fierce and hideous fiends. The fact that he is sometimes armed with a colourful bow and flower arrows, and that his daughters are pleasure, love, and desire, indicate that the Mara of Buddhist legend is none other than Kamadeva, the god of love. This episode is frequently depicted in relief sculpture at early Buddhist sites and represents the conflict between enlightenment and desire in a dramatic form. [Fig. 2.3]

---

[34]For good introductions to early Buddhism, see Rupert Gethin, *The Foundations of Buddhism*, Oxford and New York: Oxford University Press, 1998; Peter Harvey, *An Introduction to Buddhism: Teachings, History and Practices*, Cambridge: Cambridge University Press, [1990], 2012. On Jainism, see Padmanabh S. Jaini, *The Jaina Path of Purification*, Delhi: Motilal Banarsidass, 1979; Paul Dundas, *The Jainas*, London and New York: Routledge, 1992.

Fig. 2.3: Mara attacks Siddhartha as the latter calls on the earth as witness, schist, Gandhara

The core of the Buddha's doctrine is expressed in the Four Noble Truths: there is suffering (dukkha); it has a cause (samudaya); it can be suppressed (nirodha); and the way to achieve this and to attain liberation is following the Eight-fold Path (magga) consisting of right view, intention, speech, action, livelihood, effort, mindfulness, and concentration. The reasons for suffering include desire, attachment, greed, pride, aversion, and ignorance. Buddhism accepts the idea of transmigration and rebirth but rejects the idea of the atman. The ultimate goal of the teaching of the Jaina saints too is the attainment of nirvana or liberation. Nirvana (it literally means blowing out, dying out, or extinction) does not mean physical death; it refers to the extinction of desire, attachment, greed, hatred, ignorance, and the sense of I-ness, and breaking free from the cycle of birth and death. [Fig 2.4]

Jaina philosophy conceives of an infinite number of jivas (sentient essences, life monads, or souls) whose original state is one of perfection and omniscience. In Jaina philosophy, karma is considered as material. Karma particles are attracted towards the jiva due to its association with the passions, desire, and hatred. So desire is a reason for the jiva's state of bondage. Liberation requires stoppage of the influx of fresh karma particles towards the jiva and the shedding of already accumulated karma particles. This can be achieved through a transformation of consciousness and conduct, till the jiva is restored to its original state of perfection.

Thus, the suppression, elimination, and ultimate transcending of desire of all kinds, including sexual desire, was part of the basic philosophy of Buddhism and Jainism. It was not just sexual acts, sexual desires and thoughts too had to be eliminated. These concerns are reflected in the rule of celibacy for members of the sangha and chastity for the laity.

Fig. 2.4: Tirthankara Parshvanatha, sandstone, Uttar Pradesh, c. sixth century CE

In Jainism, the great vows (mahavratas) for monks have their counterparts in the lesser vows (anuvratas) for the laity. [Fig. 2.5] The first three vows for the latter—non-violence (ahimsa), truth (satya), and non-stealing (asteya)—are the same as those for members of the sangha, but the last two—celibacy (brahmacharya) and non-possession (aparigraha)—are replaced by chastity and limiting one's wants. In early Buddhism, sexual intercourse, killing living beings, theft, and false proclamation of superhuman powers were considered the most serious offences that could be committed by a monk or nun. According to the Pali Vinaya Pitaka, they were parajika offences, that is, extremely serious offences which merited expulsion from the monastic order.

Fig. 2.5: Jaina monk walking along a riverbank, ink and colour on paper by Basavana, c. 1600

Buddhist texts discuss the nitty-gritty of managing sexual urges in graphic detail.[35] Treatises for novices discuss masturbation and nocturnal emissions. The latter was not a cause for punishment but it was emphasized that enlightened monks go to sleep in a mindful state and do not emit semen in their sleep. Nuns too were recognized as having sexual urges, and punishments were laid down for nuns who sought to pleasure themselves or other women. And yet, for pragmatic reasons, monastic communities did not adopt a zero-tolerance approach towards sexual transgressions. Early Buddhist texts tell the story of a monk named Nandika who was seduced by a woman while meditating in the forest. He was stricken with remorse and immediately went to the Buddha and confessed. In one version of the story, he is exiled. But in another, the Buddha says that because Nandika was repentant and had confessed, this was not an offence warranting expulsion, and that this verdict should form a precedent for similar cases in the future. The story shows that the rule-makers grappled with the problem of monastic desire. They recognized that not all monks were able to live up to the highest standards of conduct and conceded that in certain situations, rather than throwing them out of the sangha, they should be given a second chance. In Nandika's case, it could be argued that it was a sensible decision, because he is said to have ultimately attained enlightenment.

Renunciation seems to have been incorporated into the Brahmanical tradition as a response to discussions within Brahmanical circles as well as to Jainism and Buddhism. It was built into the image of the ideal Brahmana and incorporated into the third and fourth stages of the model of the four ashramas or life stages. The sannyasi was supposed to avoid injuring creatures through thought, word, or action and was to stay in one place during the monsoon (such details suggest the influence of Jainism and Buddhism). The brahmacharya and sannyasa life stages were associated with celibacy. But in Dharmashastra, it was

---

[35] J. Duncan M. Derrett, 'Monastic Masturbation in Pāli Buddhist Texts', *Journal of the History of Sexuality*, vol. 15, no. 1, January 2006, pp. 1–13.

the householder stage that was considered the most important.[36] The idea of vanaprastha soon faded away and sannyasa was never considered obligatory. So although the Brahmanical tradition incorporated the idea of renunciation, this incorporation was never complete or unequivocal.

This is clear from the Mahabharata. The epic talks in many places about the goal of heaven, but it also talks about moksha-dharma. It puts forward two alternative paths—the pravritti marga and nivritti marga. The former involves embracing life and its joys and pleasures. The latter rejects worldly life and pleasures and involves leading a life of abstention and contemplation in order to attain moksha. Yudhishthira, who epitomizes dharma and kingship, is torn between these two paths and has to be repeatedly cajoled to stay on track and fulfil his duties as king.

The Bhagavad Gita contains one of the most powerful expressions of the Brahmanical tradition's engagement with renunciation. As mentioned in Chapter 1, its idea of desireless action emphasizes the eternal nature of the atman (self) and the importance of following one's varna-dharma. The ideal state is one of equanimity, beyond desire and attachment, but this does not require giving up one's worldly life, because, as the Bhagavad Gita states, it is not actions but the fruits of action that should be renounced.

> Renunciation indeed, O Arjuna, is difficult to attain without yoga; the sage who is disciplined in yoga quickly attains Brahman.
>
> He who is devoted to yoga, whose self is purified, whose self is subdued, whose senses are conquered, whose self has become the self of all beings, is not tainted even when acting.[37]

This was a radical reinterpretation of renunciation. Provided one attained a state of complete detachment and self-control, one could be a renouncer while living in the world and performing one's social duties.

---

[36]Patrick Olivelle (ed.), *Gṛhastha: The Householder in Ancient Indian Religious Culture*, New Delhi: Oxford University Press, 2019.
[37]Bhagavad Gita 5.6–7; Sargeant, *The Bhagavad Gītā*, pp. 82–83.

The conflicts between the life of the householder and renouncer, and between desire and detachment were debated vigorously over the centuries.

The sensuous and sensual in religion and art

In sharp contrast to the austere world of religious texts, the religious monuments of ancient India usually throng with the joy and exuberance of human life. According to the renowned art historian Vidya Dehejia,

Fig. 2.6: Mithuna couple, terracotta, Uttar Pradesh, first–second century CE

'premodern India's attitude of acceptance—indeed, celebration—of the sensuous bodily form, both sacred and profane, is unparalleled.'[38] The sensuous refers to that which is aesthetically pleasing to the senses, the sensual to that which is related to amorous or sexual pleasures, while the erotic has stronger and more direct connections with sexual desire.

Early Buddhist sites such as Sanchi, Amaravati, and Nagarjunakonda have many relief sculptures of amorous couples, referred to by art historians as mithuna figures. [Fig. 2.6] These images are not connected specifically with Buddhism but were part of a larger stratum of Indian ideas associated with auspiciousness and beauty. Their presence in a sacred space was considered entirely appropriate by the planners, artists, donors, and monks. Apart from amorous couples, there are sensuous female figures, identified as yakshis or shalabhanjikas, entwining their limbs around the sinuous trunks of trees and clinging to their branches.

---

[38]Vidya Dehejia, *The Body Adorned: Dissolving Boundaries Between Sacred and Profane in India's Art*, Ahmedabad: Mapin, 2009, p. 24. Read this book for a wonderful exploration and explication of this issue. For a detailed discussion of ancient erotic art, see Devangana Desai, *Erotic Sculpture of India: A Socio-Cultural Study*, New Delhi: Tata McGraw Hill, 1975.

[Fig. 2.7] They are connected with the idea of dohada, which literally refers to the cravings of a pregnant woman, but in this context, refers to the idea that a tree longs for the touch of a beautiful woman which will enable it to flower. The woman-and-tree motif thus fuses the feminine with nature, beauty, and fertility.

Relief sculptures of men and women drinking and having a good time are found in Gandhara and Mathura art. There are many ancient images of lovers [Fig. 2.8]. Mithuna couples are depicted on the doorways of shrines of all religious denominations. But what about the depictions of graphic sex (maithuna), for instance, terracotta plaques found at sites such as Chandraketugarh, Tamluk, and Kaushambi which show couples having sex, even orgies? Did such plaques have a ritual significance? Is this ancient pornography used for sexual arousal and stimulation? Or were they matter-of-fact renderings of a universal, mundane human activity?

The non-discerning viewer of ancient Indian art may think that most of the human figures—especially the voluptuous women—are nude. As a matter of fact, diaphanous robes often give an *illusion* of nudity. (The Jaina Tirthankaras are an exception, as they are supposed to be naked, to reflect their complete renunciation.) The idealized human body in ancient sculpture, as pointed out by Dehejia, is the body adorned, adorned with clothes and ornaments. It should also be remembered that the icons of deities that were enshrined in the sanctum of temples were further embellished with clothing and ornaments as part of temple rituals. But there is no doubt that bodies in ancient art—whether of ordinary men and women, gods and goddesses, demigods, even saints—are usually beautiful and very often sensuous. [Figs. 2.9, 2.10, 2.11] (The fierce Tantric goddesses are exceptions.) In ancient art and texts, physical beauty is seen as a concomitant of political power (kings) as well as spiritual power (of deities, Buddhas, bodhisattvas, and Tirthankaras).[39] However, the idealized bodily forms in ancient Indian art should not be seen as direct reflections of what ordinary people actually looked like.

---

[39]See Dehejia, *The Body Adorned*, Chap. 2.

Ancient India: Culture of Contradictions

Fig. 2.7: Chanda yakshi, sandstone, Bharhut

Fig. 2.8: Lovers, sandstone with limestone wash, Rajasthan, tenth century

Fig. 2.9: Celestial dancer, sandstone, Madhya Pradesh, eleventh century

Fig. 2.10: Goddess Ganga, Kailasanatha temple, Ellora, eighth century

Tapas can refer both to the heat of desire and the heat of asceticism. Asceticism, especially of the yogic type, is often connected with celibacy and the retention of semen. But as is well-known, the ancient rishis were not expected to be celibate. The idyllic ashramas in the forest often have married rishis—Agastya and Lopamudra; Arundhati and Vasishtha; Renuka and Jamadagni; Ahalya and Gautama—to mention just a few. In fact, the relationship between the rishis and sex was complex. On the one hand, they could burst into a terrible rage if their austerities were disturbed by seductive nymphs (this is what happened when Menaka disrupted Vishvamitra's austerities). On the other hand, the sages provided a powerful seminal resource (literally) for procreation. As mentioned earlier, in the Mahabharata, Vyasa was called on to impregnate the sisters Ambika and Ambalika and Dhritarashtra and Pandu were the offspring. Sages did not necessarily practice sexual abstinence.

Neither did the gods. The Hindu gods are in many ways akin to humans in their personalities and relationships; this in no way diminishes their greatness. The gods and demigods have consorts. Indra has a wandering eye and is punished for seducing Ahalya. Shiva's asceticism and amorous activity both produce great heat and the gods have to intervene. We have seen how Kalidasa's *Kumarasambhava* describes the lovemaking of Shiva and Parvati. Some of the most exquisite sculptures at Ellora and Elephanta depict the divine couple in stone. [Fig 2.12] The renderings are loving, tender, and sensuous. The relationship between Krishna and the gopis (cowherd girls) is celebrated in texts, paintings, and songs. The love between Krishna and Radha is described in beautiful Sanskrit verse in the twelfth century by Jayadeva in his poem, the *Gita Govinda*. [Fig. 2.13]

Apart from gods who love, there is a god *of* love. Kamadeva is first mentioned in the Atharva Veda and becomes more important in the Puranas, where he has various names—Madana (intoxicator), Manmatha (agitator of the mind), and Ananga (bodiless). His vehicle is a parrot, and his banner bears the emblem of a makara (crocodile). [Fig. 2.14] Rati (sexual delight) and Priti (affection) are his wives and Vasanta (spring) is his friend. Kamadeva is linked with women and the spring festival, a popular festival marked by revelry and licentiousness. But he never became a major god, nor did he become a focus of worship. In fact, on one famous occasion, Shiva put him in

Fig. 2.11: Queen Sembiyan Mahadevi/Parvati, bronze, Tamil Nadu, tenth century

Fig. 2.12: Ravana lifting Mount Kailasa with Shiva and Parvati seated on it, Kailasanatha temple, Ellora

his place by reducing him to ashes for daring to disturb his asceticism.

The connection between religion and love is best reflected in the relationship between devotee and god in the bhakti tradition. Although the language of eroticism is sometimes used to express a devotee's love for god, this love is qualitatively different from that involved in human relationships—it is more lofty and intense, and it is spiritually uplifting. In the case of women saints, love for god leaves no room for loving or marrying a mortal man. Take, for instance, the song of the Alvar saint Andal [Fig. 2.15]:

> Does it smell like camphor
>   Or the lotus flower?
> Is the sacred mouth coral-red
>   Sweet to the taste?
> I ask you in my yearning

Fig. 2.13: Krishna and Radha strolling in the rain; opaque water colour, gold, and ink on paper, Jaipur, c. 1775

For the taste and smell
Of the tusk-bearer Madhava's mouth—
Tell me, white conch, sea-born![40]

---

[40]From the Periyazhwar; P. S. Sundaram (trans.), *The Azhwars: For the Love of God*, New Delhi: Penguin Books, 1996, p. 46.

Fig. 2.14: Kamadeva, stone, Kashmir, eighth century

Fig. 2.15: Andal, copper alloy, Tamil Nadu, fourteenth century

Sex and ritual in Tantra

Apart from mithunas (amorous couples), some ancient Indian temples also have representations of maithuna (sexual intercourse). This is especially so in temples of the early medieval period, for instance those at Khajuraho, Konarak, and Bhubaneswar.[41] The Khajuraho temples, built under the patronage of the Chandela kings, include shrines dedicated to Shiva and Vishnu. The maithuna reliefs are not small or surreptitiously hidden away; they are large, prominent, and in your face. Little is left to the imagination in the depictions of twosomes, threesomes, orgies, oral sex, masturbation, and bestiality. Ascetics and aristocrats can be recognized in some of them. Such scenes are also found in Jaina temples such as the Parshvanatha temple at Khajuraho. Although their appearance in a religious context may offend modern sensibilities about

---

[41]For a detailed discussion, see Devangana Desai, *Erotic Sculpture of India*, especially Chapter 4.

sacred space, this was not the case for the people who designed and built these temples or the devotees who worshipped here.

Sexual images in temples have been interpreted in various ways—as auspicious symbols, as fertility symbols endowed with magico-religious potency, or as devices to ward off the evil eye. They have been variously described as reflecting an increasing decadence in the aesthetic tastes of royalty; an invitation to the beholder to transcend desire and reach a higher spiritual plane; and as representing Tantric sexual rites or influence. The explanation may lie in a combination of factors of which Tantra is the most important.

Tantra is extremely complex and difficult to define. It is not a single religion, but a set of diverse ideas and practices represented in sects belonging to different religious traditions; it had a powerful impact not only in India but across Asia.[42] Tantra is especially prominent in its Shaiva manifestations. Shaiva sects with formal initiation rituals belonged to one of two different but overlapping paths—the Atimarga and Mantramarga.[43] The Atimarga (outer path) was restricted to Brahmanas; initiates became celibate ascetics whose goals were purification and liberation. Mantramarga (mantra path) or full-fledged Tantric Shaivism was open to all social groups, and members could choose to be ascetics or householders. Its aims were the acquiring of siddhis (supernatural powers), the transformation of the soul, and liberation. Mantramarga included exoteric and esoteric traditions. In the exoteric Mantramarga, the forms of worship of Shiva and the offerings made to him are similar to those in Brahmanical rituals. In the esoteric branch of the Mantramarga, the main deities are fierce gods known as Bhairavas or fierce female deities; offerings include alcoholic and blood offerings; and there are

---

[42] For an excellent, lucid overview of Hindu Tantra, see André Padoux, *The Hindu Tantric World: An Overview*, Chicago and London: University of Chicago Press, 2017. On Buddhist Tantra, see Ronald M. Davidson, *Indian Esoteric Buddhism: A Social History of the Tantric Movement*, New York: Columbia University Press, 2002.

[43] Alexis Sanderson, 'Saivism and Brahmanism in the early medieval period', Gonda lecture 2006, pp. 1–3; available at https://www.academia.edu.; Sanderson, 'How Public was Śaivism', Keynote Lecture at the Symposium [on] Tantric Communities in Context: Sacred Secrets and Public Rituals, Vienna, February 2015, pp. 3–5; available at https://www.academia.edu; Padoux, *The Hindu Tantric World*, pp. 30–31.

sexual rites. As pointed out by the Tantra scholar André Padoux, a further distinction can be made between hardcore esoteric Tantra (associated with secret elements, transgressive ideas and practices, including sexual rituals) and softcore Tantra, which percolated in a powerful way into mainstream religious life in a form that was often not recognized as being specifically Tantric.

In Tantra, godhead is understood as involving the union of a masculine and feminine aspect. Shakti (energy) is conceived of as feminine and is central to the Tantric view of the universe and liberation. Tantra has a strong ritualistic and yogic element. The aim of hatha yoga is to awaken the kundalini energy that lies coiled like a serpent in the body, drawing it upwards to unite with the supreme. Tantra has many deities, male and female, often very fierce. When they appear in pairs, their iconography often has clear sexual imagery. [Fig. 2.16] (Tantric goddesses will be discussed in Chapter 3). The idea of puja in Tantra involves propitiating the deity and, according to the medieval commentaries, transforming the worshipper into the deity. Rituals are often associated with the pancha-tattva (five elements) namely—mada (alcohol), mamsa (meat), matsya (fish), mudra (parched grain), and maithuna (sexual intercourse).

Rituals involving sex, including collective sexual rites, are one of the distinctive features of Tantra and were to be performed by qualified initiates according to fixed rules.[44] Texts such as Abhinavagupta's *Tantraloka* (tenth century) explain kama not as pleasure but as a kind of passion that is a gateway to transcending the self and uniting with god. For the male initiate, sex also involves acquiring the energy of the female partner. Unlike in other systems of thought, where the emission of semen is seen as a loss of male virile power, in Tantric rituals associated with deities such as the Yoginis, the orgasmic fluid from the ritual sexual union was to be offered to the deities and then consumed by the worshippers.[45]

---

[44]David Gordon White, *Kiss of the Yoginī: 'Tantric Sex' in its South Asian Contexts*, Chicago and London: University of Chicago Press, 2003, pp. xii, 7.
[45]Padoux, *The Hindu Tantric World*, pp. 87, 92–93.

Fig. 2.16: Kali and Bhairava in union, watercolour on paper, Nepal, eighteenth century

Tantra had a powerful impact on religions across the board, including on Buddhism and Jainism. While the groups of Tantric adepts and practitioners may have been small, they acquired a large following, including in royal courts. This made Tantra a powerful presence in religious, social, and political life. The widespread impact of Tantra seems to be the major reason for the strong sexual imagery in Indian religious art of the early medieval period.

The poetic denigration of desire

Poetry contains not only the most exquisite celebrations of desire but also its most eloquent denigration. The roots of the latter lie in the strong renunciatory traditions which have been discussed earlier in this chapter.

The tension between desire and detachment is expressed most graphically in Bhartrihari's *Shataka-trayi* which consists of the *Niti-shataka*, *Shringara-shataka*, and *Vairagya-shataka*—a hundred verses on wise living, love, and renunciation. Like other ancient poets and playwrights, this fifth century poet is known through legend rather than biography. One story describes him as a king who initially immersed himself in pleasures and then turned away from them due to the unfaithfulness and fickleness of women.

Bhartrihari's love poems mark a radical reversal of the usual treatment of shringara in Sanskrit poetry. A woman's body, praised so eloquently by other poets, is grotesque. Desire is not beautiful but disgusting:

> Gaunt, blind, lame, shorn of ears and tail;
> mangled, putrid, covered with worms;
> starved, wizened, wearing an alms bowl shard
> on his neck—a dog will still follow a bitch.
> Passion smites even those bereft of life.[46]

Love is a transient, meaningless episode in the drama of life:

> For one short act, a child; next act, a boy
> In love; then poor; a short act to enjoy
> Status and wealth: till in the last act, Man,
> Painted with wrinkles, body bent with age,
> Ending the comedy which birth began,
> Withdraws behind the curtain of life's stage.[47]

---

[46] Bhartrihari, *Shataka-traya*, Prologue 2; Barbara Stoller Miller (trans.), *The Hermit and the Love-thief: Bhartrihari and Bilhana*, New Delhi: Penguin Books, [1978], 1990, p. 29.
[47] J. Brough (trans.), *Poems from the Sanskrit*, Harmondsworth: Penguin Classics, L 198, 1968, No. 14.

The solution, Bhartrihari's *Vairagya-shataka* suggests, is to give it all up.

> For humans sense pleasures flicker
> Like lightning flashing amid the canopy of cloud
> Life is fragile as water clinging
> To the edge of the wide-buffeted lotus.
> Fickle are the yearnings of youth.
> Reflect on this right now,
> And fix your mind in meditation,
> Easy to achieve by those perfected in concentration and resolve.[48]

◆

We do not know what the average ancient Indian thought about love and sex. But texts and art reflect their celebration, denigration, sublimation, and transcendence. Ancient literature in Tamil, Prakrit, and Sanskrit is permeated with the sentiments of love and the excitement of passion. Technical treatises contain the kama-experts' analysis of pleasure. Ancient art (mostly found in religious spaces) celebrates the human body and the love of man and woman, its representations ranging from subtle sensuality to the frankly erotic. Pleasure was recognized as a legitimate goal of human existence, to be pursued with a sense of balance and in harmony with other goals such as dharma and artha, even moksha. Extreme love was justified only when it formed a template for a higher love—love for god. The love between devotee and deity was visualized as reciprocal, intense, sublime, a path to a higher spiritual goal. Here, there was no possibility of excess. In Tantric ritual, sex was divested of its associations with desire or pleasure.

These diverse perspectives which attached different kinds of positive value to love, sex and/or desire coexisted with a powerful tradition that viewed all these, indeed the body itself, as sources of bondage and suffering. The control of sexual impulses and acts was central to several (though not all) ascetic systems and was a cornerstone of Jaina and

---

[48]*Vairagya-shataka*, 35, Greg Bailey (trans.), *Love Lyrics by Amaru & Bhartihari*, New York: New York University Press, 2005, p. 161.

Buddhist monastic practice. One could be a good Jaina or Buddhist by following the teachings laid down for the laity. But one could not attain liberation from samsara, that is the cycle of birth and death, without giving everything up and joining the monastic Order. Liberation required transcending *all* forms of attachment and desire. Renunciation cast its shadow (or light) across the centuries and still inspires awe and respect in India today. It is visible in the figure of the monk, sannyasi, yogi, and sadhu. Some of these men—and women—have dedicated their lives to following a difficult higher calling. Others have acquired large business empires and, in some cases, even criminal records.

It would be a bit reckless to make generalized statements about present-day 'Indian attitudes' towards love and sex, let alone try to explain how these have changed over time. Love has not gone out of fashion but its representations have changed drastically. Love and longing are favoured themes in contemporary literature, art, folk tales, music, dance, film, and theatre. Gen Y's search for love is perhaps best expressed in the increasing recourse to dating apps that give the illusion that love is just a click or swipe away. However, the celebration of the amorous and the sensual is accompanied in the public domain, especially among the middle class, by an extreme prudery when it comes to norms of social behaviour (especially female behaviour). The body (especially the female body) is considered a distraction, to be covered and concealed from the male gaze. Sex is to be discussed in a furtive manner or not at all, and has its proper place only within marriage. Love and pleasure are not usually connected with marriage, and if they are, are supposed to follow, not precede it. Some of these ideas and attitudes are rather different from what ancient literature and art suggest. If the second century BCE Chanda Yakshi[49] were magically transported from Bharhut to twenty-first century Delhi and brought to life, she would smile in disbelief. She would also be told to cover up.

---

[49]Go back to Figure 2.7 to see Chanda.

3

GODDESSES AND MISOGYNY

In 1970, a Hindi film called *Purab aur Pashchim* became a hit. The film was directed and produced by Manoj Kumar, who was also the hero. The heroine Priti, played by Saira Banu, is born and brought up in London. She has long, loose blonde hair, drinks, smokes, and wears miniskirts. At the end of the film, she repents for her evil ways, gives up drinking and smoking, ties her hair up in a bun, dons a sari, and goes to the temple. She has realized that Indian culture, embodied in the hero Bharat's values and virtues, is vastly superior to Western culture. Much has changed since the 1970s, but the stereotype of the good Indian woman is still going strong and forms one of the important elements in the idea of 'Indian culture'.

One of the many contradictions in India is the prevalence of the worship of powerful goddesses within a social system which advocates and inculcates a subordinate, male-centred life for women. The social reformers of the late nineteenth and early twentieth centuries were greatly interested in what they called the 'position of women' in ancient India. So were historians. A. S. Altekar presented the Vedic age as a golden age for women on the basis of references to goddesses in the Rig Veda, women sages in the Upanishads, and women participating with their husbands in yajnas.[1] According to Altekar, it was the entry of the non-arya woman into the arya household (and later, Muslim invasions) that led to the decline in the position of women. The idea of a time long ago when women occupied an exalted position in society could be used to claim civilizational superiority during a period of humiliating colonial rule. It was also used as an argument to improve the situation

---

[1]A. S. Altekar, *The Position of Women in Hindu Civilisation: From Prehistoric Times to the Present Day*, Delhi: Motilal Banarsidass, [1938], 1991.

of Indian women in the late nineteenth and early twentieth centuries, when practices such as child marriage, sati, and low levels of female literacy pointed to the urgent need for social reform.

Over the last few decades, feminist historians have shifted the focus from discussing women in isolation to an analysis of gender, that is, the culturally defined roles associated with men and women.[2] Of course we now know that it is necessary to look beyond gender binaries and to include transgender people as well. Women are not a homogeneous category. Their historical experience varied depending on rank, class, caste, occupation, and age. Rather than talking in generalities about 'the position of women' at a particular point of time, it is more useful to ask more specific questions such as: What were the systems of kinship and descent? How were gender roles defined? What were relationships within the household like? What customs were followed with regard to property and inheritance? How were the sexuality and reproductive potential of women controlled? How did gender intersect with class and caste? What sorts of economic activities were women involved in? How did they participate in the religious and ritual spheres? Did they have access to knowledge production and transmission? Did they exercise power or authority in the political sphere? When such questions are asked, simplistic notions about 'the position of women' dissolve to present a complex picture of the different ways in which women participated and were perceived in history.

As is the case with all subordinated social groups, a major problem in locating women's experience is the fact that almost all the written sources were produced by and for upper-class men. The Therigatha, a few poems in the Sangam corpus and *Gatha Sattasai*, and the songs of women bhakti saints are among the exceptions. The fact that women's voices are scarcely audible is itself evidence of their subordination. This chapter begins by examining the strong tradition of goddess worship

---

[2]See Uma Chakravarti, *Everyday Lives, Everyday Histories: Beyond the Kings and Brahmanas of 'Ancient' India*, New Delhi: Tulika, [2006], 2020; Kumkum Roy, *The Power of Gender and the Gender of Power: Explorations in Early Indian History*, New Delhi: Oxford University Press, 2010.

in ancient India and goes on to discuss the realities of gender relations in the religious, social, and political spheres.

Ancient goddesses

Before the gods took over, all over the world, there was a time when goddesses ruled the roost. In Palaeolithic Europe, 'Venus figurines' with exaggerated sexual characteristics represent widely prevalent fertility beliefs and rituals. In India, the site of Baghor in Madhya Pradesh has given fascinating evidence of an Upper Palaeolithic shrine going back to c. 9000–8000 BCE. This consisted of a roughly circular platform made of sandstone rubble, in the centre of which was a piece of natural stone with a striking laminated pattern. Nine other fragments of this stone were found, mostly on or near the platform. When the pieces were joined together, they formed a triangular stone, which must have been originally placed on the platform. The Kol and Baiga tribals who live in this part of the Kaimur hills today worship similar triangular stones as sacred symbols of a goddess.

In the Stone Age, the transition from hunting and gathering to agriculture and animal breeding was accompanied by increasing concerns with fertility. These are reflected in the many terracotta female figurines found at Neolithic sites, which are often routinely labelled 'Mother Goddesses'. The worship of fertility goddesses was also one of the major features of Harappan religion. Large numbers of female figurines have been found at Harappan sites. One seal shows a nude woman, head downwards, with her legs spread apart and a plant issuing from her vagina, reflecting the idea of the Earth Mother.

The habit of describing all female figurines as representations of a single great 'Mother Goddess' is an oversimplification. All ancient female figurines do not represent goddesses, not all goddesses were associated with motherhood, and not all were part of the cult of a single Great Goddess.[3] For instance, some of the Harappan female figurines may represent goddesses, while others seem to represent

---

[3] By 'cult' I mean a religious group defined by belief and practice associated with the worship of a particular deity. I am not using it in a pejorative sense.

Fig. 3.1: Terracotta goddess, third/second century BCE

Fig. 3.2: Goddess with weapons in her hair, Chandraketugarh terracotta, first century BCE–first century CE

ordinary, mortal women. The type which seems to have had a religious significance is a slim, heavily ornamented female figure wearing a short skirt and a distinctive fan-shaped headdress. These may have been images worshipped in households, votive offerings made to a deity, or part of the paraphernalia of domestic rituals.

Female figurines that seem to represent goddesses are prominent in the early historic period, from the fourth century BCE onwards. Compared to their Harappan counterparts, they are more numerous and more stylistically varied and refined. They usually have prominent breasts and broad hips and wear ornaments such as appliqué necklaces, bracelets, earrings, and girdles. Some sport a profusion of rosettes in their hair; others have elaborate headdresses consisting of a mass of conical sprouts or grass blades; still others have weapons in their hair. [Figs. 3.1, 3.2] These are not images of ordinary women. They are goddesses whose names we do not know.

Although goddess worship was an important aspect of religious practice in the subcontinent across the centuries, it became especially prominent in the early medieval period (sixth to twelfth/thirteenth centuries). The political history of this period includes the transformation of tribal chieftains into kings and the incorporation of tribal communities into state and caste society. In Orissa, inscriptions of the early Bhanjas of Khinjali mandala and the Shulkis mention the Goddess Stambheshvari, who seems to have been a tribal goddess. Shulki inscriptions also refer to Stambheshvari as the kula-devi (tutelary deity) of their lineage. In Karnataka, inscriptions of political elites in the Ganga, Shantara, and Hoysala kingdoms invoke the Jaina goddess Padmavati. In central India, the Chandelas and Kalachuri rulers may have been associated with the construction of Yogini temples.

In spite of male dominance in religious pantheons and organizations, goddess worship formed an important substratum of religious beliefs and practices in ancient India. It is best to be flexible about the category of 'goddess' and to include within it a variety of feminine figures with supramundane attributes and powers, who were objects of worship. The idea of a single Great Goddess with a capital 'G' coexisted with the idea of many goddesses with a small 'g'. While goddesses are prominent in Hinduism, they are also important in Buddhism and Jainism, and some of them moved across religious boundaries.[4] Given the great popularity of goddess worship in India over the centuries, it is only possible to discuss a few of them. Although, for the sake of convenience, the labels 'Hindu', 'Buddhist', and 'Jaina' have been used, as we shall see, in the sphere of religious practice, such labels sometimes become meaningless.

Yakshis and nagis

The category of demigods between human beings and deities included yakshas, yakshis, nagas, and nagis. In fact, the origins of bhakti (devotion), which became so pervasive in Indian religions, can be traced to the worship of these semi-divine beings. These are very old cults whose origins are difficult to determine.

Yakshas were connected with water, fertility, trees, the forest, and

---

[4]I have avoided referring to deities as Aryan or non-Aryan, because these labels tend to oversimplify complex religious processes.

Fig. 3.3: Chulakoka yakshi, Bharhut   Fig. 3.4: Sanchi Nagi

the wilderness. Their female counterparts, the yakshis (we have already encountered them in Chapter 2), were originally benign deities associated with auspiciousness and fertility.[5] The many imposing stone images of yakshas and yakshis from Mathura and elsewhere, dated between c. 300 BCE to 200 CE, indicate that they were worshipped in temples in cities and were prominent parts of the public religious landscape. The numerous small stone and terracotta images indicate that they were worshipped in a private, domestic context as well. Many of the shalabhanjikas—a generic term for sensuous sculptural representations of women grasping the branch of a tree—found in religious establishments across the subcontinent, were actually yakshis. They are especially prominent at early Buddhist sites such as Sanchi and Bharhut, and inscriptions at the latter site give some of their names. [Fig. 3.3]

---

[5]See Ananda K. Coomaraswamy, *Yakshas*, New Delhi: Munshiram Manoharlal, [1928], 1980; R. N. Misra, *Yaksha Cult and Iconography*, New Delhi: Munshiram Manoharlal, [1979], 1981.

The worship of serpents was another important aspect of religious worship from very early times in India. Nagas and nagis (snake deities and their consorts) were associated with water and fertility. [Fig. 3.4] Like yakshas and yakshis, they too were originally the focus of exclusive worship. Large images of nagas and the remains of an ancient naga temple have been found at Mathura.

In the early centuries CE, yakshas, yakshis, nagas, and nagis were gradually dethroned from their position as major foci of worship in the urban, public domain, but their worship continued in the domestic sphere, as is evident from small stone and terracotta statuettes. They were displaced by new religious ideas and practices, the most influential of which were associated with the worship of the gods Shiva and Vishnu and the goddess Durga.

Hindu goddesses

Although the Rig Vedic hymns are dominated by gods, there are a few goddesses. These include Ushas, goddess of dawn, who is invoked in twenty hymns. Representing the victory of light over darkness, she is also a generous goddess who bestows wealth. Aditi is invoked as a mother, who bestows freedom from sickness, harm, and evil. Other Rig Vedic goddesses include Raka (a benevolent, bountiful goddess), Sinivali (who bestows children), Prithvi (the earth goddess), Vach (goddess of speech), and Sarasvati (representing the river of this name). Goddesses really come into their own in the Puranas, which detail their personalities and exploits.[6]

Lakshmi

Shri and Lakshmi seem to have originally been two separate goddesses who, at some point, merged into one as Shri Lakshmi. The Shri Sukta,

---

[6]On Hindu goddesses, see David Kinsley, *Hindu Goddesses: Vision of the Divine Feminine in the Hindu Religious Tradition*, Delhi: Motilal Banarsidass, [1986], 1987; John Stratton Hawley and Donna Marie Wulff (eds.), *Devī: Goddesses of India*, Delhi: Motilal Banarsidass, [1996], 1998; John Stratton Hawley and Donna Marie Wulff (eds.), *The Divine Consort: Rādhā and the Goddesses of India*, Delhi: Motilal Banarsidass, [1982], 1984.

a supplement to the Rig Veda, describes Shri as having the form of a moon-like golden-coloured deer decorated with ornaments of gold and silver, and also invokes her as Lakshmi. 'Shri' means well-being or prosperity and the goddess of this name may have originally been a fertility goddess. 'Lakshmi' means sign, token, or mark, and the goddess with this name was associated with the signs of prosperity and luck, and hence wealth.

At Sonkh in Mathura, a relief carving of Lakshmi has been found on an architectural fragment in a second/first century BCE context. Lakshmi is also represented on a large number of stone images of this period at Mathura. Another early depiction occurs on a terracotta plaque found in an apsidal temple at Atranjikhera (Etah district, Uttar Pradesh) at a level dated to c. 200–50 BCE.

The history of Vaishnavism involved the gradual coming together of initially independent cults of various deities.[7] By the third/fourth century CE, Shri Lakshmi had been absorbed into the Vaishnava pantheon as the consort of Vishnu. The Mahabharata and Ramayana know her in this role and the Puranas further elaborate on her association with Vishnu. One of the most frequent and most striking representations of Shri Lakshmi in sculpture is in her Gaja Lakshmi form (gaja means elephant): the goddess sits or stands on a lotus, flanked by two elephants who pour water over her from pitchers held in their upraised trunks. Between the second century BCE and second century CE, Gaja Lakshmi appears on coins of the Shunga king Jyeshthamitra; of the Scytho–Parthian kings Azes II and Azilises; and of the Kshatrapa kings Rajuvula, Shodasa, and Toranadasa. Later, she appears on Gupta coins. Apart from being the consort of Vishnu, Lakshmi was a prominent goddess in her own right, associated with good fortune, including that of kings and cities. [Fig. 3.5]

A female figure seated on a lotus, flanked by elephants, is a frequent sculptural motif at Buddhist sites such as Sanchi, Bharhut, and Bodh Gaya. [Fig. 3.6] Some art historians identify her as the Buddha's mother Maya, but the very specific iconography clearly points to Gaja

---

[7] See Suvira Jaiswal, *The Origin and Development of Vaiṣṇavism*, New Delhi: Munshiram Manoharlal, [1967], 1981.

Ancient India: Culture of Contradictions

Fig. 3.5: Lakshmi, Kailasanatha temple, Ellora

Fig. 3.6: Gaja-Lakshmi, Sanchi

Fig. 3.7: Lakshmi, Raja Ravi Varma, lithograph print, 1894

Lakshmi. The references to Lakshmi's form being carved on doors in the Sangam text *Pattuppattu* indicate that this goddess was associated with auspiciousness in South India as well. Lakshmi was one of many ancient goddesses who crossed religious and spatial boundaries. [Fig. 3.7]

Durga and the Shakta tradition

The epics and Puranas provide details about the personality and feats of the goddess Durga. The Harivamsha (a supplement to the Mahabharata) addresses her by various names and connects her with the hills (especially the Vindhyas), rivers, caves, forests, gardens, and animals. It refers to her being worshipped by tribes such as the Shabaras, Barbaras, and Pulindas.[8] She is said to represent death and is fond of wine, meat, and sacrifice. She personifies the virginity of young girls and the good fortune of married women. She pervades the universe and is a saviour in the face of all kinds of dangers. In the Puranas, Durga was an important part of the idea of the Great Goddess.

The Puranas brought together many goddesses and presented them as different manifestations of a single Great Goddess, Devi or Shakti, representing the female principle. As in the case of Vaishnavism, the deities who were brought under a single umbrella were originally the focus of independent worship.[9] The Devi-Mahatmya, which was incorporated into the Markandeya Purana by about the seventh century, praises the Great Goddess and narrates her many victories. These include a dramatic encounter with the buffalo demon Mahisha, who was tormenting the gods. The Goddess emerged from the combined concentrated energy of all the gods, and defeated the demon after a fierce battle. In this aspect, she is known as Durga Mahishasuramardini (Durga, slayer of the demon Mahisha). [Figs. 3.8. 3.9] The Devi-Mahatmya also contains many verses in praise of the Goddess. She is said to sustain the entire universe. Her various manifestations include Lakshmi, Sarasvati, Narayani, Katyayani, Durga, Bhadrakali, Ambika, and the Matrikas (Mothers). In the last canto of the Devi-Mahatmya, the Goddess announces that she will appear from time to time in the world in order to destroy demons and evil.

---

[8] In ancient texts, Shabaras and Pulindas are associated with the Vindhyas, and the Barbaras with the northwest. It is notable that these tribes are routinely included in the pejorative category of mlechchha.

[9] For a discussion of how this process unfolded in Bengal, see Kunal Chakrabarti, *Religious Process: The Puranas and the Making of a Regional Tradition*, New Delhi: Oxford University Press, 2001.

Fig. 3.8: Durga Mahishasuramardini, Mahabalipuram

Fig. 3.9: Durga Mahishasuramardini, stone, Badra, Central Northeastern style, ninth century

The Kalika Purana, an important Shakta text that was composed in the area of Assam or Bengal, reflects the diverse forms of the worship of Devi. The Goddess is described as having both a benign and a terrifying form and can be worshipped in two ways—dakshina-bhava (the right method) and vama-bhava (the left method). The right method consists of regular rites and rituals; the left method includes rituals involving the use of alcohol, meat, and sexual rites. The Kalika Purana also contains details of the performance of the Durga Puja festival, which is a major festival in Bengal today.

Sculptural evidence indicates the popularity of the worship of Durga Mahishasuramardini from a very early period. For instance, a large number of stone Durga images, including as Mahishasuramardini, belonging to the period c. 200 BCE–300 CE, have been found in the Mathura area. A stone Matrika plaque seems to have been the central cult image in a small temple at Sonkh (in Mathura) and a large number of terracotta plaques depicting Durga Mahishasuramardini were found in and around it.

Some of the most impressive sculptural representations of Durga Mahishasuramardini were made by sculptors of the early medieval period. Many of them show a multi-armed goddess with a lion as her mount, piercing the buffalo demon with her spear. Pallava period sculptures (sixth to ninth centuries) from South India depict a many-armed, weapon-wielding goddess, standing on a buffalo, framed by kneeling devotees shedding blood and cutting off their own heads. She can be connected both with Durga Mahishasuramardini as well as a South Indian goddess named Korravai. Many Chola period temples have relief images of Durga as Nishumbhamardini (slayer of the demon Nishumbha), where the goddess is accompanied by a stag.

Architectural and sculptural remains from various parts of India reflect the widespread worship of the Matrikas (seven or eight in number) and the Yoginis, initially the foci of independent worship, who came to be associated with Durga.[10] [Figs. 3.10, 3.11, 3.12] The Puranas describe the seven mothers—Brahmani, Maheshvari, Kaumari, Vaishnavi, Varahi,

---

[10]See Anamika Roy, *Sixty-four Yoginis: Cult, Icons and Goddesses*, New Delhi: Primus, 2015.

Fig. 3.10: Yogini, stone, Musée Guimet

Fig. 3.11: Yogini Hayagriva, stone, eleventh century

Fig. 3.12: Yogini Chamunda, marble, Rajasthan, ninth century

Indrani, and Yami (Chamunda)—as the energies of various gods who assisted Devi in fighting demons. The Yoginis, eventually reckoned as sixty-four in number, are described as attendants or manifestations of Durga in her battle against the demons Shumbha and Nishumbha. The worship of the Matrikas and Yoginis was popular in central and eastern India. Yogini images have been found in hypaethral (roofless) temples at Ranipur Jharial and Hirapur.

The epics and Puranas contain many stories reflecting the close connection between Shaivism and Shaktism. Legends describe the resurrection of Shiva's wife Sati as Uma and the difficult penances she performed to regain her husband. The sacred places associated with Devi are known as pithas. There are various explanations of their origins. One talks of a great sacrifice that was held by Sati's father, Daksha, to which he did not invite his daughter and son-in-law. Sati went anyway, was insulted by her father, and died of grief. A furious Shiva destroyed the sacrifice, beheaded Daksha, and then went on a rampage, carrying Sati's body over his shoulder. So great was the impact of this that the other gods were forced to intervene. Brahma, Vishnu, and Shani entered Sati's body and dismembered it gradually. Every place where a piece of her body fell became a pitha. The goddess is believed to live in each of these spots in some form, along with her husband, Bhairava. The number of pithas increased over time and this reflects an expansion in the sacred geography associated with the goddess. The Kamakhya temple in Guwahati is one of the famous Shakta pithas. Here, the goddess is represented by a cleft in a rock and is offered animal sacrifices. There is an annual celebration at the time when the goddess is supposed to be menstruating.

Kali is one of the most fierce Hindu goddesses. She has an independent identity but is also connected with Durga and Shiva. She is usually represented as a bloodthirsty deity with a frightening physical form—emaciated, dark, and naked; wearing a necklace of human heads; with long hair, nails, and teeth; her tongue protruding from her mouth. She is said to frequent battlefields and cremation grounds. She is connected with the wild tribes of the forest. In the Devi-Mahatmya, she participates in Durga's battle against the demons Shumbha and Nishumbha. She emerges from Durga's forehead and kills the demons

Fig. 3.13: Kali, Kalighat watercolour, graphite, and ink on paper, 1800s

Chanda and Munda with her bare hands. At a later point in the battle, Durga calls on Kali to help her deal with the demon Raktabija. This demon has the power to reproduce himself instantaneously every time drops of blood from his body fall to the ground. Durga and her helpers, the Matrikas, find themselves helpless in killing him because more and more Raktabijas emerge from the blood from the wounds they inflict on him. Kali comes to the rescue—she sucks the blood from Raktabija's body and devours his countless clones.

In other myths, Kali is associated with Parvati, Sati, or Sita. Sometimes, Kali and Shiva are depicted as engaged in a frenzied dance together, sometimes competing with each other. In a well-known representation, Kali is shown dancing on Shiva's prostrate body.

[Fig. 3.13] The story behind this is that on one occasion, when Kali was engaged in wild, bloodthirsty behaviour on the battlefield, Shiva appeared and lay down before her in order to calm her and put an end to her violent and destructive activity. Unlike Parvati, who is a pacific consort of Shiva, Kali represents the wild and dangerous aspect of the divine feminine. The goddess became especially important in Tantra and in Bengal Shaktism.

As mentioned in Chapter 2, the union of masculine and feminine is central to the Tantric view of the world and of liberation. Woman is the source of shakti (power) and goddesses play an important role. Although the Shaiva Tantric sects have powerful goddesses, Shiva is usually considered as metaphysically above them. But in the Tantric Trika sect, the three goddesses Para, Parapara, and Apara are considered higher than Shiva. In Tantra, deities often come in pairs of male and female such as Shiva and Shakti, Durga and Bhairava, Tripurasundari and Bhairava, Kubjika and Navatman.[11] In the Yamala Shakta Tantras, the different forms of the Goddess dominate their male consort and are often depicted as seated on his shoulder. Like their male counterparts, Tantric goddesses are often fierce. Although sometimes invoked as mother, their personality is far from maternal. Even the Matrikas, who sometimes hold children, are fierce and not especially maternal in temperament. In Tantra, while women can be initiated, attain magical powers, and participate in sexual rites, they cannot be the main performers of rituals. This shows that the importance attached to the feminine principle in Tantra did not translate into a high level of leadership roles for women.

Radha

Radha is a goddess who has a primary connection with the god Krishna. As one of the gopis (cowherd girls) she has an intense love for Krishna, but she is not usually considered his spouse. There are stray references to Radha in earlier texts such as the Matsya, Varaha, and Linga Puranas. She is not mentioned directly in the Harivamsha, or in the Vishnu and

---

[11]Padoux, *The Hindu Tantric World*, pp. 49–59.

Fig. 3.14: Radha pining for Krishna, opaque watercolour and gold on paper, folio from *Gita Govinda*, c. 1775–80, attributed to Kangra or Guler, Panjab Hills

Bhagavata Puranas.

The Bhagavata Purana, an important Vaishnava text, was composed in South India in the ninth or tenth century. Book 10, the Krishna-charita, gives a detailed account of Krishna's life—his birth and his childhood with his foster-parents, Nanda and Yashodha; his cowherd life in Vrindavan; his miraculous exploits such as killing Putana and overcoming the serpent Kaliya; and his relationship with the gopis. The text speaks in particular of one gopi with whom Krishna has a special connection, but does not name her. In Krishna bhakti, the gopis' love for Krishna, their longing for him, and their grief at their separation from him, is used as a metaphor for the relationship between devotee and god.

Jayadeva's celebrated twelfth century lyric poem, *Gita Govinda*, brought Radha into the limelight. This work is known for its high literary quality and powerful eroticism, and describes Radha's intense feelings of sorrow and longing for Krishna and her desire to meet him. Radha's love is presented as the epitome of viraha (love in separation). [Fig. 3.14] The love between Radha and Krishna was elaborated on in the Brahmavaivarta Purana, which considers Radha as Krishna's Shakti and elevates her to the status of a cosmic goddess.

The Tamil epic *Shilappadikaram* mentions cowherd girls performing the rasa-lila at Madurai and singing songs about Krishna and Pinnai. Pinnai may represent the later Radha.

Buddhist goddesses

While the importance of goddess worship in Hinduism is well known, its importance in Buddhism and Jainism is not as recognized. In the history of Indian Buddhism, the period c. 200 BCE–300 CE is associated with the emergence of new ideas and practices usually referred to, for the sake of convenience, under the umbrella term Mahayana.[12] The highest goal in early Buddhism was becoming an arhat (one who has attained nibbana). In Mahayana, the highest goal was attaining Buddhahood. The bodhisattva is one who has attained great wisdom, but due to his compassion for others, refrains from taking the final step into nibbana, choosing instead to actively engage with the world in order to help others attain this goal. Great importance is attached to devotion to bodhisattvas and Buddhas who, although technically not gods (gods were given a lower position), were the foci of worship.

Goddesses have an important place in early Buddhism, Mahayana, and Tantric Buddhism.[13] Consider the description of an important event in the hagiography of the Buddha—his enlightenment. When the meditating Siddhartha is seated under the Bodhi tree, on the verge of enlightenment, the demon king Mara and his hideous, ghoulish army attack him and try to disrupt his meditation. At this point, Siddhartha calls on Prithvi, the earth goddess, to bear witness to his worthiness to attain enlightenment. Prithvi gives her testimony in the form of a powerful roar that drives Mara away. As mentioned earlier, relief

---

[12]The terms Mahayana ('the greater vehicle') and Hinayana ('the lesser vehicle') were coined by the Mahayanists. Needless to say, non-Mahayanists would not have considered or described themselves as followers of a lesser, that is, inferior path.

[13]For an excellent discussion which combines a close examination of textual and visual sources, see Miranda Shaw, *Buddhist Goddesses of India*, Princeton: Princeton University Press, 2006.

sculptures of Gaja Lakshmi appear at Buddhist monastic sites such as Sanchi. Another Buddhist goddess is Hariti, who is said to have been converted by the Buddha from a bloodthirsty, child-devouring demonic yakshi to a benevolent, maternal figure.

In Mahayana Buddhism, female deities are benevolent saviours and protectors who embody Buddhist virtues.[14] In Prajnaparamita texts, knowledge is visualized in feminine form, as a deity called Prajnaparamita. This goddess is described as the source of the omniscience of all Buddhas and the mother of all Buddhas. She embodies and bestows perfect wisdom. In Pala period sculptures, she is associated with lotus motifs, her hands often joined in the teaching vyakhyana mudra. The expanding pantheons in Mahayana Buddhism included many other goddesses such as Parnashavari (associated with the forest and healing), Marichi (a warrior goddess associated with the dawn), Janguli (protectress from snake bite), Sarasvati (associated with learning), and Vasudhara (bestower of riches).

The best-known Buddhist goddess is Tara. She started out as an attendant of the bodhisattva Avalokiteshvara but rose swiftly to reach the pinnacle of the Mahayana pantheon in early medieval times, being recognized as a Buddha. Tara is the feminine personification of transcendent wisdom and extraordinary compassion, and is believed to have a great capacity to relieve people's suffering. She is described as born out of Avalokiteshvara's teardrop (he was shedding tears of despair at the enormous task of liberating all sentient beings), from a lotus that grew in his tears, or from his heart. She is a saviour who protects people from eight great bhayas (fears)—lions, elephants, fires, serpents, robbers, drowning, imprisonment, and demons. She has multiple emanations that help her perform her salvific work. Tara inherited Prajnaparamita's epithet of 'Mother of all Buddhas'. Many Tara stotras (hymns), composed from the seventh century onwards, elevate her to the position of a companion of Avalokiteshvara, describe her as mother of all the Buddhas, and associate her with love and compassion. In Tantric Buddhism, Tara came to be considered the shakti of the

---

[14]For details, see Miranda Shaw, *Buddhist Goddesses*, pp. 155–354.

Ancient India: Culture of Contradictions

Fig. 3.15: White Tara, Bhutan

Buddha or an emanation of one of the Buddhas.

Tara is depicted as a beatific, benevolent deity, either white or green, in paintings in monasteries in the western Himalayas such as at Alchi and Tabo as well as in Bhutan. [Fig. 3.15] Many Pala period bronzes depict her as Khadiravani Tara or Shyama Tara, considered to be an emanation of the Dhyani Buddha Amoghasiddhi.[15] A terrifying form of the goddess is Mahachina Tara or Ugra Tara (Fierce Tara), an emanation of the Buddha Akshobhya. She has four arms and stands on a corpse with a sword and chopper in her right hands and a lotus and skull in left hands.

Tantric Buddhism has a number of goddesses known as Dakinis. They are fierce and wild, and are associated with bone ornaments and skulls. They include Vajrayogini, Nairatmya, Simhamukha, and the fiercest goddess Chinnamunda, who is shown carrying her own decapitated head, with blood streaming from her neck. These are powerful deities, often explicitly described as Buddhas, and practices

---

[15]The Dhyani Buddhas are a group of five eternal celestial Buddhas.

directed towards them are said to be capable of leading to liberation.

Jaina goddesses

A visitor to the spectacular Dilwara temples in Mount Abu, Rajasthan, will notice that although the main and subsidiary shrines contain images of the Tirthankaras, the walls and ceilings are carved with beautiful, sensuous female figures. Texts, inscriptions, and visual representations in temples testify to the importance of goddess worship in Jainism.[16] The goddesses are visualized as living in three different realms—the upper, middle, and lower. In the upper realms are goddesses such as Sarasvati and Lakshmi, shared by Hinduism and Jainism. In the middle realm are the sixteen Tantric vidyadevis, associated with magical or occult powers and practices. In the lower realm are the yakshis, attendants of the twenty-four Tirthankaras.

The dividing lines between yakshi, vidyadevi, and goddess are difficult to draw. In fact, it is the yakshis of the lower realm—Ambika, Padmavati, and Jvalamalini—who were the most popular Jaina female divinities, especially from the sixth century onwards. Although the texts describe them as attendants of the Tirthankaras, they were extremely important in actual religious practice. [Fig. 3.16]

The goddess Ambika is associated with childbirth and is shown seated on a lion, accompanied by her two sons. [Fig. 3.17] Padmavati seems to have originally been a snake goddess (she is the consort of the naga king Dharnendra) who later became the attendant of Parshvanatha, the twenty-third Tirthankara. The Shantara dynasty of the Karnataka region describes her as their kula-devi. Jvalamalini is the Digambara yakshi of Chandraprabhu, the eighth Tirthankara. She is clearly a Tantric goddess. Some of the goddesses presided over tirthas—for instance, Ambika at Girnar and Padmavati at Shravana Belgola. Images of goddesses appear prominently in early medieval Jaina temples in Tamil Nadu.

In Jainism, devotion to goddesses cannot lead to enlightenment, but it can help in attaining worldly goals such as prosperity, power, and

---

[16]See John Cort, 'Medieval Jaina Goddess Traditions', *Numen*, vol. 34, no. 2, December 1987, pp. 235–55.

Fig. 3.16: Digambara yakshi Kushmandini, schist, Karnataka, c. 900

Fig. 3.17: Ambika, Ellora

even victory in philosophical debates. So although they were not the main focus of worship, goddesses did have a strong presence, endowing the austere atmosphere of Jaina temples with beauty and warmth. The Tirthankaras are aloof, unmoving, and do not intercede in human affairs. The goddesses, on the other hand, are accessible and can be approached for the granting of worldly desires. Hence, although their formal status was far below that of the Tirthankaras, goddesses have been the focus of devotion for Jainas across the centuries.

Sarasvati, the goddess of learning, who is often considered a Hindu goddess, also has a place in the Buddhist and Jaina pantheons. Her earliest sculptural image is in fact found in a Jaina context at Kankali Tila in Mathura. Shri or Lakshmi, goddess of wealth, is found at Buddhist sites and is worshipped by Hindu and Jaina merchants alike. Even when they have Hindu antecedents, Jaina goddesses have distinct personalities. Sometimes there is a radical personality makeover. As in Buddhism, Jainism too has stories of the conversion of fierce goddesses into pacific and benevolent ones. The violent, bloodthirsty goddess Chamunda

Fig. 3.18: Shiva Ardhanarishvara, copper inlaid with garnets and emerald, with traces of paint, Nepal c. 1000

is said to have been turned into a benevolent, vegetarian goddess due to the influence of a Jaina monk. Nilakechi is another violent goddess who was 'converted'; not only is she supposed to have renounced her violent ways, she also devoted herself to the propagation of Jaina virtues and the refutation of Buddhist doctrines and practices.

In medieval South India, there are striking similarities between the representations in temple sculptures of Hindu and Jaina goddesses, for instance, between Ambika and Parvati, and between Padmavati and Durga Mahishasuramardini.[17] Jaina and Hindu goddesses were given similar honorifics and were worshipped in the same manner. In fact, such shared elements in religious practice are in striking contrast to the sharply defined religious boundaries suggested in texts.

The importance of goddess worship in ancient India, across religious boundaries, across regions, across elites and ordinary people, shows the ability of societies to visualize and worship divinity in feminine form. The Ardhanarishvara (the lord who is half woman) form of the great god Shiva is androgynous, that is, half male, half female. [Fig. 3.18] But is there a direct correlation between a society's ability to visualize

---

[17]Leslie Orr, 'Identity and Divinity: Boundary-Crossing Goddesses in Medieval South India', *Journal of the American Academy of Religion*, vol. 73, no. 1, March 2005, pp. 9–43.

divinity in feminine form and gender relations? Does the worship of goddesses translate into a situation of social equality—or superiority—for real women?

The world of real women

All societies known so far in history have been patriarchal, that is, ultimate power and authority within the family and society at large have been vested in men. A truly matriarchal society—one in which women wield ultimate social and political power—is not yet known. But there are significant differences between societies which recognize descent through the male line (patrilineal kinship systems), those which recognize descent in the female line (matrilineal kinship systems), and those which recognize descent both in the male and female line (cognatic or bilateral kinship systems). In India, patriliny dominates, but there are a few pockets of matriliny, for instance among the Khasi, Garo, and Lalung communities in the Northeast, the Nairs of Kerala, and the people of Lakshadweep. The fact that matriliny is not the same thing as matriarchy should be clear from the fact that in these societies, the management of property is usually in the hands of men.

In patrilineal caste societies, strict control over women's sexuality and reproductive potential is essential for the transmission of property and for the maintenance and perpetuation of the endogamous caste structure. The strengthening of patriarchal authority within the household and the emphasis on the chastity of women are the means of ensuring such control. But there are many varieties of patriarchy which offer different degrees of autonomy to women. For instance, tribal patriarchal societies may give more freedom to women than others. Social norms that valorize sons and curtail the freedom of women, which we tend to think of as culturally 'Indian', are actually typical of patrilineal societies. The picture is quite different in matrilineal societies. And if we compare India with Sri Lanka, Indonesia, Thailand, or the Philippines, where many communities follow bilateral kinship systems, we get a very different picture. These are, broadly speaking, patriarchal societies but as a result of the fact that descent and property are transmitted both through women and men, the extreme forms of discrimination seen in India against women (reflected, for instance, in dowry killing, female infanticide, and neglect of the girl child) do not exist.[18] So when it comes to gender relations, the nature of the kinship system seems to be more important than religion.

As today, in ancient times too, there were many different types of kinship, marriage, and household systems in different parts of the subcontinent. Most of the textual evidence, however, pertains to patriarchal, patrilineal societies, and this gives us a somewhat skewed picture. And yet, even in the societies represented in texts, women can be seen not only as subordinated individuals (which they were) but as active participants in history.

Inequality and oppression are easy to recognize in the larger social and economic spheres but are less recognized within the family. This is because the family is the site of many different kinds of intimate emotions and experiences—of love, affection, and support, as well as hate, conflict, and even violence. But the heart of social history is to be located in relationships within the family and household.

Women and marriage in Sanskrit texts

In Vedic texts, marriage is considered essential for the continuation of the patrilineage. Only a married man, accompanied by his legitimate wife, can become the yajamana (sacrificer). Womanhood is associated with wifehood and motherhood. The grihapati (male head of the household) had control over the productive resources of the household unit and the reproductive potential of his wife. Rituals emphasized the importance of ties with the pitris (patrilineal ancestors). Post-puberty marriages seem to have been the norm and there are references to women choosing their

---

[18]See Leela Dube, 'Kinship and Gender in South and Southeast Asia: Patterns and Contrasts', 9th J. P. Naik Memorial Lecture, 1994, see http://www.cwds.ac.in/wp-content/uploads/2016/09/Kinship-and-Gender.pdf. On the family, see A. M. Shah, *The Family in India: Critical Essays*, New Delhi: Orient Longman, 1998; and Patricia Uberoi (ed.), *Family, Kinship and Marriage in India*, Oxford in India Readings in Sociology and Social Anthropology, T. N. Madan (gen. ed.), New Delhi: Oxford University Press, 1993.

husbands and remarrying if the husband died or disappeared. There are occasional references to unmarried women, for instance, the sage Ghosha.

Vedic texts praise women in various ways. The Shatapatha Brahmana states that the wife is half her husband and completes him. The Brihadaranyaka Upanishad mentions a ritual for obtaining a learned daughter. On the other hand, women were for the most part excluded from the study of the Vedas. The number of hymns attributed to women sages in the Rig Veda is small, and there are no women priests. While women participated as wives in sacrifices performed by their husbands, they did not perform sacrifices in their own right; nor do they appear as givers or receivers of dana or dakshina. Menstruation was considered dangerous and polluting. A menstruating wife was not supposed to participate in sacrifices. According to the Taittiriya Samhita, when Indra killed Vishvarupa, son of the god Tvashtri, he transferred one-third of the stain of killing a Brahmana to women. This 'stain' is said to have taken the form of women's periods.

An ideal woman was supposed to be docile and obedient. According to the Shatapatha Brahmana, a good woman is one who pleases her husband, delivers male children, and never talks back to her husband. The desire for sons is reflected in many hymns. A ritual called the pumsavana was believed to ensure the birth of a male child. The Atharva Veda contains charms for changing a female foetus into a male one. So there is clear evidence of a preference for sons over daughters.

Dharmashastra texts reflect the strengthening of the patriarchal nature of the family, an increasing subordination of women, and greater emphasis on their chastity. They recommend that marriages should generally take place within the varna, but anuloma marriages, where the man was of a higher varna status than the woman, were accepted. There are references to polygyny (one man having several wives), for instance, in the discussion of the property rights of a man's sons born of various wives.

Dharmashastra classifies marriages into eight types: brahma, daiva, arsha, prajapatya, gandharva, asura, rakshasa, and paishacha. The brahma marriage is one in which a father adorns and honours his daughter with garments and ornaments, and gifts her to a man who is learned in the

Veda and of good conduct. The daiva marriage (which applies only to Brahmanas) is when a father adorns and honours his daughter with garments and ornaments and gives her in marriage to an officiating priest in the course of the performance of a sacrifice. The arsha marriage involves the gift of a daughter after taking a pair of cattle (a cow and bull) or two pairs, in order to fulfil customary law, not as a sale of the daughter. The prajapatya marriage is one where the father gifts the daughter after saying to the couple, 'May both of you perform your religious duties together', and after he has honoured the groom with the appropriate ceremonies. The asura marriage is one in which a girl is given away by the father after the bridegroom hands over as much wealth as he can afford to the bride and her relatives. The gandharva type is a union between a man and woman through mutual love and consent. The rakshasa type is when a woman is forcibly abducted from her home, her relatives often being beaten or killed. The paishacha form is when a man has sex with a girl while she is asleep, intoxicated, unconscious, or mentally disordered. The dharma texts considered brahma the best and the paishacha the worst. This indicates a recognition of variations in marriage practices.

The anxiety to marry girls off as early as possible was connected to the great importance attached to maintaining female chastity and producing children. While earlier texts seem to be of the view that girls should be married at or near the time of attaining puberty, later Dharmashastra texts advocate pre-puberty marriages. Every menstruation a girl had was seen as a missed opportunity of conceiving a child and it was the duty of a father to find a good match for her at the proper time.[19]

In matters of inheritance, male heirs, especially sons, took precedence. There is however a category of property—stridhana—over which the Dharmashastra experts assert that wives had rights. Stridhana means 'women's wealth' and refers specifically to certain special kinds of movable property given to a woman on various occasions during her lifetime. These include presents (jewellery, clothes, household articles, etc.) given by her parents at the time of marriage and by her relatives (father, brothers, others) on other occasions. Stridhana was supposed

---

[19]For details, see Kane, *History of Dharmaśāstra*, vol. 2, part 1, pp. 438–47.

to be passed on from mother to daughter.

The *Manu Smriti* praises women. It states that the gods rejoice where women are revered, and that no ritual bears fruit where they are not. A family where women are unhappy swiftly meets its ruin, but the one where women are content prospers. The text states that the wife cannot be sold or repudiated, and that she cannot be treated as chattel, since she is obtained from the gods and not received like cattle or gold in the market. The husband is supposed to support the wife in all circumstances, provided she is faithful.

But the *Manu Smriti* also talks of the inherently fickle nature of women (stri-svabhava) and the need to keep them under control.

> Day and night men should keep their women from acting independently; for, attached as they are to sensual pleasures, men should keep them under their control. Her father guards her in childhood, her husband guards her in her youth, and her sons guard her in her old age; a woman is not qualified to act independently.[20]

A woman was to be completely devoted and obedient to her husband under all circumstances. Even if the husband was totally devoid of virtues or good qualities and a slave to lust, a good woman should always worship her husband as though he were a god. A wife could be abandoned by the husband if she was diseased, cruel, addicted to alcohol, treacherous, insubordinate, barren, a spendthrift, or harsh in speech. But for women, lifelong monogamy was the rule. Although the *Manu Smriti* refers to widow remarriage, it disapproves of it and recommends a life of extreme austerity and abstinence for widows.

So the *Manu Smriti* is a complex text which makes pro-women as well as misogynistic statements. The contradictions can be explained in various ways: the gap between theory and practice; the juxtaposing of different opinions; the context in which the statements are made; and the point sought to be emphasized. But its overall emphasis is on the subordination and control of women within the framework of the patriarchal, patrilineal family.

---

[20]*Manu Smriti* 9.2–3; Olivelle, *Manu's Code of Law*, p. 190.

The importance of women's chastity and their absolute obedience to their husbands is emphasized in other normative Brahmanical texts as well. The *Arthashastra*, for instance, lays down fines for women who leave their home without good reason. Adultery is, of course, considered a serious crime but even lesser misdemeanours, such as going out with women friends or not opening the door to the husband, invite punishments in the form of fines. Interestingly, the *Arthashastra* states that accompanying a man on the road is no offence in the case of the women of dancers, wandering minstrels, fishermen, fowlers, cowherds, vintners, and others who give freedom to their women. This suggests that the Brahmana composers of such texts were aware of the existence of other models of feminine social behaviour.

The portrayal of women in Sanskrit kavya has been discussed in Chapter 2. In the plays, kings have shifting love interests and many wives. It is worth recapitulating that Sanskrit drama is bilingual. Men and upper-class characters speak Sanskrit. Women (regardless of their status) and lower-class characters speak Prakrit. In this manner, although it reveals the difference between high and low within the category of woman, kavya also treats them as a homogeneous category and clubs them with lower classes. This kind of clubbing is also reflected in the fact that women and Shudras are sometimes spoken of in the same breath in Brahmanical texts.

While Sanskrit texts suggest a tendency towards greater social control over women's sexuality and agency over time, the extent to which they reflect prevailing social practices can be debated. They are normative texts, representing the ideas of upper-class Brahmana males. To get a better idea about what was happening on the ground, it is necessary to examine what other sources say.

Laywomen and nuns in early Buddhist texts

Patriarchal ideas, including a preference for sons over daughters, which are visible in Brahmanical texts, are found in Buddhist texts as well. Parents are said to want sons because they add to family possessions, continue the family line, inherit the father's property, and pay homage to the ancestors. The Tipitaka reflects stereotyped ideals of the submissive and obedient woman whose life revolves around her husband and sons. Buddhist texts also contain many negative images of women as temptresses and creatures of passion. It is not surprising that a tradition that set such store on monastic celibacy perceived women as a threat.

At the same time, Buddhism accepted the possibility that women could attain the highest goal—nibbana. A bhikkhuni sangha (monastic Order of nuns) was created during the Buddha's lifetime. The texts suggest that the Buddha was not keen to establish a sangha for women but ultimately gave in to pressure from his disciple Ananda and his aunt and foster-mother Mahapajapati Gotami. While doing so, he is said to have made the gloomy prediction that on account of women being admitted into the sangha, the dhamma would decline in 500 years instead of 1,000. The sangha was not open to pregnant women, mothers of unweaned children, rebellious women who associated with young men, and those who did not have their parents' or husbands' permission to join. The Tipitaka contains several references to learned nuns. While women could attain salvation, their capability for attaining Buddhahood directly (without first being born as a man) was not initially accepted.

The Therigatha (Songs of the Sisters) is a collection of seventy-three poems attributed to seventy-two nuns who had reached a high level of spiritual attainment. Some of the poems describe their experience of nibbana. Some tell of their experiences before joining the sangha. These include unhappy marriages and tragedies such as the death of a child. Chanda, a young girl from a Brahmana family, found herself destitute when her parents died in an epidemic. A nun named Patachara gave her some food, taught her the doctrine, and initiated her into the Order. Patachara herself was born in the city of Shravasti in a banker's family. She got married and had two children, both of whom died. Thereafter, she became a wanderer and joined the sangha. The first two verses of her song in the Therigatha express her longing for nibbana, building up to a description of the instant she experienced it.

When they plough their fields
and sow seeds in the earth,
when they care for their wives and children,
young Brahmanas find riches.

But I've done everything right
and followed the rule of my teacher.
I'm not lazy or proud
Why haven't I found peace?
Bathing my feet
I watched the bathwater
spill down the slope.
I concentrated my mind
the way you train a good horse.

Then I took a lamp
and went into my cell,
checked the bed,
and sat down on it.
I took a needle
and pushed the wick down.

When the lamp went out
my mind was freed.[21]

Within the sangha, nuns did not have the same status as monks. They were supposed to observe 'eight important conditions', which included the following: regardless of a nun's seniority, she was to greet even a junior monk with great deference. Under no circumstances was a nun to revile or abuse a monk. Monks could admonish and give advice to nuns, but not vice versa.

Later Mahayana texts contain negative as well as positive images of women and femininity.[22] In some places, women are portrayed

---

[21] Susan Murcott (trans.), *The First Buddhist Women: Translations and Commentaries on the Therigatha*, Berkeley: Parallax Press, 1991, pp. 33–34.

[22] See Diana Y. Paul, *Women in Buddhism: Images of the Feminine in the Mahayana Tradition*, Berkeley: Asian Humanities Press, 1979.

as mysterious, elusive, sensual, dangerous, and weak in body and mind. In other places, they are described as wise, maternal, gentle, compassionate, and creative. Women's sexuality is seen as threatening to others and to their own spiritual aspirations, and there are several stories of women tempting and destroying the celibacy and mindfulness of monks. Mahayana texts were divided in their opinion regarding women's potential to follow the path leading to bodhisattvahood. Although a few suggest that gender was irrelevant, most present two alternative paths to attaining bodhisattvahood for women. One was rebirth as a man, the other was through a miraculous sex change. At the same time, as we have seen in an earlier section, goddesses and female Buddhas did eventually become important parts of the Mahayana pantheon.

By the standards of the sixth and fifth centuries BCE, the Buddha opened up a significant space for women's spiritual aspirations. And yet, it should be noted that all the available information about the sangha during these centuries is about the bhikkhu sangha (the Order of monks). Evidence regarding the bhikkhuni sangha is largely confined to its establishment and references to nuns as donors in inscriptions. All the great monastic centres of ancient India known from texts and inscriptions were centres of male monasticism. Although nuns (along with other women) appear very often as donors at male monastic centres, there is not a single inscription recording a donation to the bhikkhuni sangha. The story of the decline and disappearance of the bhikkhuni sangha is repeated in other Asian Buddhist countries as well. The stiff resistance faced by nuns from monks in their attempts to revive their Order in recent times suggests that monks played an important role in the decline of the bhikkhuni sangha in ancient times.

Women and salvation in early Jainism

Like Buddhism, Jainism too had a monastic Order for women. The traditional Jaina account of the growth of the sangha during the lifetime of Mahavira in fact gives greater prominence to women. According to the Kalpa Sutra, when Mahavira died, there were 14,000 monks and 36,000 nuns, 159,000 laymen, and 318,000 laywomen. A total of 1,400 women and 700 men are described as having attained salvation during Mahavira's lifetime. We need not take the numbers literally, but the larger numbers of women monastics and laity compared with men in these listings are striking.

In the early centuries CE, the Jaina sangha came to be divided into the Digambara and Shvetambara sects. Whether or not women could attain liberation became an issue of a thousand-year long debate between them.[23] The issue of nudity was central to this debate. Digambaras considered clothes as possessions and associated them with passion, sexual desire, and shame. However, they did not approve of nuns practising nudity. A woman's body was thus an obstacle to her attaining salvation. There was also an idea of the inferiority of the female body, and its association with negative features:

> In the teaching of the Jina a person does not attain moksha if one wears clothes.... Nudity is the path leading to moksha. All other paths are wrong.
>
> The genital organs of the woman, her navel, armpits, and the area between her breasts, are said [in the scriptures] to be breeding grounds of subtle forms of life. How can there be [full] renunciation for a woman?
>
> Their minds are not pure and by nature they are not firm in mind or in body. They have monthly menstruation. Therefore, for women there is no meditation free from fear.[24]

Nuns were respectfully addressed as aryika or sadhvi (noble or venerable woman) but were regarded more like celibate laywomen who had achieved a significant degree of spiritual progress. According to the Digambaras, a woman had to be reborn as a man before she could attain salvation.

---

[23] See Padmanabh S. Jaini, *Gender and Salvation: Jaina Debates on the Spiritual Liberation of Women*, New Delhi: Munshiram Manoharlal, [1979], 2001; and 'Jaina Debates on the Spiritual Liberation of Women', in Jaini's *Collected Papers on Jaina Studies*, Delhi: Motilal Banarsidass, 2000, pp. 163–97.

[24] From Kundakunda's Suttapahuda (c. second century CE); as cited in Jaini, 'Jaina Debates on the Spiritual Liberation of Women', p. 166.

The Digambara arguments for refusing to accept women's capacity to attain salvation were systematically and vigorously rebutted by the Shvetambaras. According to them, wearing or not wearing clothes was optional and women could attain moksha. (Shvetambara monks and nuns both wear white clothes.) Monks and nuns of this Order took the same vows and in theory were considered on a par with each other. Monastic protocols however reveal an element of inequality, similar to that which existed within the Buddhist sangha. No matter how senior a nun and howsoever junior a monk, she had to offer him respectful salutation. Nuns could confess their misdemeanours to monks and be censured by them, but not the other way around.

Was it possible for a woman to become a Tirthankara? According to the Shvetambaras, yes. Malli, their nineteenth Tirthankara, was a woman. Digambara and Shvetambara texts both hold that women are not capable of experiencing the worst forms of undesirable volitions, so they can never be born in the seventh and lowest hell. But they also consider misdeeds and negative propensities such as cheating, greed, unpredictability, and cunning to be responsible for rebirth as a woman. Even the Shvetambara tradition about Malli ascribes her birth as a woman to cheating in a previous birth.[25] And Malli never became a popular focus of worship. Only one ninth century image of this Tirthankara has so far been found.

The denial of the possibility of salvation may have been responsible for the declining number of Digambara nuns.[26] However, the prospect of salvation was not in itself an assurance of the long-term survival of a women's monastic Order, as is clear from the disappearance of the Buddhist bhikkhuni sangha among the Theravada communities of Sri Lanka and Southeast Asia.

---

[25] She was a king named Mahabala who was born as a princess named Malli due to a fault that he had committed. The Digambaras reject this tradition completely. Their nineteenth Tirthankara is a man named Mallinatha, born into a royal family as a prince, not a princess. After taking the vows of a Digambara monk, he eventually became a Tirthankara.
[26] Jaini, *Gender and Salvation*, pp. 26–27.

Women, work, and chastity in early South India

A very different women's world emerges in Tamil Sangam poems. Apart from featuring in poems of love and lament, women also appear as workers.[27] They work in the fields, planting seeds, weeding and husking, and winnowing paddy. They are involved in rearing cattle and sheep. Spinning, bleaching, and washing clothes are other womanly activities. The *Purananuru* mentions a potter woman of Venni who was also a poetess. Women were engaged in basket-making and pith-work. Those living on the seashore participated in catching and selling fish, the extraction and selling of fish oil, and making and selling salt. Women are also mentioned in connection with making and selling toddy made from fermented rice. Garland-making and flower-selling are other occupations associated with them. Women also appear as foster-mothers or wet nurses, bards, dancers, and bodyguards employed by kings.

In Chapter 1, mention was made of ancient Tamil society's belief in sacred forces called ananku which were supposed to inhabit various objects. Ananku was closely associated with women. A chaste woman's ananku was under control and had auspicious potential. Women were considered impure during menstruation and for a certain number of days after childbirth. Widows were considered extremely inauspicious and dangerous and were supposed to lead a life of self-denial and austerity.

Sati—the immolation of a woman on her husband's funeral pyre—is an extreme practice connected with the idea of a woman's chastity and fidelity to her husband in a highly patriarchal society. Vedic texts and Dharmashastra do not mention sati. The earliest textual references occur in the Sanskrit epics. The Uttarakanda of the Ramayana (generally considered a later addition to the text) refers to the mother of the female ascetic Vedavati committing sati on her husband's death. In the Mahabharata, Madri, one of Pandu's wives, commits sati when he dies, but Kunti does not. The four wives of Vasudeva (Krishna's father) are said to have killed themselves on his death. The five wives of Krishna kill themselves on his death. But none of these instances occur in the

---

[27]Vijaya Ramaswamy, 'Aspects of women and work in early South India', in Kumkum Roy (ed.), *Women in Early Indian Societies*, New Delhi: Manohar, [1989], 1999, pp. 150–71.

context of war. In the Stri Parva of the Mahabharata, the widows of the heroes who die at Kurukshetra mourn and lament; they do not commit sati. The earliest eyewitness account of the practice occurs in a Greek source, the *Bibliotheca Historica* of Diodorus Sicilus (first century BCE).

Sangam poems suggest the practice of sati in early historic South India. A poem talks of a loyal wife who follows her husband into death. She

> wanders toward the burning ground, her hair streaming wet and falling loose down her back while her large eyes are filled with grief!....
> Though she, in the vast well-guarded palace of her husband where the eye of the concert drum is never silent, has only been alone for a while, she is fleeing her young years that make her tremble with the sweetness of life![28]

There is also material evidence. From about the third century BCE, there is evidence of memorial stones that commemorate a heroic, premature death.[29] These stones are usually uninscribed and have scenes carved on them. The simplest ones have a single scene, showing a warrior battling against his adversary. The more complex ones have several panels, showing the hero in battle, his being carried to heaven by apsaras, and his residing in a celestial abode in the company of his preferred god or saint. Associated with hero stones is the practice of commemorating satis by setting up sati stones. These vary in composition and complexity, but can be identified by their representation of an outstretched right arm, bent at the elbow, adorned with bangles, the palm of the hand facing outwards. Bangles signify that the sati is not to be considered a widow. The additional motifs of the sun and the moon indicate that her fame would last forever. [Figs. 3.19, 3.20]

At Nagarjunakonda in Andhra Pradesh, archaeologists discovered

---

[28]George L. Hart and Hank Heifetz, *The Puranānūru: Four hundred Songs of War and Wisdom: An Anthology of Poems from Classical Tamil*, New Delhi: Penguin Books, [1999], 2002, *Purananuru* 247, p. 152.

[29]See S. Settar and Gunther D. Sontheimer (eds.), *Memorial Stones: A Study of their Origin, Significance and Variety*, Dharwad: Institute of Indian Art History, Karnatak University and Heidelberg: South Asia Institute, University of Heidelberg, n.d.

Fig. 3.19: Sati Stone, Bhojpur, Madhya Pradesh

Fig. 3.20: Sati Stone, Government Museum, Chennai

further significant evidence of the practice of sati. There was a damaged brick complex next to the river which seems to have been connected with royal funerary rituals. Here was found a limestone carving of what looks like a princess or queen lying dead. There was also a slab with a carving of a woman about to jump from a ladder placed between four fires. Two stone slabs in the adjoining pillared hall had the word sva-medha (self-immolation) inscribed on them. Although there is no indication that these acts were connected with warfare or the death of the husband in war, we can assume that they were.

The experience of women bhakti saints

As discussed in Chapter 1, in the early medieval period, the Alvar and Nayanmar saints of South India gave new expression to Vaishnava and Shaiva devotion. Most of the saints were men. There were three women Nayanmars—Karaikkal Ammaiyar, Mangaiyarkkarasiyar, and

Fig. 3.21: Karaikkal Ammaiyar, copper alloy, late thirteenth century

Isainaniyar. Andal was the only woman Alvar. The male saints were not recluses or ascetics; most of them were married and lived a social life. The situation with the female saints was, however, different.

In her hagiography, the Nayanmar saint Karaikkal Ammaiyar is said to have originally been a beautiful woman named Punitavati. [Fig. 3.21] Her husband was terrified when he discovered her unusual powers, which were the result of her extraordinary devotion to Shiva; he abandoned her and married another woman. Punitavati prayed fervently to Shiva to transform her into an ugly demoness as she had no need for beauty. Shiva granted her desire and transformed her into an ugly, emaciated woman. Thereafter, she became known as Karaikkal Ammaiyar. This is one of her songs:

Sagging breasts and swollen veins,
protruding eyes, bare white teeth.
Skeletal legs and knobbly knees
has this female *pey* [ghoul].
She lingers, weeps, and wails
and wanders aimless in the forest—
There, holding fire but cool of limbs
with matted hair in all directions
Shiva dances his cosmic dance....[30]

Karaikkal is said to have gone on a pilgrimage to Mount Kailasa. As she did not want to defile the path to the sacred mountain with her feet, she walked on her hands into the god's presence. The songs of Karaikkal were never set to music nor sung in temples, probably because they were considered too dark and forbidding.

The fact that a few women figure among the bhakti saints of early medieval India is significant, but on the whole, the leadership was predominantly male. As far as larger participation is concerned, it can be noted that mathas (Shaiva monasteries) did not admit women. And it was only among the Shrivaishnavas at the time of Ramanuja (eleventh century CE) and with the increasing impact of the Virashaiva movement from the twelfth century onwards that women devotees were given a greater participatory role in Vaishnava and Shaiva bhakti.

Akka Mahadevi was a Virashaiva saint who lived in the twelfth century. According to her hagiography, a wandering mendicant initiated her when she was a small girl and told her that she would be married to Shiva. She grew into a beautiful woman, and was married to a chieftain named Kaushika. One of her conditions for the marriage was that her husband should not disturb her devotion to Shiva. When he broke this promise, Akka walked out of her marriage and home, her naked body covered only by her long hair, her nudity a symbol of a complete rejection of all social conventions. She wandered around till she joined a group of Shaiva saints. Akka's vachanas (lyrical sayings) in Kannada express

---

[30] *Tiruvalankadu Mutha Tirupadikam*, verse 1, *Tirumurai* 11; trans. cited in Dehejia, *Slaves of the Lord*, p. 118.

her intense love for Shiva, sometimes in erotic terms and sometimes in a more abstract manner.

> When the body becomes your mirror,
> how can it serve?
>
> When the mind becomes Your mind,
> what is left to remember?
>
> Once my life is Your gesture,
> how can I pray?
>
> When all my awareness is Yours,
> what can there be to know?
>
> I became You, Lord, and forgot You.[31]

The hagiographies and songs of women bhakti saints indicate that there was a fundamental difference in the experience of bhakti for men and women.[32] In the case of male saints, there was no contradiction between the life of a householder and devotion towards their god. However, social expectations and the female body impinged on the path of the bhaktin. Youth and beauty were a burden and devotion to god could not be combined with marriage and family life. Throughout history, women who have pursued their spiritual calling have risked being labelled deviants. The claims of women to asceticism and salvation have frequently been contested.

Women as religious patrons

Despite the marginal presence of women in religious pantheons and leadership, hundreds of inscriptions found in different parts of India record religious gifts made by royal and non-royal women. These show

---

[31] Trans. Jane Hirshfield; cited in Andrew Schelling (ed.), *Love and the Turning Seasons: India's Poetry of Spiritual and Erotic Longing*, New Delhi: Aleph Book Company, 2014, p. 61.
[32] See Vijaya Ramaswamy, *Walking Naked: Women, Society, Spirituality in South India*, Simla: Institute of Advanced Studies, 1997; Uma Chakravarti, 'The world of the bhaktin in South Indian Traditions—the body and beyond', Uma Chakravarti, *Everyday Lives, Everyday Histories: Beyond the Kings and Brahmanas of 'Ancient' India*, New Delhi: Tulika, [2006], 2020, pp. 275–92.

that women were active patrons and participants in the religious sphere, that they enjoyed a certain amount of authority within the family, and some control over their family's economic resources.

In the western Deccan, women from various social backgrounds made donations to the Buddhist sangha during the early centuries CE. At Sanchi in central India, during c. 200 BCE–200 CE, 380 donations were made by men and 344 donations by women.[33] Further, the 252 gifts made here by members of the sangha include 129 by monks and 123 by nuns. Several collective gifts were made by nuns and upasikas (laywomen) of certain places. Women also figure in many Sanchi relief sculptures.

At Nagarjunakonda (in Andhra Pradesh), inscriptions of the Ikshvaku kings, who ruled in the lower Krishna valley in the third and fourth centuries, indicate that it was not kings but women of the royal household who were most active in making religious donations. A stupa called the mahachaitya was an important royal ceremonial centre in the city and women of the royal household were responsible for financing its construction.[34] The most prominent patron was Chamtisiri, sister of the king Chamtamula. A non-royal woman named Bodhisiri was another important patron here as well as at other Buddhist monastic establishments.

The evidence of women's patronage is even greater in Jainism. Early Tamil–Brahmi inscriptions in Tamil Nadu and Kerala record donations made by women and men of varied social backgrounds for the excavation of caves where Jaina monks and nuns lived. At Mathura, between c. 300 BCE to 1000 CE, women donors outnumbered male donors by almost three times. Many of these gifts were made by laywomen at the request of Jaina nuns.[35]

---

[33] Upinder Singh, 'Sanchi: The History of the Patronage of an Ancient Buddhist Establishment', Upinder Singh, *The Idea of Ancient India: Essays on Religion, Politics, and Archaeology,* New Delhi: SAGE, 2016, pp. 3–42.
[34] See Upinder Singh, 'Nagarjunakonda: Buddhism in the "City of Victory"', Upinder Singh, *The Idea of Ancient India: Essays on Religion, Politics, and Archaeology,* New Delhi: SAGE, 2016, pp. 43–72.
[35] See Kanika Kishore Saxena, *Before Krsna: Religious Diversity in Ancient Mathura,* New Delhi: Oxford University Press, 2021, p. 256.

There is substantial evidence of women's patronage towards Hindu, Jaina, and Buddhist establishments in Tamil Nadu between c. 700–1700.[36] In the Chola kingdom, women donors included queens, nuns, temple women, women belonging to the family of chieftains, and wives of landowners, merchants, and Brahmanas. Queen Sembiyan Mahadevi was a great patron of Hindu temple building in the tenth century during the reigns of her husband, Gandaraditya, and her son, Uttama I. Women gave money for the construction of temples, making of images, provision of lamps, flowers, and food for the deity, and providing for the performers of temple services.

Politically powerful women

Ancient Indian texts consider kingship to be essentially a male preserve; women usually figure as 'fillers' when male heirs were unavailable. But women were considered politically relevant by the composers of the Mahabharata and Ramayana. In the Ramayana, Kaikeyi almost succeeds in diverting the royal succession to her son Bharata. In the Mahabharata, the Kurukshetra war is an all-men's affair, but Draupadi is an active participant in debates among the Pandavas on whether or not to go to war; she is a vocal member of the pro-war party.

The *Arthashastra* too recognizes women as politically relevant figures. Kautilya takes it for granted that in normal circumstances, it is men who rule. He does not consider women as heirs, but as producers of heirs. However, he envisages the possibility of a woman occupying the throne in times of political transition, for instance, when a king has died or is on his deathbed and the minister has taken over the throne to maintain order and continuity. In such a situation, the options before the minister include putting a prince, princess, or pregnant queen on the throne. Further, while arguing for the superiority of utsaha-shakti (the power of energy) over prabhu-shakti (the power of might), Kautilya states:

---

[36]Leslie Orr, 'Women's Wealth and Worship: Female Patronage of Hinduism, Jainism, and Buddhism in Medieval Tamil Nadu', in Mandakranta Bose (ed.), *Faces of the Feminine in Ancient, Medieval, and Modern India*, Delhi: Oxford University Press, 2000, pp. 124–47.

> Those who possess might—even women, children, the lame and the blind—have conquered the earth by winning over and purchasing those who possess energy.[37]

Kautilya describes female guards (along with eunuchs, hunchbacks, dwarfs, and hunters) as part of the protective security cordon around the king, an important function, considering that Kautilya's king lives in constant fear of assassination. But he has much more to say about how women pose serious threats to the king's life. In contrast to the depictions in Sanskrit kayva, in the *Arthashastra*, the antahpura (harem) is a place of danger.

> The king can protect the kingdom only when he is protected from those close to him and from enemies, but first of all from his wives and sons.[38]

The royal family is not a happy family. Lovers, queens, and sons are ambitious, ruthless, and dangerous. To drive home his point, Kautilya cites several instances of kings who were killed by their queens.

Of course, the *Arthashastra* is a normative text and describes a potential state. To what extent do women appear as active political agents in the political history of ancient India? Across the centuries, the narrative of ancient Indian political history seems to be a story of kingdoms and empires ruled by men. Women figure as pawns in matrimonial alliances and as producers of heirs. But there is evidence of women of royal households exercising power and authority. The Satavahana and Ikshvaku kings used matronyms (that is, they were named after their mothers) and inscriptions show that women of the royal family were influential figures. The political importance of matrimonial alliances in ancient India is reflected in the portrayal of queens on certain Gupta coins and the mention of queens in Gupta genealogies in inscriptions. But there are also instances of powerful queens in ancient India who exercised political power directly.

---

[37]*Arthashastra* 9.1.9; Olivelle, *King, Governance and Law in Ancient India*, p. 349.
[38]*Arthashastra* 1.17.1; Olivelle, *King, Governance and Law in Ancient India*, p. 88.

In the fifth century CE, a marriage alliance cemented the relationship between the Guptas who held sway in the north and the Vakatakas who ruled in the western Deccan. The Vakataka ruler Rudrasena II was married to Prabhavatigupta, daughter of the Gupta emperor Chandragupta II. Vakataka inscriptions reveal that Prabhavatigupta exercised political authority during the reign of her husband. When he died, his sons Divakarasena, Damodarasena, and Pravarasena were minors, and Prabhavatigupta became de facto ruler. Divakarasena did not live long enough to ascend the throne, but his younger brothers Damodarasena and Pravarasena (II) did, and the queen mother continued to hold the reins of power. Prabhavatigupta made grants of land and her inscriptions give the Gupta genealogy before that of the Vakatakas.

There were other women who ruled. In the Eastern Chalukya dynasties, Vijayamahadevi became ruler after the death of her husband, Chandraditya. The Kadamba queen Divabbarasi ruled till her minor son attained majority. Several queens ascended the throne in the Bhauma–Kara dynasty of Orissa—Prithivimahadevi (also known as Tribhuvanamahadevi), Dandimahadevi, Dharmamahadevi, and Valkulamahadevi. While these women became rulers due to the absence of a male heir, Prithivimahadevi's accession was probably also linked to the influence of her father, who belonged to the powerful Somavamshi dynasty.

Kalhana's twelfth century *Rajatarangini* mentions three women rulers of Kashmir—Yashovati of the Gonanda dynasty, Sugandha of the Utpala dynasty, and Didda of the Yashaskara dynasty. Didda had the longest and most eventful tenure, exercising political power continuously for almost fifty years.[39] She was influential during her husband Kshemagupta's reign, was regent for her minor son Abhimanyu, and in 980–81 CE, ascended the throne to rule Kashmir in her own right. Kalhana states that Didda was aided in her rise to power by the minister Naravahana, who established her rule over the entire kingdom

---

[39]For a discussion of these and other queens, see Devika Rangachari, *Invisible Women, Visible Histories: Gender, Society and Polity in North India (Seventh to Twelfth Century AD)*, New Delhi: Manohar, 2009.

and made her comparable to Indra.

> She, whom none believed had the strength to step over a cattle track—the lame lady—traversed, in the manner of the son of the wind [Hanuman], the ocean of the confederate forces.[40]

Didda founded towns and built temples and monasteries. Kalhana describes how she killed her son and three grandsons before ascending the throne. Although killing rivals must have been routine in politics, Kalhana disapproved of a woman doing such deeds. He describes Didda as merciless, lacking in moral character, and easily swayed by others. He thought that this was partly because of the fact that she was a woman:

> Even in the case of those who are born in high families, alas! The natural bent of women, like that of rivers, is to follow the downward course.[41]

Nevertheless, Kalhana did acknowledge Didda as an important figure in Kashmir's political history.

◆

Across the centuries, the idea of the feminine as embodying fertility, auspiciousness, and plenitude coexisted with the idea of women as having negative and destructive potential. The ambivalence towards women had multiple roots—attitudes towards the woman's body, sexuality, and procreative potential; the patrilineal obsession with the production of sons; the need to control women's behaviour in order to perpetuate the caste system; and the perception of female sexuality as a threat both to male celibacy and virility.

In the religious sphere, although the central foci of veneration and religious authority remained male, female deities had a strong presence. The story of goddess worship in India is not one of diminishing significance, but of increasing vibrancy and importance. 'Goddess culture' formed a strong, continuing aspect of popular belief and practice, cutting

---

[40]*Rajatarangini* 6.226; R. S. Pandit (trans.), *Kalhana's Rājataraṅgiṇī: The Saga of the Kings of Kaśmīr*, New Delhi: Sahitya Akademi, [1935], 1968, p. 248.

[41]*Rajatarangini* 6.316; Pandit, *Kalhana's Rājataraṅgiṇī*, p. 256.

Fig. 3.22: Bharat Mata poster

across sectarian identities and divides. From the nineteenth century onwards, the nation too has been visualized as a goddess, Bharat Mata. [Fig. 3.22] Even today, in villages across the length and breadth of India, apart from the female deities known from texts, goddesses of childbirth and disease are worshipped to provide succour for everyday concerns and anxieties.

However, goddess worship did not and does not translate into empowerment for real women. Within patriarchal social structures, women have always faced different degrees of subordination, depending on their class and caste and on the prevailing kinship structure. Many texts indicate increasing efforts to control and confine women within the bounds of the family and household. But the continuing attempts to control and discipline women suggest that norms and rules were not always followed and hence had to be hammered home, century after century. The statements about the proper behaviour of women and wives in many ancient texts sound depressingly familiar and similar to attitudes prevailing in India today, but then as now, there were women who did not conform and who dared to strike their own path.

Male-dominated social and political systems offer certain spaces within which upper-class women can exercise their agency in various ways, but these spaces are very narrow for non-elite women, whose experiences of subordination and oppression are qualitatively different and are largely undocumented in the sources of ancient times. Even today, in the countries of South Asia, although some women have managed to break through the glass ceiling and have made it to the top of their professions, although there have been women presidents, prime ministers, and political leaders, gender equality is still a distant dream. The golden age for Indian women does not lie in the past but in the future.

4

VIOLENCE AND NON-VIOLENCE

In February 2020, the National Museum in New Delhi announced an event called 'Historical Gastronomica: The Indus Dining Experience'. The idea was to offer a specially researched and curated experience of what the ancient Harappans ate. At the last minute, due to some furore, the non-vegetarian dishes, which included fish in turmeric stew, meat fat soup, and lamb liver with chickpea, were struck off the menu. What remained included khatti dal (sour lentils), black gram stewed with jaggery and sesame oil, and a special Indus Valley khichri. The reasons given for the sudden change included the fact that the museum housed many images of gods and goddesses and a Buddha relic, and that it was visited by many international dignitaries. The implication was that 'Indian culture' is, and always has been, vegetarian.

All over the world, the hunting scenes that dominate Stone Age art indicate that prehistoric folk ate meat. Early farmers too supplemented their grain and vegetable diet with non-vegetarian food. While it is possible that some Harappans may have preferred vegetarian food, there is overwhelming evidence that many of them did not. Bones of wild animals found at Harappan sites include those of deer, pig, boar, sheep, goat, ass, pig, tortoise, and fish. There are also remains of domesticated animals such as humped and humpless cattle, buffalo, sheep, and goat. Cut marks and traces of charring on the bones indicate that they were killed for food. Recent studies of lipid residue on Harappan pots confirm what has been known for a long time—that apart from grain, vegetables, lentils, and fruit, the Harappans ate meat.[1]

---

[1] Akshyeta Suryanarayan, Miriam Cubas, Oliver E. Craig, Carl P. Heron, Vasant S. Shinde, Ravindra N. Singh, Tamsin C. O'Connell, and Cameron A. Petrie, 'Lipid residues in pottery from the Indus Civilisation in northwest India', *Journal of Archaeological Science*, vol. 125, 2021, pp. 1–16.

So why did Harappan food habits make newspaper headlines? It is because food is not just what we consume to survive, it has enormous cultural meaning. What people eat is connected with how they understand life and how they understand the world. It is connected with economic status and social aspirations. It is a basis of religious and cultural identity. Commensality—rules for inter-dining and the giving and accepting of food and drink—is an important feature of caste society. It is not only what one eats, but also what *other* people eat that sometimes becomes an important basis of demarcating communities, including religious communities. We know this from the strong views on beef and pork held by many Hindus and Muslims respectively.

Vegetarianism is often conflated with non-violence. There is a widespread popular belief that till the advent of Muslim rulers, 'Indian culture' was essentially non-violent. Ashoka, the Buddha, and Mahavira are the icons of ancient non-violence. But were ancient Indians non-violent? The question itself is complex. How do we define violence? Apart from violent actions, what about violent speech, thoughts, emotions, and intentions? What about the various forms and theatres of violence in the political, social, religious, and environmental spheres? What about public and private, visible and hidden violence? In all cases, the line between justified force and unjustified violence is difficult to draw and depends on perspective. Violence is difficult to define.

The very fact that contemporary Indian society is replete with violence of all kinds should demolish the theory that there is something inherently non-violent about Indians. Some of the evidence for violence in ancient India is so obvious that we may wonder why we never noticed it. Some has to be prised out because the sources are past masters at concealing violence and transforming it into something else—something desirable, necessary, even beautiful. This chapter will examine the incidence and the ideas related to violence and non-violence in ancient India. It will go on to examine the different strands of the powerful countercultures of non-violence.[2]

---

[2]For a detailed discussion of political violence, with special reference to punishment, war and the forest, see Singh, *Political Violence in Ancient India*.

The violence of the state

Like inequality, violence too has always been a part of human history, although its forms, scale, and intensity have varied. The advent of the state ushered major changes in the structures for its perpetuation and control. The theory that the Harappan civilization was a peaceful culture held together by tradition rather than force can be questioned on the basis of finds of weaponry and walled citadels. In later centuries too, cities continued to be surrounded by fortification walls, indicating the need for defence against military attack.

As discussed in Chapter 1, Rig Vedic hymns contain many references to violent conflicts among the arya tribes and between the aryas on the one hand and dasas and dasyus on the other. Later Vedic royal rituals such as the rajasuya, ashvamedha, and vajapeya, which included ritual contests between the king and his kinsmen, must have been scripted on the lines of actual, bloody contests for power. Aryavarta, a land inhabited by the culturally superior aryas, was distinguished from that of the uncivilized people of the east. The aryas also distinguished themselves from mlechchhas or barbarians, a category that included foreigners and tribals. Apart from the textual references to warfare, weapons found at archaeological sites in various parts of India in second and first millennium BCE contexts indicate the endemic nature of war.

The sixth/fifth century BCE was not only the age of Mahavira and the Buddha; it was also a period of warring states. The sixteen mahajanapadas (great states) included rajyas (kingdoms) and ganas or sanghas (oligarchies) which were constantly engaged in internecine war. This was a period of military transition when hereditary warriors were being increasingly replaced by a recruited and salaried class of soldiers. The story of the rise of the kingdom of Magadha in eastern India is a bloody one. Bimbisara, king of the Haryanka dynasty, had the title 'Seniya' (one who has an army). He is said to have been killed by his son Ajatashatru, and the latter's four successors were also patricides. The short-lived Shaishunaga dynasty that followed met a violent end. Then came the Nandas. Mahapadma, the first Nanda king, was militarily successful and expanded the Magadhan kingdom. Dhanananda, the last

Nanda ruler, was greedy, cruel, and unpopular and was overthrown by Chandragupta Maurya. Chandragupta and his son Bindusara fought wars to expand the Maurya empire. The third Maurya king, Ashoka, is known in history for his pacifism and patronage of Buddhism, but the four-year gap between his accession and consecration and the reference in Buddhist texts to his killing ninety-nine brothers (clearly hyperbole!) suggest a prolonged and violent succession struggle. When the curtain rises on the political history of early historic South India in the third century BCE, it reveals the Chola, Chera, and Pandya kings warring among themselves and with many less powerful chieftains.

It would be tedious (and unnecessary) to list all the wars fought in ancient India. The pervasiveness of violence and war is woven into the history of the rise and fall of dynasties, kingdoms, and empires over the centuries. There is no eye-witness reportage, but it can be assumed that ancient wars involved killing, looting, and raping. This is what armies have often been known to do, across cultures, across time. There is no such thing as a non-violent war. Ancient warfare would also have involved capturing prisoners of war and reducing them to slavery. The functions of the prashasti (praise of the king) in royal inscriptions include giving an impression of smooth and seamless political transitions; concealing violent intra-dynastic conflicts; celebrating the king's military victories and omitting his defeats; and tempering his martial image and achievements with pacific and benevolent attributes. So the increase of political violence was accompanied by increasingly sophisticated attempts to legitimize, invisibilize, and aestheticize it.

Apart from warfare, certain forms of coercion and violence were, and still are, inherent in the state. Throughout history, states have been based on the systematic appropriation of economic and human resources from subjects. There may be no agricultural tax in India today, but in ancient Indian agrarian societies, rulers took a share of the surplus agricultural produce in the form of taxes. Extracting taxes on a regular basis involved coercion and the threat or actual use of force. The harnessing of labour for state projects also involved coercion.

Theories of the origin of kingship in the Aggana Sutta of the Buddhist Digha Nikaya and the Shanti Parva of the Mahabharata highlight the relationship between the king and his subjects. They describe people handing over taxes to the king in return for his performing certain duties, especially maintaining social order and preventing crime and violence. Many texts describe one-sixth of the produce as the king's share and advise the ruler to be fair and moderate while levying taxes. This fiction of a voluntary social contract between the king and his subjects deliberately conceals the coercion that was involved in making farmers pay taxes.

Violence was also inherent in the interactions of ancient Indian states with forest people. The expansion of agriculture, cities, and states involved a steady clearance of forests, but the most massive forest clearance took place in the middle of the nineteenth century as a result of population increase, commercial farming, and the expansion of the railways. Till then, states lived cheek by jowl with forest tribes. Extracting and controlling valuable economic and military resources like wood, ivory, and elephants involved a steady encroachment on forest habitats and constant conflicts with forest people.[3] The forest was an important object of the exploitation and violence *of* the state; but it was also a constant source of violent challenge *to* the state. The term mlechchha included tribals as well as foreigners and presented them as a threat to 'civilized' people. But it could also be used to justify the use of violence *against* tribals and foreigners. One of the theories of the origins of kingship in the Mahabharata (discussed later in this chapter) mentions the Nishada and indicates a recognition of the political importance of forest tribes.

While ancient texts conceal the coercive element involved in taxation and the state's interface with forest people, they loudly proclaim that the king's use of danda (literally the rod; by extension, force or punishment) is essential to maintain social order. A favoured metaphor for chaos in ancient texts is matsya-nyaya, literally, the law of the fish, a situation where the big fish eat the small fish, that is, where the mighty oppress

---

[3]For a detailed discussion of the many different ways in which the forest was understood in ancient India, see Singh, *Political Violence in Ancient India*, Chap. 5. Also see Thomas R. Trautmann, *Elephants and Kings: An Environmental History*, Ranikhet: Permanent Black, 2015.

the weak. We do not know the details of the mechanisms for settling civil and criminal disputes in ancient times, but the development of a judicial system (howsoever rudimentary) gave the state and its agents the right to adjudicate civil and criminal disputes and to impose punishment, even death. The king's rod is said to inspire fear in people and prevents them from committing crimes. But all ancient texts emphasize that a ruler must use the rod in accordance with the principles of justice.

The power of the state to punish subjects is discussed in great detail in the *Arthashastra*. Although there is little evidence suggesting that the 'laws' contained in this text were actually used in civil or criminal cases, they are important for the history of legal ideas. The system of criminal and civil law in the *Arthashastra* involves judges, with the king theoretically presiding over the justice system at a higher level. Punishments include fines, confiscation of property, exile, corporeal punishment, mutilation, branding, torture, forced labour, and death. Torture is both a punishment and a means of acquiring information during interrogation and includes striking, whipping, caning, suspension from a rope, and inserting needles under the nails. The *Arthashastra* also refers to capital punishment, distinguishing between shuddha-vadha (simple death), and chitra-vadha (death by torture). The latter refers to painful deaths which may have involved public spectacle. They include burning on a pyre, drowning in water, cooking in a big jar, impaling on a stake, setting fire to different parts of the body, and tearing the body apart by bullocks.

To be fair to him, Kautilya was not, as is often imagined, an advocate of unrestricted or wanton state violence. In line with the larger ancient Indian political discourse, he argues that the king's punishment must be rooted in vinaya (discipline). A ruler who imposes wrongful punishment cannot escape punishment himself. If used indiscriminately, unfairly, out of anger or malice, the rod destroys the king. In the absence of institutional checks, the political theorists sought to control the king's propensity to exercise brute force by warning of the disastrous consequences of excessive force and by emphasizing the need for rulers to be wise, educated, disciplined, and receptive to good advice.

Given the pervasiveness of warfare and the force or threat of force implied in systems of taxation and justice, violence can indeed be described as an intrinsic part of human history, and ancient India is no exception.

War was central to ancient Indian political culture

Beyond the pervasiveness of warfare in ancient Indian political history, I would like to suggest that war was *central* to ancient Indian culture (as it was to many other cultures).[4] It is impossible to imagine the Sanskrit epics—Mahabharata and Ramayana—without war. The oldest Tamil literature, the Sangam poems, also reflect a warrior ethos. In these and other texts, war forms a context within which many other important issues are discussed—human relationships, social duty, the goals of life, happiness, death and its aftermath, heaven and hell, and the relationship with the gods. The ideas and values represented in such texts must have percolated down to various strata of society.

Puram poems and hero stones

The puram poems of the Sangam corpus attach great value to a heroic death. Bravery in battle was an attribute of masculinity, cowardice a source of shame. The spirit of a warrior who died in battle was believed to dwell in paradise. Consider the following poem, supposed to have been written by a poetess:

> Many said,
> That old woman, the one whose veins show
> on her weak, dry arms where the flesh is hanging,
> whose stomach is flat as a lotus leaf,
> has a son who lost his nerve in battle and fled.
> At that, she grew enraged and she said,
> 'If he has run away in the thick of battle,
> I will cut off these breasts from which he sucked,'
> and, sword in hand, she turned over fallen corpses,

---

[4]For a detailed discussion of war in ancient Indian thought, see Singh, *Political Violence in Ancient India*, Chap. 4.

groping her way on the red field.
Then she saw her son lying there in pieces
and she rejoiced more than the day she bore him.[5]

Bodies of warriors who did not die in battle were cut with swords before the funerary rites, in order to simulate death in battle. At times, kings who had been defeated in war committed ritual suicide through starvation, accompanied by their near and dear ones. A poet describes King Kopperuncholan performing this act after defeat in war; he is grief-stricken that the king had not asked him to accompany him into death.[6]

Sangam poems speak of memorial stones known as natukal and virakal set up in honour of heroes who had died fighting. These stones were decorated with garlands and peacock feathers; the warrior's weapons were sometimes placed beside them. The spirit of the dead hero was believed to reside in the stone and it was worshipped with ritual offerings of rice balls, liquor, and animals.

Apart from poetry, hero stones (mentioned in Chapter 3) commemorating the death of men in battles proliferated over the centuries, not only in South India, but also in other parts of the subcontinent. The events they commemorated were usually not the large-scale wars celebrated in royal inscriptions but small-scale local events, often cattle raids, that were important in the life and historical memory of villagers and local communities. These stones consist of one or more carved panels and are usually uninscribed. It is not easy to date them, but the practice seems to go back to the third century BCE. [Figs. 4.1, 4.2] More elaborate hero stones make their appearance in the third and fourth centuries CE, for instance at Nagarjunakonda in the Krishna valley. Here, at the site of the ancient Ikshvaku capital of Vijayapuri, there are a large number of memorial pillars commemorating the heroic death of army generals and groups of soldiers.

---

[5] *Purananuru* 278; the song of Kakkaipatiniyar Nachchellaiyar; George L. Hart III (trans.), *Poets of the Tamil Anthologies*, p. 199. It is interesting that this poem, with its graphic glorification of a heroic death, was composed by a woman.
[6] *Purananuru* 219; Hart, *Poets of the Tamil Anthologies*, p. 186.

Fig. 4.1: Hero stone outside Vidisha Museum, Madhya Pradesh

Fig. 4.2: Ekasar hero stone, Mumbai; note the naval battle in the lowest panel

Although the details of the beliefs and customs associated with them must have varied across time and regions, the thousands of hero stones found in various parts of India reflect the pervasiveness of ideas of masculinity and honour that valorized a violent, heroic death.

War and dharma

The close connection between war and social values is expressed more eloquently in the various tellings of the Mahabharata and Ramayana, which had great cultural impact across India and Southeast Asia. [Fig. 4.3] The Mahabharata was probably woven around the memory of an actual conflict between warring kin and reflects the rivalry that must have commonly existed among ruling elites. The war at Kurukshetra is said to have been one of many episodes of conflict between gods and demons, a dharma-yuddha (righteous war). This is because it was fought for Yudhishthira's right to the throne (he was the eldest son); the Pandavas were semi-divine; and the god Krishna fought on their side. But the ideas about this dharma-yuddha are accompanied by questions and doubt which bring out the problematic nature of both dharma and war. The Mahabharata combines the old idea of the Kshatriya warrior whose aim was to die in battle and attain heaven with a newer, higher goal—moksha. In the epic, war becomes a setting that triggers discussion and debate about many other profound issues, especially dharma. All important issues *have* to be sorted out in the face of possible death on the battlefield, after which no further discussion and debate would be possible.

The relationship between war and dharma is best illustrated in the Bhagavad Gita, which brings together many diverse philosophical strands to create a new synthesis. The narrative setting of the battlefield is dramatic. Arjuna stands in his chariot and sees his kin, teachers, and friends arrayed before him. His mouth goes dry, his body feels weak and tremulous, his bow slips from his hands. He is assailed by a terrible confusion. Killing is not the problem; that is what Kshatriyas do. It is the killing of one's own people (sva-jana)—one's close relatives, teachers, and friends—that is problematic. The killing of kin leads to the destruction of

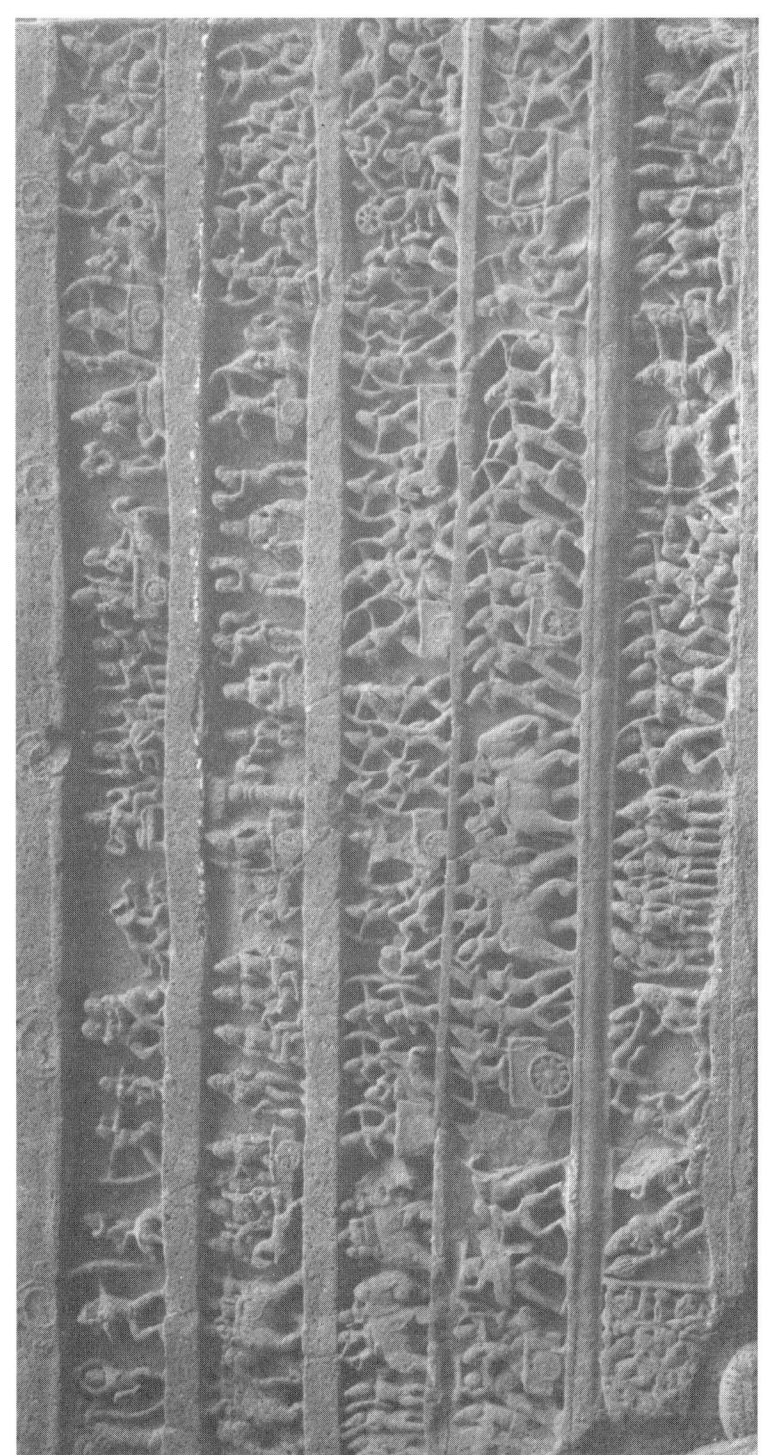

Fig. 4.3: Mahabharata panels, Kailasanatha temple, Ellora

the kula (lineage), the corruption of its women, and social chaos. Surely, fighting such a war would be a papa (great sin). Arjuna expresses these misgivings to his charioteer, Krishna. He puts away his bow and arrows, sits down in his chariot, and says that he will not fight.

The rest of the Bhagavad Gita consists of Krishna's teaching to Arjuna. One must follow one's dharma (sva-dharma), that is the dharma of the varna one belongs to. A warrior who dies fighting in such a dharma-yuddha will attain heaven and eternal fame. Turning away from battle will result in shame and infamy, which is much worse than death. Killing the enemy is not something to feel sorrowful about because death is inevitable. In any case, it is only the physical body of the enemy that is killed; the embodied self (atman) is indestructible and eternal.

> Weapons do not pierce this (the embodied Self), fire does not burn this, water does not wet this, nor does the wind cause it to wither.
> This cannot be pierced, burned, wetted or withered; this is eternal, all pervading, fixed; this is unmoving and primeval.[7]

A wise man performs his duty with complete mastery over his senses, unconcerned about their consequences. This is desireless action.

Krishna also uses the argument of bhakti. If Arjuna seeks shelter in him (Krishna), is absorbed in him (Krishna), in return, he (Arjuna) will be set free from all sin. Arjuna's doubts are removed and he picks up his bow and arrows, ready to fight. The Pandavas ultimately win the war at Kurukshetra, but it is after a great deal of slaughter, and they do not live happily ever after. Although the Mahabharata contains a powerful philosophical justification of war, it also contains in its eleventh book, the Stri Parva, a powerful lament on its consequences.

While the Mahabharata war is fought between two confederate armies for the sake of a kingdom, in the Ramayana, none of the princes hanker for the throne. Rama goes to war to rescue his beloved wife Sita, who has been abducted by Ravana, the demon king of Lanka. This war too is presented as another round of the conflict between the

---

[7] *Bhagavad Gita* 2.23-24; Sargeant, *The Bhagavad Gita*, pp. 30–31.

Ancient India: Culture of Contradictions

Fig. 4.4: Mahabharata battle, Paithan school, ink and colour on paper

gods and demons. Rama and his three brothers are parts of Vishnu. Rama's birth as a man is part of a divine plan to kill Ravana, who has created mayhem by obstructing the activities of the gods, Brahmanas, gandharvas, yakshas, and sages. But this war is very different from the one fought at Kurukshetra. Rama and Lakshmana set out for the island of Lanka seated on the shoulders of the vanaras Hanuman and Angada, their army consisting almost entirely of vanaras. The vanaras are monkeys only in appearance—they are actually the sons of various gods and have been created in order to help Rama defeat Ravana.

Both epics have the idea of a code of honour in battle but acknowledge the occasional need to resort to unfair practices to achieve one's goals. Rama transgresses the warrior's code when he shoots the vanara Vali in the back while the latter is fighting Sugriva. But by and large, Rama is presented as compassionate even towards his enemies. The practice of deceit for the sake of victory is much more pronounced in the Mahabharata, and it is practised by both sides. [Figs. 4.4, 4.5] The

Fig. 4.5: Bhima defeats Duryodhana, Folio from *Razmnama* (a Mahabharata translation commissioned by Akbar); ink, watercolour, and gold on paper, early seventeenth century

Pandavas rattle and then kill Drona by announcing that Ashvatthama—the name of Drona's son, but also that of an elephant that Bhima had killed for the deceit—is dead. Karna is killed while trying to free his chariot wheel from the mud. Bhima kills Duryodhana by giving a low blow to his thigh. As the Pandavas shamefacedly watch Duryodhana die, recalling all their transgressions of the warrior's honour code, Krishna offers a justification. The Kauravas were militarily stronger and could not have been defeated in fair fight; that is why he had devised these strategies.

> You should not take it to heart that this king [Duryodhana] has been slain, for, when enemies become too numerous and powerful, they should be slain by deceit and stratagems. This is the path formerly trodden by the gods to slay the demons; and a path trodden by the virtuous may be trodden by all.[8]

Dharma is complicated. Nothing illustrates this better than what transpires over eighteen days at Kurukshetra. War is the stage on which many questions related to human existence are asked and answered, often inconclusively.

War as a natural part of politics

The importance of war in ancient Indian politics is clear from the fact that political theorists discuss it in great detail. War is the subject of Book 10 of the *Arthashastra* but is also a prominent subject of discussion in several other books. In fact, it seems that the analysis of war was one of Kautilya's important contributions to the discussion of statecraft. The theory of the raja-mandala (circle of kings) presumes the existence of multiple warring states, vying for political supremacy. Kautilya advises the vijigishu—the king desirous of victory—on how to overreach his rivals and become the hub of the circle of kings, that is, to attain paramountcy.

The theory of the circle of kings is connected to the six measures (gunas) of inter-state policy and the four expedients (upayas). The six measures are peace/treaty (sandhi), war/initiating hostilities (vigraha), staying quiet (asana), initiating a military march (yana), seeking shelter (samshraya), and the dual policy of peace or treaty with one king and war against another (dvaidhibhava). The four expedients are an important part of governance as well as the conduct of inter-state relations; they

---

[8]Mahabharata 9.55.61–62; Smith, *The Mahābhārata*, pp. 560–61.

comprise pacification (sama), giving gifts (dana), force (danda), and creating dissension (bheda).

Apart from military strategy, the *Arthashastra* has a great deal to say about the organization of the army. It talks of the four-fold army (chaturanga-bala) consisting of infantry, cavalry, chariot wing, and elephant corps. It lists six types of troops (bala)—hereditary (maula), hired (bhrita), banded (shreni), ally's (mitra), alien (amitra), and forest (atavika). Hereditary troops are considered the best and forest troops the worst. Battle arrays, siege tactics, salaries, and keeping soldiers happy and loyal are important issues that are addressed. Kautilya talks of the harassment and oppression of the people as a result of war. According to him, the harassment inflicted on the people by another's army is worse than that inflicted by one's own army. The harassment by the enemy's army afflicts the entire land, ruins it through plunder, killing, burning, destruction, and deportation. The destruction of the enemy's crops in the course of the march is mentioned. Plunder is part of warfare and Kautilya suggests how to divide it up among confederate armies. But according to Kautilya, war must never be waged without a careful cost-benefit calculation. If the gains of war and peace are likely to be similar, the king should opt for peace, because war has many negative results.

Kautilya gives a basic three-fold classification of war—prakasha-yuddha (open war), kuta-yuddha (crooked war), and tushnim-yuddha (silent war). Open war is when fighting takes place at a designated and announced time and place. Crooked war involves creating fright, sudden assault, striking when there is an error or calamity on the enemy's side, and retreating and then striking at the same place. All these tactics have the element of sudden, unexpected attack. Silent war includes pretence, ambush, and luring the enemy's troops with the prospect of gain. It involves the use of trickery, secret practices, and instigation. There is also a fourth type of war—mantra-yuddha (diplomatic warfare). This involves discussion, persuasion, and negotiation with the enemy, as opposed to military action. Kautilya talks of three kinds of victors. The dharma-vijayi (righteous victor) is satisfied with submission. The lobha-vijayi (greedy victor) is satisfied with the seizure of land and goods. The asura-vijayi (demonic victor) is only satisfied with seizing the enemy's land, goods, sons, wives, and life. But apart from this passing reference to dharma-vijaya, the *Arthashastra* is more concerned with victory than honour.

While Kautilya has no compunctions about the use of force to attain political ends, he also warns of its dangers. Going against the other experts, he argues that mantra-shakti (the power of counsel) is superior to prabhu-shakti (military might) and utsaha-shakti (the power of energy). He also suggests that the results of war can be achieved through other means, including marriage alliances, buying peace, and assassination. Other recommended ways of dealing with enemies include the use of poison, magic, spells, and charms. Kautilya views judicious force as one of the many ways whereby the vijigishu can achieve his political aims, but force should always be a last resort. A ruler's greatest weapon is his intellect.

Many centuries later, another political theorist, Kamandaka, wrote a work titled the *Nitisara*. This too discusses war. It details the uncertain and possibly disastrous results of war, especially one launched hastily without due consideration and consultation. Kamandaka lists sixteen types of war that should not be fought. War is a risky business and should hence be avoided by a prudent king. 'As victory in war is always uncertain, it should not be launched without careful deliberation.'[9] War, Kamandaka asserts, has inherently disastrous doshas (qualities). While Kautilya urges caution in war, Kamandaka expresses stronger reservations. But war is still considered an integral part of politics and the aim is carefully calculated military victory.

The aesthetics of war

Political theorists deliberated on the nature and conduct of war. Poets, playwrights, royal biographers, and composers of royal inscriptions celebrated the military prowess and victories of kings. Through an elegant sleight of hand, they divested war of its ugliness and violence and presented it as something necessary, desirable, even beautiful.

---

[9]*Nitisara* 10.24; Rajendralala Mitra (ed.), *The Nītisāra, or The Elements of Polity by Kāmandaki*, revised with English translation by Sisir Kumar Mitra, Calcutta: Asiatic Society, [1861] 1982. Bibliotheca Indica series, no. 179; translation mine.

Fig. 4.6: Allahabad Pillar

Two examples of this stand out—the Allahabad pillar inscription of Samudragupta and the *Raghuvamsha* of Kalidasa.

A remarkable sandstone pillar, presently standing in the Allahabad Fort, bears inscriptions of four emperors—a set of six edicts and two minor pillar edicts of the Maurya emperor Ashoka; a prashasti (paneygyric) of the Gupta emperor Samudragupta; and an inscription of the Mughal emperor Jahangir. [Fig. 4.6] The inscription of Samudragupta (c. 350–370 CE) was composed by Harishena, a high-ranking official and military commander.

Samudragupta's martial qualities and achievements are described in detail in the Allahabad pillar inscription. Harishena's achievement was to give an account of Samudragupta's irresistible and spectacular wars and successes, which, at first glance, gives the illusion of his being emperor of the whole subcontinent, but on closer reading, presents a more complex and limited picture of the empire. Also striking is the way he aestheticizes war. He describes the king as one who has engaged in hundreds of battles, and whose body is beautiful on account of being covered with hundreds of scars caused by various types of enemy weapons. This is a king whose '...fame has tired itself with a journey over the whole world caused by the restoration of many fallen kingdoms and overthrown royal families.'[10] But the references to the king's many military victories are regularly punctuated by references to his non-martial qualities and achievements.

Kalidasa's *Raghuvamsha* (fourth/fifth century CE) is an extremely important and influential poetic work, which deals both with the ideals and realities of kingship. It tells the history of kings of the Ikshvaku dynasty, including Dilipa, Raghu, and Rama. The fourth canto describes the digvijaya (victory over the quarters) of Raghu. Kalidasa describes this as an elaborate clockwise military circumambulation of the subcontinent. The description is marked by great poetic beauty and elegance, with references to the landscape, trees and flowers, and the produce of various regions. By and large, Kalidasa avoids graphic descriptions of the violence of war in favour of aestheticized descriptions.

> His [Raghu's] march was clearly marked by many kings who were dispossessed, deposed or overthrown, as the march of an elephant is marked by uprooted, broken trees, devoid of fruit.[11]

And yet, notwithstanding the importance of victories in battle, Kalidasa makes it clear that great kings do not seek political paramountcy for

---

[10]B. Chhabra and G. S. Gai, *Corpus Inscriptionum Indicarum*, vol. 3, revised by D. R. Bhandarkar, New Delhi: Archaeological Survey of India, p. 217, line 23.
[11]*Raghuvamsha* 4.33; translation mine. For the text and translation of this work, see C. R. Devadhar (ed. and trans.), *Raghuvaṁśa of Kālidāsa*, Delhi: Motilal Banarsidass, 1985.

the sake of land or riches but for the sake of fame. Nor do they cling to power. After his conquest of the quarters, Raghu performs a grand sacrifice called the vishvajit (victory over the world) in which he uses up all the wealth he had obtained in his wars. Having discharged his duties, Raghu hands over the reins of power to his son Aja, retires from worldly life, and realizes the ultimate reality through the performance of yoga and meditation. The *Raghuvamsha* expresses the idea that empire involved military victories but not necessarily conquest. War is idealized and aestheticized and combined with renunciation. Its mundane objectives and violence are erased.

Violence against the state

The upheavals of ancient Indian political history indicate that kings and dynasties faced frequent challenges from rivals. Further evidence of threats of violence against the state comes from reading between the lines of texts, especially taking note of their apprehensions, insecurities, and anxieties.

One of the accounts of the origin of kingship in the Shanti Parva of the Mahabharata talks of the gods approaching Brahma and Vishnu to intervene in order to put an end to social disorder.[12] Vishnu produced a mind-born son Virajas, who was followed by his son Kirtiman and grandson Kardama. But these three men wanted to renounce the world and did not want to rule. Then came Ananga (who was a good king) and Atibala (who did not have control over his senses). They were followed by Vena, who was dominated by passion and hate and was unrighteous in his behaviour towards his subjects. The sages decided to get rid of him and stabbed him to death with blades of kusha grass. They churned his right thigh and out of it emerged an ugly man named Nishada who was told to go away because he was unfit to be king. Then they churned Vena's right hand and therefrom emerged Prithu, a man with a refined mind and an understanding of the Vedas, dharma, artha, the military arts, and politics. Prithu proved to be an exemplary ruler. Although this story cannot be considered an account of historical events, it is

---

[12]Mahabharata 12.59.1–140.

significant for the many ideas it enfolds—kings who do not want to rule, the tension between kingship and renunciation, the inferiority of forest tribes, and the justification for killing evil kings.

The Mahabharata discusses the king's duties and warns of the consequences of not performing them. A just king goes to heaven, one who is unjust goes to hell. There are other warnings as well:

> A cruel king, who does not protect his people, who robs them in the name of levying taxes, is evil [Kali] incarnate and should be killed by his subjects. A king who, after declaring 'I will protect you,' does not protect them, should be killed by his people coming together, as though he were a mad dog.[13]

So once again, as in the story of Vena, the epic sanctions the killing of bad kings. There are several stories in ancient Indian texts of evil men who are also kings being killed (Duryodhana, Ravana, and Kamsa are some of the well-known ones), but the overall attitude of the Mahabharata—indeed of all ancient Indian texts—is pro-government and pro-monarchy. Kinglessness is seen as the equivalent of anarchy.

The most comprehensive and pragmatic discussion of violence against the state occurs in the *Arthashastra*. Kautilya advocates ruthless, carefully calculated, and effective use of violence by the state in order to prevent and respond to violence against the state. Kautilya's king lives in constant fear of assassination, especially at the hands of his wives and sons. Other threats include enemy kings, neighbouring rulers, angry subjects, forest tribes, robbers, mlechchhas, and rebellious troops. Kautilya advises the king to have an elaborate espionage system and to deal firmly with revolts and conspiracies. Those who cannot be killed openly, such as high-ranking officers, should be dealt with through upamshu-danda (silent punishment), that is, secret killing. Silent punishment can also be used against hostile subjects.

Kautilya recognizes violence against the king as a serious political problem that has to be dealt with ruthlessly and effectively through pre-emptive action, punishment, and retaliation. The punishment for

---

[13]Mahabharata 13.60.32–33.

one who reviles or spreads evil news about the king or reveals secret counsel is the tearing out of the tongue. More severe crimes against the king and kingdom invite more violent punishments. Death by setting fire to the hands and head is the punishment for one who covets the kingdom, attacks the king's palace, incites forest people or enemies, or causes rebellion in the fortified city, countryside, or army. In several cases (including crimes which invite mutilation), Kautilya refers to the possibility of commuting punishments to fines. But unless there is some crucial mitigating circumstance, no commutation is suggested where the crime merits the death penalty, especially for treason or loss to the state.[14] Whether or not Kautilya's recommendations were actually applied, we know that autocracies tend to react violently to criticism and come down hard on rebels.

The *Arthashastra* contains several references to disaffection among subjects and prakriti-kopa (the anger of the people). These suggest an anxiety about the possibility of a mass rebellion of unhappy, dissatisfied subjects. But ancient Indian sources do not record a single historical instance of popular rebellion against the state. Does this mean that ancient Indians were docile and obedient, never questioning the inequities and oppression of their rulers? There are other possible reasons—the concealment of such incidents by the sources; the effectiveness of the state's coercive and repressive machinery in preventing and crushing any resistance; and the absence of collective will, resources, and organization that would have enabled the victims of state oppression to come together and revolt against the state.

Occasionally, cracks can be seen in the façade. Land grant inscriptions routinely state that the gifted village land was not to be entered by the king's troops. This only makes sense in a context of a military presence in the countryside. The fifth century Chammak copper plate of the Vakataka king Pravarasena II records the gift of Charmanka village to a thousand Brahmanas and states that the grant was to last as long as the sun and the moon endured (that is, forever). But it adds the curious caveat that

---

[14]There are some special concessions made for Brahmanas. According to Kautilya, Brahmanas who commit treason should be blinded instead of being killed.

the grant would last as long as the Brahmanas in question committed no treason against the kingdom; were not found guilty of the murder of a Brahmana, theft, or adultery; did not wage war; and did not harm other villages. If they did any of these things, the king would do no wrong in taking the land away from them. This inscription suggests that Brahmanas patronized by the king were considered capable of presenting a threat to society and to the state.

Incidents of violent rebellion are known in early medieval India, but none of them were 'popular' rebellions. For instance, the Kaivarta rebellion in eastern India in the late eleventh century was basically a revolt of politically powerful landowners. The Damara rebellion in Kashmir too involved powerful landlords, not ordinary folk. On the other hand, there are a few inscriptional references to agrarian conflicts, in some cases involving the state. For instance, a thirteenth century inscription from Karnataka states that when farmers protested against their village being converted into a brahmadeya (Brahmana village) a royal army was sent to punish them.[15] Then, as now, farmers were no match for an all-powerful state.

Social conflict and violence

Coercion, violence, and the threat of violence go hand in hand with social inequality. As discussed in Chapter 1, in the context of ancient India, the structures of inequality included class, slavery, varna, caste, untouchability, and the patriarchal family. Texts and inscriptions frequently refer to the king as maintainer of the order of varnas and ashramas, that is, protector of the social order. Actions against subjects could be justified on these grounds and could be presented as being in the interests of the subjects themselves. In the Uttarakanda of the Ramayana, Rama kills the Shudra Shambuka. The moral justification is that the latter had transgressed the varna order by performing austerities; this transgression had led to unnatural events such as the premature death of an innocent Brahmana child. So the otherwise compassionate

---

[15]R. N. Nandi, *State Formation, Agrarian Growth and Social Change in Feudal South India (c. AD 600-1200)*, New Delhi: Manohar, 2000, pp. 125–27.

Rama killed Shambuka without any hesitation in order to protect the larger social good.

Occasionally, incidents involving social conflict at the grassroots level erupted into the open. Several inscriptions from the Karnataka area point to conflict within the rural community, often over natural resources.[16] A 1230 CE inscription from Hassan taluk states that two farmers died while trying to prevent the agents of Brahmanas from cutting down palmyra trees in their village. Then, as now, water was an especially sensitive issue. A 1080 CE inscription from the same taluk refers to a conflict between a Brahmana and a farmer's family over drawing water from a village tank. An early thirteenth century inscription mentions a conflict between farmers and a chief over an irrigation tank. The chief was killed and the Hoysala king set up a hero stone in his memory and built a new tank. A 1231 CE inscription from Mannargudi, belonging to the time of the Chola king Rajaraja III, reveals the burden of compulsory labour levies on farmers. It states that the nattar (leading men of the locality) of a village complained to the Brahmana sabha and mahasabha (these were Brahmana assemblies) of the oppressiveness of various tax collectors (some armed) who were demanding the same levies. The inscription also mentions the burden of compulsory labour imposed on villagers for the repair work to be conducted in the capital city, which was located about 35 kilometres away from Mannargudi.[17]

So social conflict and violence were not absent in ancient India, but their presence has to be largely inferred from sources that muffle the voices of discontent or dissent. Such conflicts were often dealt with and diffused—though never entirely resolved—at the religious level before they boiled over. Examples of this can be seen in Jainism and Buddhism in the early period, and bhakti in later centuries.

---

[16]Nandi, *State Formation, Agrarian Growth and Social Change in Feudal South India*, pp. 125–27.

[17]Subbarayalu, 'State and Society during the Chola period', R. Champakalakshmi, Kesavan Veluthat, and T. R. Venugopalan (eds.), *State and Society in Pre-Modern South India*, Thrissur: Cosmobooks, 2002, pp. 92–94.

Gendered violence

Much of what we would consider inappropriate sexual behaviour in the post-MeToo era was considered normal in ancient times and it is not helpful to apply our standards retrospectively. It is more meaningful to try to understand how norms and transgressions were understood in ancient texts. Of course, it has to be kept in mind that standards and customs would have varied a great deal across classes, communities, and regions.

Sanskrit kavya presents an idyllic picture of polygynous royal households and harems, thronging with queens, mistresses, slaves, and servants, where women of varying rank and standing were available to kings for their pleasure and the production of heirs. However, if the aesthetic veneer is peeled off and texts are read against the grain, the image of the happy harem dissolves into something ugly. Dharmashastra, the Sanskrit epics, *Arthashastra*, and *Kamasutra* provide some entry points into this alternative picture.

Of the eight types of marriage listed in Dharmashastra texts, two—the rakshasa and paishacha—involve violence. The rakshasa (demonic) type of marriage is defined in the *Manu Smriti* as 'when someone violently abducts a girl from her house as she is shrieking and weeping, by causing death, mayhem, and destruction'.[18] The paishacha (ghoulish) marriage, considered the most evil, is when someone secretly rapes a woman who is sleeping, drunk, or deranged in mind. The rakshasa marriage is considered lawful for Kshatriya warriors and can to some extent be seen as an extension of the violent Kshatriya dharma. But gandharva, a marriage based on mutual love and desire, is also associated with Kshatriyas. So the Kshatriya was singled out for violence as well as love and sometimes the two are connected. For instance, in the Mahabharata, Arjuna abducts Subhadra by force because he has fallen in love with her.

The reference to stri-vyasana (womanizing) in the standard list of the king's vices in Sanskrit political discourse recognizes the ruler's propensity for sexual indulgence, which was considered all right in

---

[18]*Manu Smriti* 3.33; Olivelle, *Manu's Code of Law*, p. 109.

moderate doses, but problematic when it became excessive. The texts always discuss this vice from the perspective of its implications for the king, not from that of the women who were the object of the king's desire.

There are several episodes of violence against women in the political domain in the Mahabharata and Ramayana. Many refer to a woman being dragged by the hair, an act laden with real and symbolic violence.[19] Mention was made in Chapter 1 of the incident in the Mahabharata where Duhshasana violently drags Draupadi by the hair into the assembly hall and attempts to disrobe her in public. The assault is politically motivated and involves humiliating a woman in order to humiliate her husbands. Later in the epic, while the Pandavas are living in disguise in the Matsya court, Draupadi is the victim of a violent sexual assault by Kichaka (the brother-in-law of King Virata), who thinks she is a servant woman. He tries to rape her and when she resists, he drags her by the hair into the assembly. Another important incident where the cruel treatment and humiliation of a woman invites dire retribution is that of Amba and her birth as Shikhandin—neither man nor woman—in order to destroy Bhishma.

In the Ramayana, Ravana uses brute force while abducting Sita, seizing and dragging her by the hair. [Fig. 4.7] Yet he does not force himself on her, because he is in love with her and is prepared to wait until she comes to him willingly. A very different picture of Ravana is presented in the Uttarakanda of the epic, where there are many more details about his violent past and personality.[20] Here, we are told that in an earlier birth, Ravana had assaulted a virtuous Brahmana ascetic woman named Vedavati (who was none other than Sita in an earlier birth). Vedavati had immolated herself to preserve her chastity, and while doing so, had vowed that she would be born in the future as the daughter of a virtuous man, although not from a human womb, in

---

[19]See Minoru Hara, 'The Holding of the Hair (Keśa-grahaṇa)', *Acta Orientalia*, vol. 47, 1986, pp. 67–92.
[20]See Goldman and Goldman, *The Rāmāyaṇa of Vālmīki: An Epic of Ancient India*, vol. 7: Uttarakāṇḍa.

Fig. 4.7: Jaimini Roy, 'Jatayu, Sita and Ravana', tempera on paper, c. 1940

order to destroy Ravana. Ravana also rapes the apasara Rumbha while she is on her way to a rendezvous with her lover Nalakubara. When Nalakubara learns of the incident, he curses Ravana that if he ever again tried to molest a woman against her will, his head would break into seven pieces. This explains why he did not force himself on Sita. In both the Mahabharata and Ramayana, sexual assault and rape invite dire retribution. Clearly, the composers did not approve of such behaviour. But the fact that these incidents are described in graphic detail and form extremely important parts of the epic narratives suggests a recognition of sexual violence against women as a feature of the political domain.

There is one incident in the Ramayana that is, however, presented in a very different way. When Ravana's sister, the demoness Shurpanakha, propositions Rama in the forest, Rama and Lakshmana make fun of her. The angry Shurpanakha threatens to eat Sita alive. Rama orders Lakshmana to cut off her nose and ears with his sword. Bleeding and screaming in pain, she rushes to Ravana and tells him what has happened. Shurpanakha represents unbridled female sexuality which is far removed from the modest, chaste behaviour of the female protagonist and role model, Sita. Violence against such wanton women is presented as justified. In contemporary performances of the Ram-lila, while Ravana's abduction of Sita is meant to arouse the sympathy of the audience, the Shurpanakha episode is meant to arouse laughter.

The *Arthashastra* distinguishes between legitimate force and illegitimate violence against women. While discussing ways of inculcating modest behaviour in wives, Kautilya urges husbands not to say hurtful things to them, but recommends that they administer three strikes on the back with a split bamboo cane, rope, or hand. If a wife misbehaves while her husband is away and he does not forgive her, her ears and nose should be cut off (her paramour should be put to death). Kautilya also refers to punishments for violent crimes against women such as rape, causing miscarriage, and inappropriate touching. A jailer violating a married woman prisoner who is a slave or a pledge should be made to pay the lowest fine for violence. Pregnant women are not to be tortured under any circumstances. Punishments are prescribed for deflowering a courtesan's daughter, the non-slave daughter of a male or female slave, and a female slave due for redemption. Kautilya factors in consent—punishments for such offences are greater if the woman is unwilling.

The *Kamasutra* provides another perspective on the subject. Vatsyayana talks about love as a battle but since the aim of this battle is mutual pleasure, the woman's consent is especially important. Vatsyayana urges men to be gentle in their lovemaking in order to win a virgin's trust. He warns that if a man uses force in sex with a woman, she will become a man-hater. At the same time, he states that there are times when a woman's no means yes and is her way of exciting him. He suggests tricks and strategies to seduce women and, if all these fail, he recommends taking a woman by force.

The *Kamasutra* has a section on the sex life of powerful men, which focuses especially on kings.[21] Vatsyayana recommends strategies that these men can use to ensnare other men's wives. He recommends certain 'secret methods' involving subterfuge as well as force, which he says

---

[21]*Kamasutra* 5.5.

are generally used by princes. He also refers to the sexual violence of kings. While discussing four forms of slapping, he mentions the 'wedge', a kind of slap on the woman's chest, which he says is prevalent in the South. He criticizes it on the ground that it causes pain to the woman and is dangerous. Interestingly, all the specific instances he cites of the fatal use of slapping techniques during sex have to do with kings.

It should be evident that several texts of different genres discuss the use of force against women, especially by politically powerful men. In some situations, this was considered as legitimate force, in others as illegitimate violence.

Countercultures of non-violence

As is the case with social inequality, the most powerful reactions to violence in ancient India came from religion. It is not a coincidence that the sixth/fifth centuries BCE, a time when violent wars increased in number and scale in North India, was also the time when ahimsa-oriented religions came to the fore. And it is not a coincidence that the leading figures of Jainism and Buddhism came from the warrior elites. These religions represented powerful responses to certain perennial problems of the human condition as well as reactions to certain specific features of their time. The latter included the killing of animals in yajnas and the killing of men in wars. There was a close connection between renunciation and non-violence.

Jainism and Buddhism have some things in common (for instance, a monastic Order, lack of importance attached to gods, and the goal of liberation from samsara), but there are also several differences. The Jainas accept the idea of an eternal jiva while the Buddhists deny the existence of anything permanent. The Jaina path for monastics as well as laity is very rigorous. Buddhism, on the other hand, advocates a middle path, between extreme austerities and indulgence. Ethics is important in both religions, and non-violence is an important part of ethics. It is seen as something that harms both the victim and the perpetrator. Intention is important in both religions but is taken to greater lengths in Jainism.

Jainism and Buddhism made non-violence a central cultural

issue, something which their competitors had to address. Apart from advocating refraining from violence, they also put forward the positive ideas of caring and friendship with all beings.

Extreme non-violence: Jainism

The hagiographies of the Jaina Tirthankaras emphasize their strong commitment to non-violence. The twenty-second Tirthankara Neminatha is said to have decided to renounce the world when he heard the cries of animals being killed for his wedding feast. The twenty-fourth Tirthankara Mahavira is said to have stayed perfectly still while in his mother's womb, so as to not cause her any discomfort or distress; but he moved a bit when he sensed that she was anxious about whether he was alive.

Jainism's emphasis on non-violence is connected with its theory about the nature of the world. In this theory, reality consists of three basic categories—sentient (i.e., that which has consciousness), material, and that which is neither sentient nor material. The sentient category is represented by the jiva (soul). Jivas are supposed to be infinite in number; they transmigrate due to karma, which is thought of as consisting of material particles.

In the Jaina pyramid of life, there are four main forms of existence—deva (gods), manushya (humans), naraki (hell beings), and tiryancha (animals and plants).[22] The animal and plant category is divided into smaller sub-categories on the basis of sense faculties. The lowest one comprises single-sense bodies. The lowest of these are nigodas, tiny organisms that only have one sense, that of touch. They are born together in clusters and their life lasts a fraction of a second. The nigodas are supposed to inhabit the bodies of plants, animals, and people. Above the nigoda, slightly higher in the scale, are single-sense organisms that inhabit the various elements. These are the earth bodies, water bodies, fire bodies, and air bodies. Plants are higher in the scale—although they only have one sense, that of touch, they have a more complex structure and a longer life. Animals are still higher, as they have two to five senses.

---

[22]For details, see Padmanabh S. Jaini, *The Jaina Path of Purification*.

Those with five senses are divided into those totally dependent on instinct and those with powers of reasoning. Karma connects animals and humans in a great chain of being and becoming. A human birth is considered superior to animal birth, but humans can be born as animals and vice versa. Life is everywhere.

There is a direct relationship between non-violence, a virtuous life, and liberation from the cycle of rebirth. The Triratna (three gems) of Jainism are right faith, right knowledge, and right conduct. As mentioned in Chapter 2, there are five mahavratas (great vows) for monks and nuns which are modified into anuvratas (lesser vows) for the laity. Ahimsa is the first vow for both renunciants and the laity. It is not only actions but the emotions and intentions behind actions that count. Because injuring others draws on negative emotions and passions, it is detrimental to the achievement of salvation. Violence harms the victim and the perpetrator. But all killing is not the same. Harming organisms with different numbers of senses has different value. Intentional, premeditated violence (sankalpaja himsa) is distinguished from the less serious violence that occurs in the course of performing an acceptable occupation (arambhaja himsa)—for instance that of a surgeon or farmer. Even less serious are acts of violence committed purely in self-defence. Not only violent acts, violent speech and thought too are to be avoided. Modes of speaking must be measured and moderate; negative, exploitative words should not be uttered about fat men or animals, big trees, ripe fruits, or vegetables. Negative speech must be replaced by positive speech.

Laypersons are supposed to avoid harming beings with two or more senses, but monks and nuns are expected to take non-violence to the highest possible levels. Jaina texts contain detailed rules to avoid injuring life through actions, speech, and thought. Monks and nuns must, of course, not injure or kill animals, but they must not even point at them lest they frighten them. They should refrain from harming even single-sense beings and element bodies. They should not dig the earth lest they kill earth bodies. They should avoid bathing, swimming, or walking in the rain, lest they kill water bodies. They should not light or extinguish flames, to avoid harming fire bodies. They should not

Fig 4.8: Jaina saint Bahubali performing austerities in perfect stillness; Ellora

fan themselves to avoid harming air bodies. They must try not to walk on greenery or touch living plants to avoid harming vegetable bodies. Digambara monks carry a small broom which they use to brush away insects before sitting down so that they do not harm them. The Jaina emphasis on non-violence is truly remarkable. [Fig. 4.8]

Jaina doctrine considers the desire for food as a source of bondage. Because consuming food involves killing, eating is a cause of violence.[23] The problem is that food is necessary in order to live. The Jaina response is to try to minimize this violence as much as possible through a series of dietary rules. Eating any kind of meat is strictly forbidden. Even if an animal has not been killed for the express purpose of eating but has died a natural death, its meat is not to be consumed because dead flesh is considered a breeding ground for nigodas. The Shvetambaras made some exceptions—for instance, meat could be eaten in a time of famine or to cure an illness. Jaina dietary restrictions extend beyond animals. Figs, honey, and alcohol are forbidden because nigodas are supposed to be especially present in sweet and fermented substances. Root plants such as garlic, onions, turmeric, radish, and carrots are to be avoided because they are believed to contain many living organisms and digging the earth harms living beings. Dairy products are allowed. Vegetables that do not contain seeds, such as grains, lentils, and green leafy vegetables are all right. Eating fruits with one seed is permitted but eating those with many (for instance, brinjals or figs) is not. Refraining from eating—fasting—is considered highly meritorious among Jainas. There was a debate among the Shvetamabaras and Digambaras on whether or not a kevalin (enlightened being) continues to eat in order to survive. Shvetamabara texts assert that he subsists on morsels of food, while the Digambaras assert that he does not experience ordinary human sensations such as hunger or thirst.

Given the centrality of non-violence in Jainism, it is not surprising that the jobs which necessarily involve violence, such as hunting and fishing, are to be shunned. The six approved occupations are governing, writing, farming, imparting knowledge, trade, and crafts. Of these, governing and agriculture potentially involve injuring life (governing can involve warfare, tilling the soil kills insects) and therefore also get

---

[23]Padmanabh S. Jaini, 'Fear of Food: Jaina Attitudes on Eating', in Jaini, *Collected Papers on Jaina Studies*, Chap. 16, pp. 281–96; and Padmanabh S. Jaini, 'Ahiṁsā: A Jaina Way of Spiritual Discipline', in Padmanabh S. Jaini (ed.), *Collected Papers on Jaina Studies*, pp. 3–19.

ruled out. Trade is likely to cause less injury and remains a preferred occupation for Jainas. The most meritorious kind of death for a person, whether renunciant or layperson, involves entering death by fasting and meditating (there are various types of ritual death, including sallekhana). These are highly regulated ritual practices connected with non-violence and are not considered ordinary suicide.

Surprisingly, the strong emphasis on non-violence did not necessarily translate into a proscription of war. Jaina attitudes towards war include criticism, ambivalence, tacit acceptance, and justification. Mahavira rejected the idea that soldiers who die fighting bravely go to heaven and predicted that almost all such soldiers would be reborn in lower realms of existence. Much of the story literature emphasizes that even killing in self-defence leads to hell. For instance, in the Jaina Ramayana, Lakshmana kills Ravana, and both go to the same hell due to their violent acts. And yet, violence for the sake of self-defence (virodhi himsa) is sometimes justified as a last resort.

Jaina monks are known to have prophesied victory or defeat for kings as they embarked on military campaigns. Kings professing faith in Jainism were not pacifists. Kharavela, the Chedi dynasty king who ruled in Kalinga, boasted in the same breath of his gifts to Jaina monks and his military victories. In later centuries, many Jaina kings, ministers, and generals planned and participated in wars. Kings and generals of the Kadamba, Western Ganga, and Hoysala dynasties who had Jaina leanings, fought as hard to protect and expand their dominion as those with other religious affiliations. [Fig. 4.9] Chamundaraya, the famous tenth century general of the Western Ganga dynasty, was as renowned for his ferocity on the battlefield as for having patronized the building of a colossal statue of the Jaina saint Bahubali at Shravana Belgola (in modern Karnataka). It is possible that kings and generals who performed sallekhana may have done so to atone for violence they had committed during their lifetime.

Fig 4.9: Jaina hero stone panel, Cave 32, Ellora, tenth/eleventh century

Moderate non-violence: Buddhism

Non-violence was an important part of the ethical code for members of the Buddhist monastic Order and the laity. [Fig. 4.10] In early Buddhist texts, all acts of killing are not the same. They depend on several factors, including the size and virtue of the victim.[24] Killing humans is worse than killing animals; killing an animal is worse than killing an insect. Killing

---

[24]Rupert Gethin, 'Can killing a living being ever be an act of compassion? The analysis of the act of killing in the Abhidhamma and Pali Commentaries', *Journal of Buddhist Ethics*, vol. 11, 2004, pp. 71–174. Also see Rupert Gethin, 'Buddhist monks, Buddhist kings, Buddhist violence: On the early Buddhist attitudes to violence', in John R. Hinnells and Richard King (eds.), *Religion and Violence in South Asia: Theory and Practice*, London and New York: Routledge, 2007, pp. 62–82.

Fig 4.10: Meditating Buddha, sandstone, Sarnath Museum, fourth/fifth century CE

a criminal is not as serious an offence as killing a virtuous man. Other factors are the intensity of the desire to kill and the amount of effort used to do so. The Buddhist emphasis on ahimsa involved a critique of Brahmanical animal sacrifices on the grounds that they were violent and useless. Hunting, selling, or trading in meat were forbidden to the laity. Apart from killing animals, injuring them, or having sexual contact with them was also forbidden. Compassion and loving kindness were to be extended to all beings, including animals.

Many Buddhist Jataka stories feature forest animals. The ones that occur most often are monkeys, elephants, jackals, lions, and deer. The bodhisattva frequently appears as an animal, sometimes as king of his species. The animals of these stories have human-like emotions, cognition, and rationality. They also have potential for spiritual progress and attainment, though not to the same degree as humans. Some stories emphasize that animals should not be killed (in sacrifice, hunting, or for food) and should be treated with respect and compassion. The animals themselves often appear as spokespersons for this cause. For instance, the Nigrodhamiga Jataka tells the story of Banyan Deer, who offers himself for slaughter to the king, in order to save a pregnant doe. The king is impressed and spares them both. But Banyan Deer insists that the king should extend his protection to all the four-footed animals, birds, and fish in the park.

The Buddhist emphasis on ahimsa did not necessarily entail vegetarianism. In fact, the Buddha is said to have refused to make vegetarianism mandatory when urged to do so by his cousin Devadatta. Monks and nuns were not forbidden from eating meat or fish, provided certain conditions were met—they should not see, hear, or suspect that the animal in question was killed specifically for their eating. Monks were to accept all food offered to them, without showing any desire or preference. Further, refusing meat would deprive the donor of the merit arising from the offering. There are, however, certain exceptions. Monastics could not accept meat that was raw or not thoroughly cooked. The flesh of a human, elephant, snake, dog, horse, lion, tiger, leopard, hyena, or bear was not to be eaten under any circumstances.

The Buddha was not a vegetarian. His last meal is said to have been at the home of a blacksmith named Chunda and he was offered some kind of meat, possibly pork.[25] He is supposed to have fallen ill after the

---

[25]The term for the food is 'sukara-maddava' (Digha Nikaya 16.4.17), which has been translated in various ways, including as pork, truffles, or some kind of mushroom. See

meal and this eventually led to his death. Even today, there are debates among Buddhists about vegetarianism. The current (fourteenth) Dalai Lama is not a vegetarian[26] and monastic food practices vary considerably across the world.

What was the Buddhist attitude towards war? The positive results of compassion in the course of war are exemplified in the story of a battle between the gods and demons. Overwhelmed by the demons, the gods withdraw towards the north, chased by the demons. As the chariots of the gods move into the forest, Sakka (Indra) tells his charioteer Matali to be careful not to disturb the birds:

> Avoid, O Matali, with your chariot pole
> The bird nests in the silk-cotton woods;
> Let's surrender our lives to the asuras [demons]
> Rather than make these birds nestless. [27]

The charioteer turns the chariot around. The demons think that the gods had returned to confront them and flee in fear. The gods win due to Sakka's compassion.

In the Mahasilava Jataka, King Mahasilava refuses to fight or resist when he is attacked; instead, he loads his enemies with presents. In the Seyya Jataka, the bodhisattva, born as the king of Banaras, opens the city gates to his enemy. In both cases, there is a positive outcome due to the king's extraordinary virtues. But there are many other Jataka stories where good kings, even bodhisattvas, fight wars. In the Bhojajaniya Jataka, the bodhisattva is a royal war horse, who dies after participating in a war with exceptional bravery and determination.

According to the Vinaya Pitaka, soldiers could only join the sangha if released by the king. Monks were not supposed to visit the battlefield,

---

Peter Harvey, *An Introduction to Buddhist Ethics*, Cambridge: Cambridge University Press, 2000, pp. 159–62 for a discussion of this issue and of different dietary practices among Buddhists living in different parts of the world.

[26]The Office of His Holiness the Dalai Lama, 'Third Day of Teachings Preliminary to the Kalachakra Empowerment', 7 January 2017.

[27]Bhikkhu Bodhi trans., *The Connected Discourses: A Translation of the Saṁyutta Nikāya*, Boston: Wisdom Publications, 2000, Book 1, 325; 6 (6), 892.

except in special circumstances, for instance, if a kinsman was lying there on the verge of death. And yet, some Buddhist texts contain arguments that appear to justify killing, violence, and war. Certain Mahayana and Vajrayana texts seem to condone the idea of killing out of compassion. For instance, there is the story of a bodhisattva who killed a dacoit who was about to kill 500 bodhisattvas. This is said to have been done out of compassion—killing one man saved many lives and the dacoit was saved from going to hell.[28]

Non-violence in Brahmanical texts and Hinduism

In the Vedas, food is the basis of life; the world consists of food and eaters of food. The classification of animals is based on several overlapping criteria—gramya (domesticated) and aranya (wild); those that could and could not be sacrificed; those that could and could not be eaten.[29] Wild animals are not to be eaten or sacrificed. Generally, it is the domesticated four-footed animals that are described as food. The two-footed animal—man—is the eater. Vedic texts refer to meat eating and to the offering of animals such as goat, sheep, and oxen to the gods in sacrifices. At the same time, the cow is referred to as aghnya (not to be killed).

While the precept of non-violence is not central to the Vedic tradition, later ritualistic texts are concerned about violence in the sacrificial arena. They deal with the problem by sacralizing, justifying, modifying, and euphemizing this violence.[30] The method of killing

---

[28]*Upāyakauśalya Sūtra*, cited by Gethin, 'Can killing a living being ever be an act of compassion?', p. 189. Also see Lambert L. Schmithausen, 'Aspects of the Buddhist attitude towards war', *Violence Denied: Violence, Non-Violence and the Rationalization of Violence in South Asian Cultural History*, Jan E. M. Houben and Karel R. van Kooij (eds.), Boston: Brill, 1999, pp. 45–68.
[29]Brian K. Smith, *Classifying the Universe: The Ancient Indian Varṇa System and the Origins of Caste*, New York and Oxford: Oxford University Press, 1994, Chap. 8.
[30]See Henk W. Bodewitz, 'Hindu ahiṁsā and its roots', and Jan E. M. Houben, 'To kill or not to kill: the sacrificial animal (yajña-paśu)? Arguments and perspectives in Brahmanical ethical philosophy', Houben and van Kooij (eds.), *Violence Denied*, pp. 17–44, 105–83.

animals through strangulation so that they did not cry out seems to have emerged from this concern.

While discussing animal sacrifice, the *Manu Smriti* asserts that himsa (violence) that is sanctioned by the Veda and is well-established in mobile and immobile creation, should be understood as ahimsa.[31] It distinguishes between what *appears* to be violence and *true* violence. The implication is that means must be considered in relation to ends. Where injuring or killing can be established as necessary, meaningful, or even beneficial, it should not be considered violence. On meat-eating, the *Manu Smriti* presents different views. The first is that the god Prajapati created this whole world as food, and meat could be eaten on certain occasions, for instance, when it was sacrificially consecrated, offered by a Brahmana, or when a person's life was at risk. The other view is that killing animals outside the sacrificial arena (for food) should be avoided as far as possible because it harms animals. The *Manu Smriti* seems to favour the second view. It states that there is no fault in eating meat, drinking liquor, or having sex as these are natural activities; but abstaining from these activities brings great rewards. The fact that there are contradictory statements about meat-eating in the *Manu Smriti* indicates that it was a subject of debate.

In the Brahmanical tradition, non-violence is a part of samanya-dharma or sadharana-dharma—the dharma common to all, regardless of varna, gender, and social status. This dharma is not, however, as important as varna-dharma. The idea of non-violence also features in the Dharmashashtra model of the four life stages. The brahmachari was supposed to avoid causing injury to living beings. The grihastha was supposed to perform the pancha-mahayajnas (five great sacrifices) every day in order to expiate for the injury caused in various daily activities. These five great sacrifices were sacrifices only in name. They consisted of the study and teaching of the Veda, offerings to the ancestors, offerings made into the fire, oblations to all beings, and honouring guests. This indicates an awareness of the problem of violence in everyday life and the use of ritual to atone for it.

---

[31]*Manu Smriti* 5.39, 5.44; Olivelle, *Manu's Code of Law*, p. 140.

As mentioned earlier, the idea of non-violence was strongly connected with renunciation. The vanaprastha (partial renunciant) was supposed to be compassionate. The vows of a sannyasi included avoiding injury to creatures through thought, word, or action. Nevertheless, there was always the question of whether conventional moral imperatives, including non-violence, remained relevant once one had attained the highest spiritual goal, namely liberation from samsara.

The text that most eloquently and effectively expresses the tension between violence and non-violence and the impossibility of absolute non-violence, especially in the political domain, is the Mahabharata. It is ironical that one of the most violent stories in the ancient world contains deep reflection (and many contradictory statements) on violence and much praise of non-violence. The two important terms are ahimsa and anrishamsya.[32] Ahimsa was the ideal for the renunciant and was impossible to practise in absolute terms while living a worldly life. Anrishamsya (non-cruelty or compassion) was an ethic for worldly life. Both terms are mentioned as the 'highest dharma' in the Mahabharata.[33] However, in spite of all this, neither ahimsa nor anrishamsya constitute the central message of the epic.

The Mahabharata is especially concerned with the violence of rulers. In his long lecture to Yudhishthira in the Shanti Parva, Bhishma warns Yudhishthira against being too soft. Nothing great can be achieved through anirshamsya. A ruler who is excessively gentle and compassionate is not respected by people and is considered unmanly. A person does not incur sin through violence in the pursuit of one's hereditary profession. The sin arising from inflicting violence as a ruler

---

[32] See Mukund Lath, 'The concept of Ānṛśaṁsya in the Mahābhārata', R. N. Dandekar (ed.), *The Mahābhārata Revisited*, pp. 113–19; Papers presented at the International Seminar on the Mahābhārata organized by the Sahitya Akademi at New Delhi on 17–20 February 1987, New Delhi: Sahitya Akademi, 1990. Lath suggests that anrishamsya was a new word and idea and was much more important in the Mahabharata than ahimsa.
[33] Alf Hiltebeitel, *Rethinking the Mahābhārata: A Reader's Guide to the Education of the Dharma King*, New Delhi: Oxford University Press, [2001], 2002, pp. 207–14. Many other things are also mentioned as the 'highest dharma'. These include truth, the Veda, following one's spiritual teacher, honouring guests, and wealth. But anrishamsya occurs most often, and like ahimsa, it too is discussed contextually and is not an absolute.

can be countered by protecting the subjects and making them prosper, giving gifts, and performing sacrifices and asceticism.

Ahimsa is an important ethic in Vaishnavism. The Narayaniya-parva of the Mahabharata advocates devotion to the god Narayana, who is also referred to as Vasudeva, Vishnu, and Hari. It does not reject Vedic sacrifice but emphasizes renunciation and non-injury and prescribes rituals that do not involve animal sacrifice. It states that in the horse sacrifice performed by Vasu Uparichara, a devotee of Vishnu, no animals were slaughtered; produce of the wilderness formed the only offerings. The Vishnu Purana states that a devotee of Vishnu does not indulge in any sort of violence. The Pancharatra and Vaikhanasa were important Vaishnava sects which combined devotionalism towards Vishnu with ascetic and yogic elements. Non-injury was an important part of the Pancharatra understanding of ritual.

Moral and pragmatic approaches to non-violence: Ashoka and Kautilya

The discussion so far should have made it apparent that by the early centuries CE, although there was a broad cultural consensus on the positive value to be attached to non-violence, the specific views varied considerably in their grounding and emphasis. This emerges clearly from a comparison of two figures who are often considered opposites—Ashoka and Kautilya. The Maurya emperor Ashoka has rightfully earned the reputation of being a remarkable king who renounced war and devoted his life to making people follow dhamma, which included non-violence. [Fig. 4.11] Kautilya, on the other hand, was a proponent of realpolitik for whom the ends justified the means and the ruthless pursuit of power justified deceit, subterfuge, and killing.[34] So it may be a bit surprising that there are several similarities in their ideas.

Both Ashoka and Kautilya associated kingship with benevolent paternalism, ensuring the welfare and happiness of all beings in this

---

[34]This section is based on my J. P. Jayaswal Lecture, 'Portraits of power: Aśoka and Kauṭilya', 31st K. P. Jayaswal Memorial lectures, 27 November 2016; published in Upinder Singh, *Portraits of Power*, Patna: K. P. Jayaswal Research Institute, 2017.

Fig 4.11: Ashoka and his consort, limestone, Kanaganahalli

world, and helping them attain heaven in the next. In Ashoka's dhamma, the appropriate conduct towards all living beings is one of compassion, gentleness, and abstention from injuring and killing. The *Arthashastra* acknowledges the ethics applicable to everyone, which include non-violence, truthfulness, purity, freedom from malice, non-cruelty, and forbearance.

Ashoka considered all living beings as part of his moral constituency, so non-violence includes non-violence towards both humans and animals. Rock Edict 1 talks of the king's attempts to curb violence towards animals in sacrifices, in certain popular festive gatherings, and in the royal kitchen. In Rock Edict 8, Ashoka announces that royal pleasure tours, which must have included hunting, had been replaced by dhamma tours. Rock Edict 2 announces positive welfare measures undertaken by the king for animals—the provision of medical treatment; the planting of herbs, root plants, and fruit trees; digging wells and planting trees along roads. The most detailed and remarkable statement about the protection of animals is in Pillar Edict 5, which contains a series of commands that were issued in the twenty-seventh year after the king's consecration. There is a ban on killing female goats, ewes, and sows who are pregnant or lactating, as well as young animals less than six months old. Animals that used to be hunted in the elephant forests were not to be killed. The killing and selling of fish in the fishermen's preserves was banned on certain specific days. Husk containing living animals was not to be burnt. Forests were not to be needlessly burnt. Living beings were not to be fed with other living beings. Cocks were not to be castrated. Bulls, goats, rams, and boar were not to be castrated on certain specific days. The branding of horses and bulls was banned on certain specific days. What this amounted to was not an elimination of violence against animals, but a regulation and reduction. Of course, it is unlikely that Ashoka or his administration would have been able to enforce these measures effectively throughout the empire.

While Ashoka's concern for animals is well known, Kautilya's is not. The *Arthashastra* lays down punishments for causing injury to humans, animals, and plants. It refers to abhaya-vanas (animal sanctuaries). Kautilya recommends that the highest fine should be imposed on those who bind, kill, or injure animals living in these sanctuaries. Those who do not take proper care of state elephants, including those who strike an elephant in an improper place, should be fined. If horses under state care were incapacitated by war, disease, or old age, they should receive food for maintenance; those no longer fit to be used in war should be used as stallions for breeding. Veterinarians should tend to elephants suffering as a result of a long journey, disease, work, rut, or old age. Hurting domesticated animals is a punishable offence. Fines are prescribed for those riding a temple animal, stud bull, or pregnant cow. Pregnant females or those with young are singled out for special consideration. A fine should be imposed on a driver of a bullock cart who injures the animals on account of a broken nose string or yoke. So both Ashoka and Kautilya extended the principle of non-injury to animals and expanded it to include measures for animal welfare.

However, there is a big difference in rationale and emphasis. Ashoka's commitment to non-violence was rooted in a moral stance based on his faith in the Buddha's teaching and his own reflections on the problem of violence. His edicts imply that the reason why violence towards other beings is to be avoided is that it injures life and leads to the incurring of papa (sin) and apunya (demerit). Kautilya's valorization of non-violence might sound hypocritical, considering the numerous places where he advocates ruthless actions involving injuring and killing human beings. But as mentioned earlier, Kautilya was not a votary of unrestrained state violence; he sanctions all measures that are necessary for the king to maintain and enhance his political power. For Kautilya, while human life has the greatest value (although this value varies depending on social status), the value of animals lies in their being an important item of private property and an economic and political resource for the state. This is why they have to be protected against injury, theft, and killing. While there are occasional glimmers of compassion that extend beyond the utilitarian frame, Kautilya's general perspective is a pragmatic one, where the chief aim is maximizing economic gain from animals, especially for the state. Ensuring their welfare is essential for this. So although both Ashoka and Kautilya talk about the protection of animals, they do so from very different points of view.

Another major difference between the ideas of Ashoka and Kautilya can be seen in their attitude towards war. Ashoka's Rock Edict 13 is a remarkable reflection on the consequences of war. It describes the king's victory in a terrible, bloody war against Kalinga (in eastern India), which occurred in the ninth year after his consecration. The inscription informs us that in this war, 150,000 people were carried away as captives, 100,000 were killed in action, and many times that number perished. This was a transformative event for Ashoka. Filled with shame and remorse, he eschewed war and devoted himself to the propagation of dhamma. Rock Edict 13 also talks about the killing, death, and deportation that accompany war in general and the nature of the injury and pain it causes. It extends the scope of war-time injury beyond those who suffer physical injury, death, or capture, to include the emotional injury caused to all those who are loved by or are attached to the direct sufferers. The king announces that he has given up military victory for dhamma-vijaya (victory through dhamma), which consists of propagating dhamma within and beyond the frontiers of his empire. Dhammic victory is the best because it leads to fruits in this world and the next. But while heralding a new idea of dhamma-vijaya, there is also an element of pragmatism in Rock Edict 13. Ashoka urges his sons and grandsons to aim at dhamma-vijaya but recommends mercy and moderation in punishment if they do engage in warfare. After exhorting the forest people to follow dhamma, he reminds them of the power he wields in spite of his repentance, and warns them not to provoke him lest they be killed.[35]

For Kautilya, war is a normal part of political life but should be waged after a clear calculation of the likelihood of victory. In his listing, the dharma-vijayi (righteous victor) is one who is satisfied with mere submission. There is a big difference between Kautilya and Ashoka's idea of righteous victory. The former is the most noble form of military victory; the latter is not a military victory at all but consists of the propagation of virtue and goodness.

While there are some similarities between Ashoka and Kautilya's vocabulary and even their ideas on non-violence, there are also significant differences arising from different premises and goals. Ashoka wanted to make people good and virtuous. Kautilya wanted to control subjects and harness their interests to those of the king. Ashoka's aim as king was to create a new world moral order. Kautilya was concerned with material rather than moral welfare, but his great achievement was to demonstrate that furthering the welfare of the subjects was in the political and material self-interest of the king.

---

[35]The fact that Ashoka's non-violence had limits is also clear from Pillar Edict 4, which grants a three-day respite to those accused of capital crimes, indicating that he did not abolish the death penalty.

Ancient India: Culture of Contradictions

◆

It is not easy to define violence, nor is it easy to draw a line between justified and unjustified force. Where that line is drawn depends on perspective. Vegetarianism was by no means the norm in ancient India but the issue of violence goes far beyond dietary habits. Like the histories of other parts of the world, India's ancient history too is replete with violence of various kinds. War is the best documented, but other forms of political and social violence can be identified or inferred. (Religious conflict and violence will be discussed in the next chapter). The intellectual reactions to violence included moral, political, and aesthetic ones. Attitudes towards the violence of the state, including war, were fairly pragmatic, even in the religions of non-violence. All textual traditions distinguish force that is necessary, proportionate, and legitimate from that which is unnecessary, excessive, and illegitimate, thereby leaving open a window for questioning the state's tyranny and coercive power.

Were ancient Indians non-violent? No. Were they less violent than people living in other parts of the world? In order to answer this question, we need a comparative global history of violence. But one thing is certain—ancient Indian intellectuals, political theorists, philosophers, and religious leaders discussed the tension between violence and non-violence more intensely than anywhere else in the world.

How is the amnesia about violence in ancient Indian history to be explained? It comes from an idealized interpretation of Indian history, from a hop, skip, and jump approach that magically connects Mahavira, the Buddha, Ashoka, and Gandhi and leaves out everything in between. It comes from the centrality of non-violence in the Indian freedom struggle. Gandhian nationalism contributed in a big way towards creating the illusion that non-violence was somehow ingrained in the Indian psyche. But even Gandhi, the modern icon of non-violence, struggled throughout his life with the problem of violence and met his end through an assassin's bullet. It is in the midst of violence that non-violence acquires its deepest meaning.

5

DEBATE AND CONFLICT

In October 2020, Tanishq, a well-known jewellery brand, released an advertisement showing an elderly woman affectionately leading her heavily pregnant young daughter-in-law to her baby shower ceremony. The young woman was evidently Hindu and the mother-in-law Muslim. The advertisement was part of a campaign for a new collection of jewellery called Ekatvam (Oneness) and was meant to celebrate oneness by showing the coming together of communities. Some praised it, others found it unacceptable. Threats of boycott and violence led to the company hastily withdrawing the advertisement, citing hurt sentiments and worries for their employees' safety.

In communally charged times, 'hurting religious sentiments' is an allegation that flies all too easily. Apart from writers, artists, and film-makers, historians too often find themselves in the line of fire of religious orthodoxies. The charges are usually based on ideas of monolithic and antagonistic religious identities. How have these ideas come to rule the roost? And how is it that in spite of the visibility of communal prejudice and conflict all around, many Indians persist in thinking of themselves as a tolerant people?

Ideas about the tolerant and assimilative nature of Hinduism first appeared in the writings of eighteenth and nineteenth century European Orientalists. Indian thinkers such as Dayanand Saraswati, Ramakrishna Paramahamsa, and Swami Vivekananda, too, talked of a tolerant Hinduism. [Fig. 5.1] In a famous speech he delivered in the World Parliament of Religions on 11 September 1893, Vivekananda declared:

> I am proud to belong to a religion which has taught the world both tolerance and universal acceptance. We believe not only in universal toleration, but we accept all religions as true. I am proud to belong

Ancient India: Culture of Contradictions

Fig. 5.1: Swami Vivekananda poster

to a nation which has sheltered the persecuted and the refugees of all religions and all nations of the earth.... I will quote to you, brethren, a few lines from a hymn which I remember to have repeated from my earliest boyhood, which is every day repeated by millions of human beings: 'As the different streams having their sources in different paths which men take through different tendencies, various though they appear, crooked or straight, all lead to Thee.'[1]

The idea of Hinduism as a religion that—in contrast to other world religions—believed in and practised religious tolerance had come to stay.

---

[1]'Address at the Parliament of Religions', see https://ramakrishna.org/vivekanandaparliament.html.

A discordant note was struck by those who drew attention to the social dimensions of Hinduism and its centuries-old association with varna, caste, and untouchability. Although a devout Hindu, Gandhi was acutely aware of this aspect; he accepted varna but rejected caste and untouchability. Ambedkar's strong critique of Hinduism and its oppression of the 'untouchables' is the best known, and over the decades, this critique has grown in Dalit writing. Notwithstanding Hinduism's poor track record on the social front, the notion that it has always been tolerant towards other *religions* is quite widespread. This is connected with the idea that over the centuries, Hinduism has amicably accepted absorption and accretion from other religions. Along with the idea of non-violence, the idea of Hinduism's tolerance has become part of a construct of 'Indian culture' and 'Indian civilization'.

In addition to the idea of an essentially tolerant, peace-loving Hinduism, there is also an idea of an essentially tolerant, peace-loving Buddhism. This is in spite of the violence in Buddhist history which extends from ancient times to the present, the most recent instance being the persecution of the Muslim Rohingya people in Buddhist-majority Myanmar and the violent political repression exercised by the military regime there. In popular perception, a peaceful, tolerant Hindu–Buddhist period is often contrasted with a violent Muslim/medieval period. As expected, the reality is much more complex.

A slippage that often takes place when talking about ancient India is to consider it equivalent to Hindu India. This is inaccurate, not only because of the internal complexities within Hinduism but also because of the existence of diverse religious and philosophical traditions. Hinduism, Jainism, and Buddhism were the most important ancient religions, but there were many religious beliefs and practices that cut across traditions or defy classification. The vast forest tracts were inhabited by tribal communities who had their own distinctive cultural identities and practices. The relationship between Hinduism and tribal religion was marked by reciprocal interaction and a constantly shifting frontier, visible, for instance, in the incorporation of tribal deities into the Hindu pantheon and the Hinduization of tribal deities and communities.[2] As discussed in Chapter 4, the historical context of these 'incorporative processes' included a great deal of conflict and violence.

We should also remember that India was part of a larger world of interactions that included Asia, Europe, and Africa. In the early medieval period, there were Muslim, Christian, Zoroastrian (Parsi), and Jewish communities in India, especially along the western coast. Across the centuries, India was a centre of both cultural influence and confluence.

The diverse range of religious ideas in ancient Indian texts include polytheism, monotheism, monolatry, and monism; these coexisted with agnosticism and atheism.[3]

Looking for and at religion in ancient India

Religions look different depending on whether you are looking at them from the inside or outside. The devout believer thinks of his or her religion as embodying timeless, eternal, and absolute truths, but the discipline of history obliges a historian to contextualize religion and to analyse it objectively as part of a historical process. A recognition of this simple, basic fact would protect historians from the accusations that are sometimes hurled against them for hurting religious sentiments while they are simply doing their job.

The Sanskrit word dharma does not mean the same thing as the English 'religion'. The concept of 'religion' is, in fact, based on the Abrahamic faiths (Judaism, Christianity, and Islam) and evidence from Eastern cultures does not always fit easily into this model.[4] Notions of

---

[2]The Jagannath cult of Orissa is a striking example of this interface. See Gaya Charan Tripathi, Anncharlott Eschman, and Hermann Kulke, *The Cult of Jagannath and the Regional Tradition of Orissa*, New Delhi: Manohar, 2014.
[3]Polytheism is a belief in many deities, monotheism a belief in one god. Monolatry refers to the worship of one god without denying the existence of others (Vaishnavism, Shaivism, and Shaktism are examples). Monism is a belief in the primacy of central principle (like brahman in the Upanishads). Agnosticism involves a refusal to take a stand on the existence of God or gods, while atheism is the denial of his/their existence.
[4]See Daya Krishna, 'Comparative Philosophy: What it is and what it ought to be', Nalini Bhushan, Jay L. Garfield, and Daniel Raveh (eds.), *Contrary Thinking:*

religious identity as singular and monolithic are also based on these monotheistic faiths.

It has been argued that philosophy and religion do not exist in India. The fact of the matter is that they do not correspond to notions of philosophy and religion in the West. Indian history shows that philosophy and religion are not necessarily separate; that religion does not necessarily involve a belief in a God or gods; that divinity can be visualized as one and many, as male, female, or both, with or without form; that beliefs in divinity coexist with agnosticism and atheism; and that there are many different ways in which politics and religion can intersect.

Unlike many other religions, Hinduism has no historical founder, canon, or organized priesthood; it is also marked by a great deal of diversity. Various attempts have been made to define it—on the basis of ideas such as samsara, karma, moksha (though these are found in other Indian religions too); as a social system based on a recognition of the authority of the Brahmanas and the systems of varna and/or jati (these too are found within Buddhism and Jainism); on the acceptance of the authority of the Vedas; as a vaguely defined 'way of life'; or based simply on birth in a Hindu family. Another perspective is that Hinduism is better understood through its parts such as Vaishnavism, Shaivism, and Shaktism, which were centred on the worship of a supreme deity. Yet another view is that Hinduism as a religious category emerged in the nineteenth century when Western observers clubbed together very diverse sects, doctrines, and customs of people who did not see themselves as part of a homogeneous religious community. According to this view, Hinduism is a category that was 'invented' by the British. Was the idea of Hinduism a foreign implant that was accepted by gullible Indians? As this is an important (and a sensitive) issue, it requires a bit of discussion.

Selected Essays of Daya Krishna, Oxford, New York: Oxford University Press, 2007, pp. 59–77. Also see Bimal K. Matilal, 'Toward defining religion in the Indian context' and 'Religion and value', in Jonardan Ganeri (ed.), *Philosophy, Culture and Religion: The Collected Essays of Bimal Krishna Matilal*, New Delhi: Oxford University Press, 2002, pp. 166–74, 175–95.

It was not an Englishman but an Indian—Rammohan Roy—who first used the word Hinduism in 1816. The word 'Hindu' is derived from the river Sindhu or Indus, and the term was initially used to refer to the land and people of the Indus valley or beyond. The earliest references to it occur in ancient Persian, Greek, and Chinese sources. Medieval Persian texts also use the word in this sense. But at some point of time, 'Hindu' became more than a geographical category; it became a religious term. When did that happen? This debate is not just about the word, but also about what it meant. In an often cited article, the historian of religion David Lorenzen has argued that a Hindu religion grounded in texts such as the Bhagavad Gita, Puranas, and commentaries on the six philosophical schools acquired shape and became a basis of identity between 1200 and 1500, through interaction with Islam.[5] The evidence for this comes from fifteenth–sixteenth century bhakti poets like Vidyapati, Kabir, and Ekanath. Even earlier, Al-Biruni's eleventh century *Kitab al-Hind* talks about Hindus as a religio-cultural category, juxtaposes Hindus with Muslims, and copiously cites the Gita, Samkhya, Dharmashastra, Puranas, and Patanjali's *Yogasutra*. Al-Biruni must have got these ideas from his Indian informants, so the process of the creation of a Hindu identity was clearly underway.[6] There is also evidence that between the twelfth and sixteenth centuries, certain philosophers began to treat the teachings of the Upanishads, epics, Puranas, and the philosophical schools that later came to be known as the six systems of Hindu philosophy as a unified whole.[7] So Hinduism as a religious

---

[5]David N. Lorenzen, 'Who invented Hinduism?', David N. Lorenzen, *Who Invented Hinduism?: Essays on Religion in History*, New Delhi: Yoda Press, 2006, pp. 1–36.

[6]One of the reasons why some historians are not willing to accept such a hypothesis is that they think that talking about Hindu–Muslim conflict in the past can be used to provide support to a Hindu communalist agenda in the present. But an anxiety to stand against majoritarian political Hindutva in the present should not be a reason to deny the existence of a Hindu identity or Hindu–Muslim conflict in earlier times.

[7]Andrew J. Nicholson, *Unifying Hinduism: Philosophy and Identity in Indian Intellectual History*, Ranikhet: Permanent Black, [2010], 2011. Nicholson highlights the pivotal role of the late-sixteenth-century Bhedabhedin (Difference and Non-Difference) Vedanta scholar Vijnanabhikshu in this process.

category was not invented by the British. It was present from the eleventh/twelfth centuries onwards.

The term Hinduism is also sometimes used with retrospective effect for earlier times, referring to a long and complex religious process, whose roots lie in the Vedic tradition, whose forms of religious practice are visible in the Puranas, and which continued to include a great deal of diversity.[8] The religion of the Rig Veda was centred around the performance of yajnas or sacrifices. It is these sacrifices, which consisted of incantations accompanying offerings made into the sacred fire, that established a connection between the world of the gods and the world of men. There are no references in the Vedas to the worship of deities in temples. While some of the gods and goddesses mentioned in the Rig Veda (for instance, Vishnu and Rudra) are known in later texts, their personalities are not fully developed. The Puranas, many of which were compiled during the fourth and fifth centuries CE, reflect features of religious practice that later came to be described as Hinduism, including the worship of deities in a temple context, the performance of vratas (vows), and pilgrimage. So for the purpose of historical analysis, a distinction can be made between Vedic religion (sometimes referred to as Vedic Hinduism) and Puranic Hinduism, even though the latter anchored itself in the former.

Religious history is ultimately about what people believe and do, about religious communities and identities. The religious space has always been an interactive one, so religions are best studied not in isolation but in their interactions with each other and within the larger social context. Apart from texts, archaeology and inscriptions also throw valuable light on these issues. Many ancient sites—for instance, Mathura, Ellora, Gaya, and Nagarjunakonda—have pluralistic religious landscapes in the sense that they reveal Hindu, Buddhist, Jaina, and other associations. This certainly indicates coexistence, but it is the

---

[8]Many historians are averse to such usage and prefer the term 'Brahmanism'. In my view, 'Brahmanism' is also a problematic term and does not fully capture the religious processes it seeks to describe. 'Hinduism' is preferable, provided we recognize all the caveats that have been discussed here.

nature of the relationships between religious communities that is crucial.

The word 'tolerance' can include a wide range of attitudes including indifference, superficial engagement, genuine dialogue, and concord. This word makes sense in a monotheistic context, especially in cultures where there was a close relationship between the state and church, and is a bit out of place in the context of ancient India. So instead of talking about tolerance and intolerance, this chapter examines issues such as philosophical dialogue and debate; classifications of philosophical schools and the astika/nastika divide; hagiographies of saints and religious leaders; royal religious policy; the relationship between Hinduism and Buddhism, and Jainism and Shaivism; and religious satire.

Ancient philosophical debates

What we see every day on television news channels should be proof enough that debate does not necessarily mean an open-minded or open-ended exchange of ideas. Like all speech acts, dialogue and debate can serve different functions—as a means of explication and elaboration, persuasion (rhetoric), polemic, asserting superiority, emphasis, affirmation, legitimation, or rejection. Historicizing debates involves looking at their contexts, patrons, participants, topics, styles, stakes, and results.

Words for discussion and debate in ancient Indian texts include samvada, vada, and sambhasha. Anvikshiki stands for logical reasoning; hetu and tarka for hypothetical reasoning. Philosophical and religious texts contain serious and sophisticated reflections on the nature, type, and format of debate. Apart from the vadin (proponent) and prativadin (opponent), there could also be prashnikas (judges). The logicians of the Nyaya school classify debates into three types—vada (constructive debate aimed at arriving at the truth); jalpa (confrontational debate aimed at establishing the superiority of one's own view, which could involve using debating tricks); and vitanda (destructive debate in which the goal is to demolish the opponent's thesis, without putting forward any thesis of one's own). The Mimamsa philosophers generally divided

Fig. 5.2: Sages deep in discussion, Kailasanatha temple, Kanchipuram

their works into five parts, which correspond to five parts of a debate—vishaya (topic); vishaya/sandeha (doubt); purvapaksha (prima facie view); uttara or uttarapaksha (response); and nirnaya (final decision). Logical reasoning and persuasion were important parts of debates, although on occasion, miracles also played a part. [Figs. 5.2, 5.3]

In the Buddhist *Milindapanha* (first century BCE–first century CE), after the learned King Milinda (identified with the Bactro-Indo-Greek King Menander) discussed and debated with representatives of various

Fig. 5.3: Ascetics conversing; Mukteshwar temple, Bhubaneshwar, c. 950–75

philosophical schools, he sought a discussion with the Buddhist monk Nagasena. The monk agreed on one condition—that Milinda should participate not as a king, but as a scholar:

Milinda: How is it then that scholars discuss?

Nagasena: When scholars talk a matter over with another, then there is a winding up, an unravelling, one or the other is convicted of error, and he then acknowledges his mistake, distinctions are drawn and contra-distinctions; and yet thereby they are not angered. Thus do scholars, O king, discuss.

Milinda: And how do kings discuss?

Nagasena: When a king, Your Majesty, discusses a matter and he advances a point, if any one differ from him on that point, he is apt to fine him, saying, 'Inflict such a punishment upon that fellow.' Thus, Your Majesty, do kings discuss.

Milinda: Very well. It is as a scholar, not as a king, that I will discuss. Let Your Reverence talk unrestrainedly, as you would with a brother or a novice, or a lay disciple, or even with a servant. Be not afraid.⁹

In the *Analects* of Confucius, conversations form the narrative frame for the Master to make authoritative moral pronouncements about the dao (way) of the junzi (gentleman), family relationships, and governance of the state. Ancient Greek plays contain considerable argument and debate on legal and moral ideas, on which the plot often turns. Plato's early aporetic dialogues conclude on an inconclusive, open-ended note. In contrast, most ancient Indian dialogues generally have a decisive conclusion. The aim was to attain a decisive victory over the opponent by proving him wrong. Discussion and debate were not confined to the realms of philosophy and religion. They permeated all aspects of ancient Indian discourse, including the disciplines of Dharmashastra, Arthashastra, Kamashastra, aesthetic theory, and the sciences.¹⁰

Discussion, debate, and disagreement are the basis for the expansion of the frontiers of knowledge. Let us look at some great debates in ancient Indian texts.

Upanishadic debates

The word samvada occurs in the Rig Veda. The Vedic hymns express many different ideas about the origins of the world. The Purusha-sukta, mentioned in Chapter 1, describes creation as the outcome of a primeval sacrifice, but there are other cosmogonies too in the Rig Veda. The Nasadiya-sukta speculates about how creation might have happened and ends on a questioning note. In the Rig Veda, the various views on creation are not presented as part of a debate; they are simply found within the same text, without an assertion of the superiority of one over the other. Dialogues and riddles are found in some Vedic hymns, and the ritualistic texts known as the Brahmanas refer to different views on various details

---

⁹Translated and cited in Esther A. Solomon, *Indian Dialectics: Methods of Philosophical Discussion*, 2 vols., Ahmedabad: B. J. Institute of Learning and Research, 1978, vol. 1, pp. 37–38.
¹⁰See Solomon, *Indian Dialectics* for a detailed and comprehensive analysis of discussion and debate in ancient and early medieval India.

Ancient India: Culture of Contradictions

of the sacrifices. But it is in the Upanishads that dialogic debate truly emerges centre stage. Debate is not only central to the Upanishads; it is also central to the reception and interpretation of Upanishadic thought across the centuries.

The knowledge that the Upanishadic philosophers sought was not for all and sundry.[11] It was a doctrine that could only be revealed to a select few; its secrecy emphasized its newness, importance, and exclusiveness. Dialogue and debate were part of the search for ultimate knowledge, but this knowledge could not be fully grasped through even the most strenuous logical reasoning. It had to be experienced. The Upanishadic debates are often crisp, sharp, and dramatic. How could they not be, considering their subject matter—the self, life, death, immortality—and their goal—moksha?

It is not all that important whether the Upanishadic debates actually happened or whether the participants were historical individuals. Apart from their content, their narrative frame, participants, and audience are important. As discussed in Chapter 1, the Upanishads are not really anti-sacrifice or anti-Brahmana. They did however shift the emphasis from sacrifice to the attainment of a new kind of knowledge. The Upanishads contain many exciting debates in which debaters use argument, humour, sarcasm, even insult. Although Kshatriyas and kings play significant roles as interlocutors and explicators, Brahmanas continue to be important, not as ritual experts but as philosophers. Brahmanas are central, and they are shown debating with their students, other Brahmanas, and kings.[12] They also feature in the audience. Some of the Upanishadic

---

[11]For overviews of issues and themes in Indian philosophy, see Jonardon Ganeri, *Philosophy in Classical India: An Introduction and Analysis*, London: Routledge, 2001; and Jonardon Ganeri (ed.), *Indian Philosophy: A Reader*, London: Routledge, 2019. For a more detailed treatment, see Karl Potter (gen. ed.), *Encyclopaedia of Indian Philosophies*, Delhi: Motilal Banarsidass, 1955–2019, of which 25 volumes have so far been published.
[12]For a good discussion of Upanishadic debates, see Brian Black, *Priests, Kings, and Women in the Early Upaniṣads: The Character of Self in Ancient India*, Delhi: Motilal Banarsidass, 2014. There are many good English translations of the early Upanishads. See, for instance, Swami Nikhilananda, *The Upanishads: A New Translation*, New York, Ramakrishna Vivekananda Centre, [1949–59], 1959; Patrick Olivelle, *The Early*

debates (known as brahmodyas) took place with much fanfare in royal courts, in the presence of kings. Reputations were on the line and the loser often had to become the acolyte of the winner. The victor not only acquired prestige but also raked in riches.

Almost all Upanishadic debates are among men. The one between the sage Yajnavalkya and the woman sage Gargi is one of the few instances where women participate. This is how it is described in the Brihadaranyaka Upanishad: Janaka, king of Videha, was performing a great sacrifice and Brahmanas had come from far and wide to attend. The king announced a spectacular prize of 1,000 cows with 10,000 gold pieces fastened to their horns for the wisest among them all. Yajnavalkya asked his pupil Shamashravas to herd the cows home. The other Brahmanas were furious at this arrogance and a philosophical contest ensued. One by one, eight debaters sparred with Yajnavalkya on issues related to sacrifice, the senses, the worlds to which great men departed, the nature of the self, the making of the universe, and the resting places of the gods and spirits. One of them was Gargi. As she shot out her rapid-fire questions and Yajnavalkya his responses, at some point, he told her, 'Don't ask too many questions, Gargi, or your head will shatter apart!' Gargi retreated, but came forward again for second round of questioning.

> I rise to challenge you, Yajnavalkya, with two questions, much as a fierce warrior of Kashi or Videha, stringing his unstrung bow and taking two deadly arrows in his hand, would rise to challenge a rival.[13]

Yajnavalkya answered her questions, revealing the imperishable brahman to be the foundation of everything. Gargi was satisfied with his answers and acknowledged defeat, telling the assembled Brahmanas that Yajnavalkya was unbeatable, and that they should consider themselves lucky if they managed to escape from him by merely paying their respects.

Vidagdha was the last interlocutor. He started well but was eventually

---

Upaniṣads: Annotated Text and Translation, New Delhi: Munshiram Manoharlal, 1998.
[13]Brihadaranyaka Upanishad 3.8.2, Olivelle, *The Early Upaniṣads*, p. 91.

stumped by a question about the atman. His head is said to have shattered into pieces. Were the violent references to exploding heads attempts to infuse drama into philosophical debates? Are they to be understood metaphorically or were philosophers defeated in debates sometimes decapitated? The jury is still out on this. We know from history that intellectuals who ask inconvenient questions sometimes have to pay a heavy price, but this is a case of someone who could not *answer* a question. In our day and age, not being able to answer a question in an examination or interview has consequences, but not such dire ones. At the very least, the Upanishadic debates show that in ancient cultures, words, riddles, and debates, especially those concerning profound matters such as the nature of reality and existence, were endowed with enormous importance.

Shramanic debates

As discussed in earlier chapters, the sixth and fifth centuries were a time of intense debate in the middle Ganga valley. Apart from Nigantha Nataputta (Mahavira), Buddhist texts mention many thinkers—Purana Kassapa, Makkhali Gosala, Ajita Keshakambalin, Pakudha Kachchayana, and Sanjaya Belatthaputta. It is through such references—usually negative and derogatory—that we get an idea of the contemporaries and competitors of Mahavira and the Buddha.

Wandering renunciants known as shramanas shared some ideas such as karma, samsara, non-violence, and the goal of liberation; but there were also significant differences in doctrine and practice. According to Makkhali Gosala, karma and transmigration existed but human effort was useless as everything was predetermined by fate. The Ajivikas observed extreme asceticism, nudity, and non-violence, but not celibacy. Purana Kassapa seems to have denied that actions had consequences and rejected the distinction between good and evil acts. Pakudha Kachchayana taught that the elements such as earth, water, fire, and air, as well as happiness, sorrow, and life were fixed and unchanging and did not affect each other. Ajita Keshakambalin was a materialist who rejected the ideas of rebirth, merit, and demerit, and argued that human actions affect nothing. Sanjaya Belatthaputta is said to have refused to take a stand on anything, earning him the label of one who wriggled about like an eel. His typical response to any question was:

> If you ask me: 'Is there another world?' if I thought so, I would say so. But I don't think so. I don't say it is so, and I don't say otherwise. I don't say it is not, and I don't not say it is not.[14]

Jaina and Buddhist texts recount multiple spirited debates. Winning was important, not only to establish the truth but also to attract patrons and followers. This must have generated some tension, even conflict. Buddhist texts state that Purana Kassapa committed suicide after he and his followers were defeated in a miracle contest by the Buddha.

In the Pali Tipitaka, the Buddha is constantly on the move, talking with all sorts of people—Buddhist monks, Brahmanas, Jainas, other rivals, gods, and lay people.[15] [Fig. 5.4] Dialogues are the frame for explaining the dhamma to monastics and laity and for demonstrating the errors of wrong views. Debates with Nirgranthas (Jainas) try to show that in spite of their austerities and espousal of non-violence, the Jainas were actually violent in thought and speech. The Buddha, on the other hand, remains cool and collected throughout. The dialogues generally end with the opponent or sceptic being completely convinced of the truth of the Buddha's teaching and taking refuge in the Buddha and the dhamma, or the Buddha, dhamma, and sangha. The first was the assertion made by lay followers, the latter by those joining the monastic Order.

The continuing hostility of Brahmanism towards shramanic religions is reflected in the grammarian Patanjali's (second century BCE) description of the relationship between Brahmana and shramana as an example of an antagonistic compound word. But the relationship between Buddhism and Brahmanas was actually quite complex. As

---

[14]Samannaphala Sutta, *Digha Nikaya*; Maurice Walshe (trans.), *Long Discourses of the Buddha: A Translation of the Dīgha Nikāya*, Boston: Wisdom Publications, 1995, p. 97.
[15]See Michael Nichols, 'Bowing to the Buddha: The Relationship between Literary and Social Dialogue in the Nikāyas', in Brian Black and Laurie Patton (eds.), *Dialogues in Early South Asian Religions: Hindu, Buddhist and Jaina Traditions*, London and New York: Routledge, 2015, pp. 173–90.

Fig. 5.4: Monks and laity listening attentively to the Buddha preaching, schist, Gandhara, late second–early third century

mentioned in Chapter 1, 'Brahmana' is used in Buddhist texts in the conventional sense as a social category, and there is sharp criticism of the low spiritual calibre and opulent lifestyle of these men. But 'Brahmana' is also used in Buddhist texts as an ideal category based not on birth but on exemplary conduct. In fact, in places, the Buddha himself is addressed as Brahmana.

Jainism: a model for inter-religious dialogue?

Dialogue and debate are prominent in Jaina canonical texts and narrative literature. In the Shvetamabara canon, doctrines are usually embedded in dialogues as the words of Mahavira, endowing them with the quality of indisputable truth. The Jina talks to rival philosophers, monks, gods, and lay people. Because he is omniscient and can read minds, on occasion, he engages in silent debate. For instance, in the Viyahapannatti, two gods come to Mahavira and ask him a question in their mind. He answers them silently in his mind. Mahavira's disciple Goyama Imdabhui is a spectator to this exchange and wants to ask Mahavira a question, but before he can open his mouth, Mahavira makes it apparent that he can read his student's mind.[16] Such dialogues result in the listener realizing the Jina's omniscience and the truth of his teaching.

Like their Buddhist counterparts, Jaina texts criticize the Brahmanas, their sacrifices, way of life, and arrogance. Like the Buddhist texts, they talk of the 'true' or ideal Brahmana, giving the word new content, shifting the emphasis from birth to conduct.

The ideas of anekantavada (doctrine of the manifold nature of reality) and syadavada (the doctrine of maybe) are of special significance in the context of religious dialogue and debate. According to Jaina doctrine, reality is manifold (anekanta). Everything that exists has three aspects— substance (dravya), quality (guna), and mode (paryaya). According to syadavada, every judgement we make is relative to the particular aspect of the object we are judging and the point of view from which we look at it. No judgement is true without qualification. Reality cannot be grasped in its entirety and complexity. All statements about it are partially true statements and should hence be prefixed with the word syat ('maybe' or 'in some respect'). The Jaina criticism of the views of other philosophical systems is that their pronouncements about reality— for instance, on whether reality is eternal or non-eternal, changing or unchanging—represent a single, partial, and extreme view of things.[17] The views of other schools are not condemned as absolutely invalid but are considered partially true statements (nayas).

It has been argued that the Jainas practise something that can be

---

[16]For details, see Anna Aurelia Esposito, 'Didactic Dialogues: Communication of Doctrine and Strategies of Narrative in Jaina Literature', in Black and Patton (eds.), *Dialogues in Early South Asian Religions*, pp. 79-98.

[17]For further details, see Jaini, *The Jaina Path of Purification*, pp. 89-106.

called intellectual non-violence.[18] The basic argument is as follows: Jaina doctrine recognizes that there are many different perspectives on truth; this translates into toleration and an acceptance of other religious viewpoints. This tolerance is rooted in the emphasis on ahimsa: just as all living beings are treated with respect, all perspectives must be treated with respect. Does this accurately describe the Jaina position? According to the scholar of Jainism John Cort, not really. Jaina texts accept that other points of view on the way to moksha are partially correct, but for the most part, are incorrect. Only the Jaina doctrine, rooted in the omniscience of the Jinas, is based on correct perception and correct knowledge. Jaina texts contain violent philosophical debates and there is a criticism of non-Jaina perspectives, especially with regard to ahimsa. Jaina libraries have many non-Jaina manuscripts, e.g., on grammar, poetics, philosophy, and ritual, including Buddhist and Brahmanical texts. These were evidently read and studied by Jaina scholars. Jaina philosophical compendia contain summaries of different philosophical schools, the earliest of which was by Haribhadra (eighth century). But although Jainas engaged with other religions (they actively engaged with the Mughals in medieval times), this did not mean that they considered other views as valid as theirs.

Upanishadic, Buddhist, and Jaina dialogues and debates express and explain their own doctrines and assert their superiority over others. Their target audience must have been fairly small. While in the case of the Upanishads, debates can be seen as a way of helping a seeker get closer to a higher truth, in the case of the Jaina and Buddhist texts, they were, in addition, directed towards creating communities of followers who were distinguished and demarcated from other communities. So dialogue and debate in ancient texts do not in themselves indicate a genuine exchange of ideas or concord. In fact, they can indicate quite the opposite.

---

[18]John E. Cort, '"Intellectual Ahimsa" revisited: Jaina tolerance and the intolerance of others', *Philosophy East and West*, vol. 50, no. 3, July 2000, pp. 324–47.

Debate and doubt in the Mahabharata

While most debates end with a winner and a loser, those in the Mahabharata often end inconclusively or on a note of doubt. The Mahabharata abounds in debates, the most important of which are about the subtlety and mysteriousness of dharma. The overall emphasis of the narrative is that one must understand one's dharma—essentially that of the varna one is born into—and strive to follow it, no matter how unpleasant it may be and how much unhappiness it may bring. Nevertheless, characters in the epic are frequently tormented about what exactly their dharma is, none more so than Yudhishthira, the eldest Pandava brother, who (ironically) has the epithet Dharmaraja (king of dharma).

Although at one level, dharma is spoken of as eternal and universal, the Mahabharata in fact suggests the existence of several dharmas. The dharmas of the four ages (Krita, Treta, Dvapara, and Kali) vary. Dharma is frequently associated with the varnas and the ashramas, but there is also a dharma of sages, of forest people, even of mlechchhas. In times of acute distress or emergency, apad-dharma (dharma in time of emergency) kicks in, and certain departures from the norm are justified. We have noted the Mahabharata example of the Brahmana sage Vishvamitra, starving in a time of famine, stealing some forbidden meat from the house of a Chandala and defending his action as being in accordance with apad-dharma. Reference has been made in earlier chapters to the dharma that applies to all, known as samanya dharma or sadharana dharma, which consists of various virtues such as truthfulness, generosity, and non-violence, but this is not as important as the dharma of the varnas. On several occasions, the Mahabharata asserts non-violence or non-cruelty to be the highest dharma. Towards the end of the Shanti Parva, the unchha vow is described as the highest dharma. This consists of a frugal life based on food acquired through gleaning, that is, gathering leftover grain from fields. The Mahabharata accepts a life of engagement with the world and also talks about the dharma of liberation from the cycle of rebirth (moksha-dharma) which requires true knowledge, control of the senses, and complete detachment. The epic composers often included contradictory statements about dharma within a dialogic frame and did not always try to reconcile the many different points of view.

One of the many exciting debates in the Mahabharata is between the philosopher king Janaka and the wandering female ascetic Sulabha, who had attained moksha.[19] Sulabha hears that Janaka had attained moksha while remaining king. Using her yogic powers, she assumes the body of a beautiful woman and appears in his court to check for herself whether this is true. She challenges Janaka to a debate and uses her yogic powers to enter into the king's being. Janaka questions her credentials to debate with him, especially on the grounds that she is a beautiful woman, and mocks and insults her. But debate they do, and their topic is whether it is possible to attain moksha while leading a worldly life or whether renunciation is an essential prerequisite. It is an extremely unusual debate as the beings of both debaters inhabit one body during its entire duration. At some point of time, Janaka falls silent, a sign that he has lost.

A powerful philosophical response to a whole range of issues related to dharma, violence, war, and renunciation in the Mahabharata occurs in the Bhagavad Gita, which has already been mentioned in earlier chapters. The Bhagavad Gita weaves together strands from the philosophies of Samkhya, Yoga, and Vedanta with the ideas of duty and religious devotion. It absorbs certain Buddhist ideas such as impermanence and suffering, and rejects certain others (for instance, the denial of the soul). It reconciles dharma and moksha. Its idea of karma-yoga emphasizes the eternal nature of the atman and the importance of following one's varna-dharma; it is the fruits of actions and not actions themselves that are to be renounced. The text contains different ideas of god—an impersonal cosmic god who is the creator, preserver, and destroyer of the world, as well as a god who is immediate and worthy of devotion. The latter idea is best described as monolatry—the worship of a god as a supreme god without denying the existence of other gods. Such a unique synthesis could only have emerged from a creative engagement

---

[19]Mahabharata 12.308.

with a variety of philosophical ideas.

Along with the Bhagavad Gita, the Mahabharata also contains the Anugita.[20] After the end of the great battle at Kurukshetra, Arjuna tells Krishna that he has forgotten everything that the latter had told him earlier and asks him to repeat it. Krishna tells him that this is not possible as he had delivered his Bhagavad Gita teaching while in a deep meditative state and cannot redo the act. But he tells Arjuna that he can give him another teaching that is essentially the same as the previous one. He proceeds to deliver the Anugita, which emphasizes knowledge and renunciation as the paths to liberation—a teaching that is rather different from the Bhagavad Gita's thrust on desireless action and bhakti!

The inconclusive nature of the dialogues and debates in the Mahabharata and the presence of diverse, contradictory ideas within the text have a great deal to do with its compositional history, which may have stretched over as many as eight centuries and involved numerous composers and redactors. It also indicates the pragmatic approach adopted by the composers, who juxtaposed many different views without trying to make them all fall in a single line. Compared to other texts, the Mahabharata dialogues actually explore different facets of complex issues and do not shirk from admitting confusion, dilemmas, and grey areas. At the same time, there are limits to the flexibility, and this is indicated in the text's hostile attitude towards the nastikas, who are discussed below.

The astika–nastika divide

The history of ancient Indian philosophical schools is not one of linear progression or neat clusters. Vedanta, for instance, was not as prominent in the first millennium as it became in the second.[21] Apart from Shankara's Advaita Vedanta and its idealist monism, there were many other Vedanta schools that criticized each other vigorously. These

---

[20]Mahabharata 14.16.
[21]Daya Krishna, 'Vedanta in the first millennium AD: The case study of a retrospective illusion imposed by the historiography of Indian philosophy', *Journal of the Indian Council of Philosophical Research*, 1996, pp. 201–07.

include the Vishishtadvaita (Qualified Non-Dualist), Dvaita (Dualist), and Bhedabheda (Realist) schools. There were many diatribes within and across these Vedantic schools. For instance, Vedantadeshika (a proponent of the Vishisthadvaita school) described Bhaskara (a proponent of the Bhedabheda Vedanta school) as a Vedantin who smelled like a Jaina. The Bhedabhedin Advaitin Vijnanabhikshu described the Advaita Vedantins as Buddhists in disguise.

Philosophers of the Samkhya and Yoga schools criticized the Vedantins and Mimamsakas for their acceptance of animal sacrifices. The seventh century Mimamsaka Kumarila Bhatta wrote in his *Tantravarttika* that the Samkhya, Yoga, Pancharatra, Pashupata, and Shakya (Buddhist) treatises on dharma and adharma were not accepted by those who know the three Vedas. The eleventh century Shaiva Somashambhu wrote that the Vedantins, Mimamsakas, and those who worshipped other gods such as Vishnu would be reborn in hells, unless they underwent a complex ritual to turn themselves into Shaivas.[22]

Several texts listing and discussing different philosophical views (these are known as doxographies) appeared in the early medieval period.[23] Their presentation of various views was usually organized to build up to an assertion of the primacy of the last school discussed—which also happened to be the one to which the composer belonged. The earliest enumeration occurs in the fifth/sixth century Tamil epic *Manimekalai*, which lists six schools according to the number of means of valid knowledge (pramanas) accepted by each of them—Lokayata, Buddhism, Samkhya, Nyaya, Vaisheshika, and Mimamsa. The heroine Manimekalai meets the proponents of various doctrines one by one, ending with a Buddhist monk, whose doctrine is presented as the best. This is not surprising considering that the *Manimekalai* is a Buddhist epic. The sixth century Bhavaviveka belonged to the Madhyamika school of Buddhism. His *Madhyamaka-hridayakarika* (Verses on the Heart of the Middle Way) presents arguments of various schools—'Hinayana' Buddhism, Yogachara Buddhism, Samkhya, Vaisheshika, Vedanta, and

---

[22]Nicholson, *Unifying Hinduism*, pp. 3–5.
[23]Ibid., pp. 144–65.

Mimamsa, but asserts the superiority of Madhyamika Buddhism at the beginning and end of the text.

Listings and orderings of various philosophical schools intersected with a binary division into astika and nastika.[24] The ambiguity of the distinction lies in the literal meaning of the two words themselves—astika is asti+ka (one who says 'it is') and nastika is na+asti+ka (one who says 'it is not'). What is being affirmed or denied (the 'it' in question) is unspecified, so the terms could be and were given varying content.

In Purva Mimamsa, a nastika is one who does not accept or perform the prescribed rituals. The *Manu Smriti* criticizes Brahmanas who use hetu (logic) to question the shruti or smriti, which are the sources of dharma, and states that such nastika denigrators of the Veda should be ostracized. The Mahabharata has much to say about nastikas who deny the authority of the Veda; their views cannot be accepted or be condoned. They should be avoided at all cost and kings are advised to go all out to eliminate them.[25]

The fourteenth century *Sarvadarshana-samgraha* lists six astika schools of philosophy. This work is ascribed to the Advaita Vedantin scholar Madhava, who was a minister in the Vijayanagara empire and later became the head of the Shringeri matha. This text juxtaposes the astika schools (Samkhya, Yoga, Nyaya, Vaisheshika, Purva Mimamsa or Vedanta, and Uttara Mimamsa) against the nastika schools (which include the Buddhists, Jainas, and Charvaka materialists). All the schools—astika and nastika—are shown to be inferior to Advaita Vedanta.

The terms astika and nastika were also used in non-Brahmanical texts but were given different content. The Jaina scholar Haribhadra's *Shaddarshana-samuchchaya* describes six schools—Buddhism, Nyaya, Samkhya, Jainism, Vaisheshika, and Mimamsa—as the astika schools which affirm the existence of the other world, transmigration, virtue, and vice. Of these, he asserts that Jainism is the best. He gives the

---

[24]See Nicholson's excellent discussion on this subject in *Unifying Hinduism*, pp. 166–84, 191–92.

[25]See Naina Dayal, 'Sūtas, Nāstikas and Retelling the Mahābhārata', in Naina Dayal and Kumkum Roy (eds.), *Questioning Paradigms, Constructing Histories: A Festschrift for Romila Thapar*, New Delhi: Aleph Book Company, 2019, pp. 196–210.

nastika label to the materialist Lokayata school. The fourth century Buddhist text Bodhisattvabhumi criticizes various types of Buddhists but reserves its strongest condemnation for those who hold a position of universal negation and say that nothing exists. Later texts identify them with Buddhists of the Madhyamika school.[26]

The dividing lines between astika and nastika are a good indicator of how proponents of different philosophical schools and religious traditions saw themselves in relation to others. While there were different views on what exactly made someone or a philosophical school or a religious group nastika, in all cases, the term had negative connotations. Nastikas were not only criticized; their views were condemned, and they were supposed to be shunned.

Vaidika orthodoxy, Shaivas, Shaktas, and Vaishnavas

In the earlier chapters, we saw the emergence and increasing popularity of religious sects based on devotion to a supreme deity. The kind of religiosity they reflect can be described as monolatry—a belief in a supreme deity without denying the existence of other deities. But across the centuries, there was a coexistence of different notions of divinity—for instance, a deity could be seen as the focus of independent worship, as a member of a larger pantheon, or one of many manifestations of a single divine being. The Puranas, which express deference to the Vedic tradition, actually reflect many new religious ideas and practices. Yajna (sacrifice) was not rejected but a new range of pious activities such as dana (pious giving), tirtha (pilgrimage), and vrata (vows) were held to be highly meritorious.

In the course of the early medieval period (sixth–thirteenth centuries), Tantra made a strong impact on religious traditions across the board. As mentioned in Chapter 2, Tantra existed in softcore and hardcore forms, and in the former, it is often not recognized as especially Tantric. Apart from the corpus of specifically Tantric works, Tantric elements are also found in certain Puranas such as the Linga, Shiva, Kalika, and Agni Puranas. Apart from deities who are seen as specifically

---

[26]Nicholson, *Unifying Hinduism*, pp. 154–55, 172–74.

Tantric, non-Tantric deities such as Shiva or Vishnu could be worshipped as a supreme god in a Tantric or non-Tantric manner. The worship of the Great Goddess, Devi, came to be deeply imbued with Tantric elements.

Vaishnavism enjoyed considerable political patronage during 300–600 CE. Subsequently, Shaivism increasingly attracted political patronage across South and Southeast Asia, so much so that the distinguished scholar of Shaivism Alexis Sanderson has described the early medieval period as the Shaiva Age.[27] The most important Tantric sects were Shaiva. There was a close relationship between the Shaiva and Shakta sects due to the close connection between the deities Shiva and Shakti. The most important early Tantric sect among the Vaishnavas was the Pancharatra. The Sahajiyas of Bengal were a later sect belonging to the Tantric variety of Vaishnavism. Tantric Buddhism, known as Vajrayana (Thunderbolt or Diamond Vehicle) or Mantrayana (Vehicle of the Mantras) combined ritual, magic, meditation, and a belief in the great efficacy of mantras in attaining spiritual perfection. The impact of Tantra on Jainism has been recognized but is less studied.

The relationship between the Vaidika Brahmanas (Brahmanas who followed the Vedic tradition) and the Vaishnava and Shaiva sects—Tantric or otherwise—was a complex one. Most of the Tantric texts were written in Sanskrit and were composed by Brahmanas who were well-versed in Brahmanical philosophical and social traditions. Tantra did not challenge the Brahmanical tradition directly. In fact, it attempted a compromise in various ways.[28] Tantric texts accept Brahmanical ritual and socio-religious norms of varna and jati but consider them as valid on a lower plane, better adapted to the Kali age, or of such little significance that there was no harm following them. They present Tantric doctrines both as a continuation of the Veda and superior to it but hold that Tantric doctrines alone could lead to spiritual advancement and liberation. The attitude of accommodation is expressed in the

---

[27]See Sanderson, 'Śaivism and Brahmanism in the Early Medieval Period', The fact that Shaivism was swiftly adapting itself to the changing needs of political elites is indicated in kings taking diksha from Shaiva raja-gurus and an increase in epigraphic references to Shaiva mathas (monasteries) between the eighth and twelfth centuries.
[28]Padoux, *The Hindu Tantric World*, pp. 8–10.

Tantraloka of Abhinavagupta (tenth/eleventh century), whose theory of uttarottaravaishishtya (progressive ascending position of doctrines) arranges various doctrines in a hierarchy, with the Vedas at the bottom and his own Tantric Trika system at the top. All systems, including the Vaidika, Vaishnava, and Buddhist, are said to have a certain validity in a limited context and all originally proceed from the supreme God Shiva, and hence deserve a certain respect. But according to Abhinavagupta, only the nondualistic Shaivism of Trika is the completely valid one and it alone can lead to the attainment of the highest goal.

So the Shaiva and Vaishnava sects (both the Tantric and non-Tantric ones) extended nominal recognition to the Vedas, the smriti texts, and to the idea of the dharma of varnas and ashramas, but held that true liberation could only be achieved by following the Shaiva or Vaishnava path respectively. (The Shaivas and Vaishnavas also held their own scriptures and paths to be superior to one another's.) But this attitude of conditional acceptance was not reciprocated.[29] Orthodox Vaidika Brahmanas reject all views that do not rest on the Veda. The seventh century *Tantravarttika* of the Mimamsaka Kumarila Bhatta describes followers of Samkhya, Yoga, Pancharatrika Vaishnavas, Pashupata Shaivas, Buddhists, and Jainas as contradicting the Veda and hence unacceptable. In a discussion of how uninvited guests should be treated, Medatithi's tenth century commentary on the *Manu Smriti* states that Pancharatrika Vaishnavas, Shaivas of any type, Buddhists, and Jainas should not be given respect; they could be offered food, but only in the manner in which it was offered to 'untouchables'. So for Vaidika Brahmanas, the Vaishnavas and Shaivas were non-Vaidikas whose scriptures were false; they were condemned and to be shunned.

The problem was that the increasing popularity of the Shaiva and Vaishnava sects and their ability to attract substantial following and patronage created a religious world where Vaidika orthodoxy had

---

[29]Alexis Sanderson, 'Tolerance, Exclusivity, Inclusivity, and Persecution in Indian Religion During the Early Mediaeval Period', John Malinson (ed.), *Honoris Causa: Essays in Honour of Aveek Sarkar*, London: Allen Lane, 2015, pp. 155–224, available at https://www.academia.edu.

to coexist with these sects, even if it 'officially' condemned them. This coexistence was especially visible in political circles. Kings who advertised themselves as worshippers of Vishnu, Shiva, the Jina, or the Buddha gave grants of land to Vaidika Brahmanas. Some kings also boasted about their performance of Vedic sacrifices. A Brahmana who followed the Vaidika traditions and rituals could also worship a supreme deity. The possibilities of coexistence are revealed in the Kaula formula: 'Kaula inside, outwardly Shaiva, and socially Vaidika'.

Some of the South Indian bhakti sects strongly questioned the Brahmanical tradition and acts of conventional religious piety. The songs of the Vaishnava Alvars and Shaiva Nayanmars valorize exclusive love for god and include a strong critique and rejection of Vaidika and Puranic religious practice. For a devotee of the lord, the performance of sacrifices and conventional marks of religious piety were meaningless. Appar asks:

> Why bathe in Ganga or in Kaveri?
> or take a holy dip at Kumari?
> Why bathe where mingle waters of the seas?
> One thing alone will to your rescue come—
> Seeing everywhere the Lord Supreme.
>
> Why chant the Vedas, follow Vedic *karma*?
> Why preach day by day the books of *dharma*?
> Why the six Vedangas learn by rote?
> One thing alone will to your rescue come—
> thinking always of the Lord Supreme.
>
> Why roam the forests, wander through the towns?
> perform strict *tapas* as in books laid down?
> why fast and starve, sit gazing at the blue?
> One thing alone will to your rescue come—
> faith in him, Lord of Wisdom True.
>
> Fetching waters from a thousand *tirtha*s
> of what avail such futile ritual act?
> Like it is to mindless fool who water brings
> and guards it safely in a leaking pot!
> One thing alone will to your rescue come—

Loving at all times our gracious Lord.³⁰

As discussed in Chapter 1, the twelfth century Virashaiva bhakti saint Basava came from a Brahmana family and at a young age rebelled against Brahmanical ritualism. The Virashaiva doctrine was anti-caste and anti-Brahmana. It rejected the Vedic tradition, sacrifices, rituals, social customs, and superstitions. Although it espoused ahimsa, it critiqued Jainism, which was highly influential in the Karnataka area. Members of the Virashaiva sect wear a small emblem of the god called an ishta-linga on their body and attach no importance to worshipping him in temples. Although loving kindness towards all is a feature of the teaching of some of their saints, the primary emphasis is on devotion towards Shiva. The core Virashaiva ideas are encapsulated in free verse lyrics known as vachanas, composed by the saints. This is one of Basava's vachanas:

The rich
will make temples for Shiva.
What shall I,
a poor man,
do?

My legs are pillars,
the body the shrine,
the head a cupola
of gold.

Listen, O lord of the meeting rivers [Shiva],
things standing shall fall,
but the moving ever shall stay.³¹

---

³⁰*Tirumurai* 5, Appar's hymn 99, vv. 2, 4, 6, 8, and 10; trans. cited in Vidya Dehejia, *Slaves of the Lord*, pp. 13–14.
³¹Basavanna 820. Trans. from the Kannada by A. K. Ramanujan, *Speaking of Śiva*, Harmondsworth: Penguin Books, 1973, pp. 88, 87. Kudalasangamadeva ('Lord of the meeting rivers') is a name with which Basavanna frequently invokes Shiva. Kudalasangama is a sacred place in north Karnataka, located at the meeting point of two rivers, a place where Basavanna is said to have attained enlightenment.

Nayanmars versus Jainas

The songs of the Shaiva Nayanmar saints contain a great deal of criticism of other religious communities, especially the Jainas. Food is a favourite basis for reproach.[32] Sambandar criticizes Jainas for secretly longing to eat meat. The songs of Appar, who is supposed to have once been a Jaina monk, talk of Jainas with their decrepit teeth, their fasting, eating in silence, and eating with both hands. Buddhists are ridiculed for their fondness for rice gruel and fine robes.

The crossfire is at its sharpest in hagiographies. Stories of the lives of great saints or teachers were a powerful vehicle for emphasizing religious values at a popular level. The twelfth century Periyapuranam (also known as the Tiruttontarpuranam), attributed to an author named Sekkilar, contains hagiographies of the sixty-three Nayanmars. Sekkilar is said to have composed the text in order to wean away his patron Chola king from an interest in a Jaina text, the Chintamani.[33]

Diatribes against followers of other religions were evidently not meant to be communicated to them but were directed inwards towards members of the Nayanmar community itself. Running down the competition and emphasizing the dividing lines was a way of forging a stronger sense of community identity. Notwithstanding the many differences between the Nayanmars and Jainas, there are also some similarities in their emphasis on asceticism and almsgiving, as well as between certain elements of Jaina and Shaiva Siddhanta philosophies, for instance, the idea of karma being material and the visualization of the state of liberation.[34] The Nayanmar hymns and hagiographies clearly indicate that for the Shaiva leadership of South India, the Jainas were the

---

[32]See Katherine E. Ulrich, 'Food Fights: Buddhist, Hindu, and Jaina Dietary Polemics in South India', *History of Religions*, vol. 46, no. 3, February 2007, pp. 228–61.

[33]The king named Anapayan in the text is identified with Kulottunga II. See Anne Monius, 'Love, Violence, and the Aesthetics of Disgust: Śaivas and Jainas in Medieval South India', *Journal of Indian Philosophy*, vol. 32, no. 2/3, June 2004, pp. 113–72.

[34]Richard H. Davis, 'The story of the disappearing Jainas: Retelling the Śaiva-Jaina encounter in medieval South India', in John E. Cort (ed.), *Open Boundaries: Jaina Communities and Cultures in Indian History*, Delhi: Sri Satguru Publications, [1998], 1999, Chap. 11, pp. 213–24.

strongest competitors for patronage and allegiance; this is why they were attacked so sharply. Inscriptions also attest to specific sites of conflict. A twelfth century inscription from Ablur records a conflict between Jainas and Shaivas which led to the demolition of a Jaina temple and the building of a Shiva shrine in its place.[35]

Interestingly, while Shaiva texts engage in diatribe against the Jainas, Jaina texts concentrate on polemic against the Buddhists. There is a story that the Jaina monk Akalanka debated with the Buddhists in the royal court at Kanchipuram and defeated them with the help of the yakshi Ambika; the Buddhists were subsequently banished from the city.[36] This indicates that from the point of view of the Jainas of South India, it was not the Shaivas but the Buddhists—with whom they shared common principles such as non-violence—who were the arch-rivals when it came to attracting followers and patrons.

Buddhists, Vaishnavas, and Shaivas

The absorptive capacity of Hinduism is displayed in the Puranas, which created pantheons that brought together numerous gods and goddesses who were initially foci of independent worship. The incorporation of the Buddha as an avatara (incarnation) of Vishnu is often cited as an example of the syncretic nature of Hinduism. The question is: what sort of incorporation was it? The Puranic description of the Buddha is anything but flattering. He is supposed to delude the wicked in the Kali age and to pave the way for the arrival of the Kalki avatara. The early Bengal Upapuranas say many negative things about Buddhists; they describe them as symbols of evil, defiling, and to be avoided. Even dreaming about them is inauspicious. The later Upapuranas offer a more positive image, describing the Buddha as an embodiment of peace and beauty, and connecting him with the compassionate aim of

---

[35]Inscriptions at Sravana Belgola refer to the Jainas appealing to the Vijayanagara king for protection from the Vaishnavas. Sanderson, *Tolerance, Exclusivity, Inclusivity*, p. 212.
[36]Leslie Orr, 'Identity and Divinity: Boundary-crossing Goddesses in Medieval South India', *Journal of the American Academy of Religion*, vol. 73, no. 1, March 2005, p. 12.

ending animal sacrifices.[37] Nevertheless, in spite of being recognized as an avatara, the Buddha was never worshipped in Vishnu temples.

Incorporative and subordinating strategies were not only adopted by the Vaishnavas; they were also adopted by the Buddhists, interestingly, more vis-à-vis Shaivism than Vaishnavism.[38] Buddhist texts narrate the Trailokyavijaya episode, where Heruka, an emanation of the bodhisattva Vajrapani, gets angry with Shiva Maheshvara and destroys him by crushing him under his left foot. He then resurrects Shiva and his consort as Uma Maheshvara and gives them a new name, Bhairava–Bhairavi, and admits them into the Buddhist fold as his followers. This event is also represented visually in many Buddhist images. Religious conflict is also reflected in the many images of wrathful Buddhist Tantric deities trampling on Hindu gods and vice versa.

Inter-religious dynamics are relevant to the debate on the decline of Buddhism in India. Various factors have been suggested for this decline—the failure of Buddhism to maintain a distinct identity in relation to the Hindu sects; an alleged 'degeneration' brought in by increasing Tantric influences; an aggressive Brahmanism/Hinduism; and the Turkish invasions. Did Buddhism slowly fade out or was it pushed out? There is a view that it was pushed out and that this involved a great deal of very real violence.[39]

The Mimamsaka Kumarila Bhatta is described in his hagiographies as defeating the Buddhists and establishing the supremacy of the Veda. Kumarila is said to have spent many years studying (undercover, so to speak) with a Buddhist teacher, and learning the doctrine in order to eventually refute it. He succeeded in defeating the Buddhists (and Jainas) in debate. The accounts of these debates are quite violent:

---

[37] Kunal Chakrabarti, 'A History of Intolerance: The Representation of Buddhists in the Bengal Purāṇas', *Social Scientist*, vol. 44, no. 5/6, May–June 2016, pp. 11–27.

[38] Abhishek S. Amar, 'Buddhist Responses to Brāhmaṇa Challenges in Medieval India: Bodhgayā and Gayā', *Journal of the Royal Asiatic Society*, third series, vol. 22, no. 1, January 2012, pp. 155–85.

[39] See Giovanni Verardi, *The Gods and the Heretics: Crisis and Ruin of Indian Buddhism*, New Delhi: Aditya Prakashan, 2018.

He defeated countless Buddhists and Jainas by means of different types of arguments in the various sciences. Having cut off their heads with axes, he threw them down into numerous wooden mortars and made a powder of them by whirling around a pestle. In this way he was fearlessly carrying out the destruction of those who held evil doctrines.[40]

Is this metaphorical violence or is it a reflection of violent religious conflicts on the ground?

There are also references to political persecution (discussed later) of Buddhism. But Buddhism did not disappear from India. The Buddhist monasteries at Sanchi and Amaravati continued to exist till the twelfth/thirteenth and fourteenth centuries respectively. The thirteenth century *Chachnama* refers to Buddhism flourishing in Sindh in the northwest. In Kashmir, the Jayendra monastery at Shrinagara and the Raja vihara at Parihasapura declined by the eleventh century, but the Ratnagupta monastery and Ratnarashmi monastery at Anupamapura flourished in the eleventh and twelfth centuries. In Bengal and Bihar, the Palas were patrons of Buddhism. Various monasteries such as Nalanda, Odantapura (near Nalanda), Vikramashila (identified with Antichak in Bhagalpur district, Bihar), and Somapuri (located at Paharpur) flourished in their kingdoms. In Orissa, remains of early medieval Buddhist stupas, monasteries, and sculptures have been found at Lalitagiri and Ratnagiri. Several Buddhist viharas were built during this period in Nepal, as well as in Ladakh, Lahul, and Spiti. It was the Tantric form of Buddhism that flourished at most of the major monastic centres. It should be noted that some of the monasteries that were established in Tibet and in the western Himalayas during these centuries have a continuous history right down to the present. So Buddhism did not completely disappear from the subcontinent, but it did decline and was relegated to the geographical, political, and cultural margins. There is much about the history of Buddhism in early medieval India, especially the reasons for

---

[40]From Anantanandagiri's *Shankaravijaya*, Jonathan Bader (trans.), *Conquest of the Four Quarters: Traditional Accounts of the Life of Śaṅkara*, New Delhi: Aditya Prakashan, 2000, p. 215.

Fig. 5.5: Fierce Buddhist deities, Bhutan monastery

dwindling lay support and patronage, that remains obscure. But although the texts may present a dramatized, exaggerated version of events, there is no doubt that religious competition and conflict are part of the story.

It is worth noting that apart from the especially fierce Tantric deities, the iconography of many Indian deities includes weapons, and their mythology involves killing, even if those being killed are evil beings. [Figs. 5.5, 5.6, 5.7] Why is there so much violence in representations of Indian gods and goddesses and in stories of their exploits? Even if these images are interpreted metaphorically—the defeat of evil, the passions, or the ego—the stark violence in them cannot be ignored.

Fig. 5.6: Bhairava, Nepal, twelfth century

Fig. 5.7: Aparajita trampling Ganesha, stone, Bihar Museum

Shankara's digvijaya

Shankara, who lived in the late eighth and early ninth centuries, was one of the most influential proponents of Advaita Vedanta. He seems to have been a relatively unknown figure during his lifetime and for several centuries thereafter. The view of Shankara as representing an aggressive Hindu assertion in the early medieval period is based on his hagiographies, the earliest of which were written many centuries after his time in the fourteenth and fifteenth centuries, during the Vijayanagara period. The best known is Madhava's *Shankara-digvijaya*, written anywhere between 1650 and 1800, which brought together material from several earlier texts.[41] Subsequently, Shankara was associated with other mathas too.[42] The hagiographies present a picture of Shankara's thought that is very different from that contained in his own works. Although a large number of texts are attributed to him, in the philosophical ones that are considered definitely his, although Shankara recognizes the existence of ishvara (god), it is the knowledge of atman and brahman which is the only path to salvation. The hagiographies, on the other hand, portray him as an ardent devotee of Shiva and as his incarnation. They are more reflective of the concerns of the hagiographers and their times than a faithful description of the life of their subject.

The basic facts of Shankara's life include the following: he was born in a Brahmana family in the Kerala region, left home at an early age to become a sannyasi, and became a student of a philosopher named Govinda, who was himself a student of the great Advaita philosopher

---

[41] For a discussion of these hagiographies, see Bader, *Conquest of the Quarters* and Mathew Clark, *The Daśanāmī Saṁnyāsīs: The Integration of Ascetic Lineages into an Order*, Leiden, Boston: Brill, 2006.

[42] Shankara is supposed to have established four or five monasteries known as the Amanaya mathas (see Clark, *The Daśanāmī Saṁnyāsīs*). Although some sort of organization for preserving and propagating Shankara's teaching emerged fairly early in the day, many scholars have argued that the mathas (including those at Shringeri and Kanchi) seem to have been established several centuries later, and were attributed to Shankara in order to endow them with prestige. The Shringeri matha, for instance, seems to have been set up in the fourteenth century, during the Vijayanagara period.

Gaudapada.⁴³ Shankara wrote numerous works, the most important of which are commentaries on the Upanishads, Bhagavad Gita, and Brahmasutras. He travelled a great deal and engaged in many debates. Other possible factual details include his father's early death; his encounter with the Mimamsaka Mandanamishra; and his own death at the early age of thirty-two. Shankara's hagiographies do not emphasize his debates with Buddhists. In fact, they give the credit for defeating the Buddhists and establishing the supremacy of the Veda to Kumarila Bhatta. In spite of Kumarila's victories, we are told that he decided to immolate himself on a slow-burning pyre of chaff to atone for his having deceived his Buddhist teacher. Shankara is said to have been passing by when the fire was ablaze and the two men had a philosophical conversation. The fact that these are not historical accounts should be clear from the fact that Kumarila lived well before Shankara.

Shankara is said to have travelled all over the country, meeting and debating with philosophical adversaries, defeating them all. The most heated debates took place with the Shaktas, tantric worshippers of Bhagavati, Shaiva dualists, Vaishnava Pancharatras, a Bhedabheda Advaitin, and Jainas. There are hardly any Vaishnava opponents. The tone and tenor of the debates vary considerably across texts, ranging from cordiality to insult. While the hagiographies make much of Shankara's debates with various great thinkers of his time, they do not usually give details of their philosophical content.⁴⁴

The fact that Shankara's debate with Mandanamishra is an important event in all the hagiographies shows that at the time when they were written (fourteenth to sixteenth centuries), Advaita Vedanta philosophers considered the Mimamsakas as their most formidable rivals. In sharp contrast to the wandering sannyasi Shankara, Mandanamishra is described as living a householder's life in a palatial mansion. Depending on the text, the debate between the two men is said to have lasted

---

⁴³See David N. Lorenzen, 'The Life of Shankaracharya', Fred W. Clothey and J. Bruce Long (eds.), *Experiencing Siva: Encounters with a Hindu Deity*, New Delhi: Manohar, 1983, pp. 155–75; G. C. Pande, *Life and Thought of Śaṅkarācārya*, Delhi: Motilal Banarsidass, [1994], 1998.

⁴⁴See Bader, *Conquest of the Quarters*, pp. 182–229.

anywhere between six and a hundred days. Mandanamishra's wife, Ubhayabharati (she is given different names in various texts, some of which describe her as none other than the goddess Sarasvati) appears as the arbiter who announces her husband's ultimate defeat. In one version, she emerges from the kitchen and challenges Shankara to continue the debate with her. He protests that she is a woman, but she cites the Upanishadic precedents of Yajnavalkya's debate with Gargi and Janaka's with Sulabha. After seventeen days of debating, Ubhayabharati changes the subject to one where she knows that she has the upper hand—love and sex. (Shankara had no experience in these areas because he had become a celibate sannyasi at a young age.) Shankara asks for a break. Using his yogic powers, he enters the body of the dying King Amaruka to learn about the arts of love, and returns to the debate, having experienced them first-hand. Ubhayabharati concedes defeat and Mandanamishra becomes Shankara's disciple.

The fact that many of Shankara's hagiographies have the word vijaya (victory) or digvijaya (victory over the quarters) in their title indicates their drawing of a parallel between world victor and world renouncer, an idea first seen in early Jainism and Buddhism. The descriptions of Shankara's extensive travels to places from the Himalayas to Rameshvaram, and from Dvaraka to Kamarupa, are reminiscent of the Puranic mapping of places of pilgrimage in various parts of the subcontinent and also of the digvijayas of great emperors.

Shankara is presented in a very different light in the texts of his rivals.[45] Hagiographies of the thirteenth century Madhvacharya, founder of the school of Dvaita (dualistic) Vedanta, refer to Shankara as Samkara (the defiled one) and describe him as the illegitimate son of a widow and as an incarnation of the demon Manimat, who was born in order to destroy Vedanta. The eleventh/twelfth century Vishishtadvaita philosopher Ramanuja summarizes and critiques the philosophy of Advaita Vedanta and also says nasty things about Shankara. The sixteenth century Tibetan traveller Taranatha describes Shankara as having been victorious over many Buddhist monks before he was defeated in a major

---

[45]Bader, *Conquest of the Quarters*, pp. 64–66.

showdown with the Buddhist philosopher Dharmakirti at Nalanda.

Does the violence in philosophical debates and religious hagiographies reflect real violence or is it metaphorical? Was the cut and thrust of the debates and the abuse hurled at adversaries matched by conflict and violence between philosophical schools and religious communities on the ground? Although the texts should not be read literally, they suggest rivalry and contest, not concord.

Royal religious policy: keeping the lid on religious conflict and blowing it off

There was no 'state religion' in ancient India. Although certain religions were in the ascendant in certain parts of the subcontinent at certain points, none succeeded in capturing the state for any length of time. Generally, royal patronage was not constrained by the ruler's personal religious beliefs but was distributed to other groups as well.

Regardless of rulers' personal religious affiliations, Brahmanas were major recipients of royal land grants across the centuries. Unlike the Jainas and Buddhists, they did not have a formal organization, but they functioned very much like an institution with a greater level of flexibility and adaptablity, forging close links with kings and courts. Although many Brahmana recipients of royal land grants are advertised in inscriptions as Vaidikas, the fact that sectarian religion continued to grow and blossom in the kingdoms of ancient and early medieval India suggests that the hostility between the Vaidika Brahmanas and sectarians expressed in some of the texts did not play out on the ground. What emerged in royal courts was a political culture marked by a significant amount of hybridity, which created a powerful model for non-elite groups. Although the ideology of kingship in India changed over time and was expressed with different nuances in different regions, this seems to have been a constant feature, with some notable exceptions (these will be discussed further on).

The earliest unequivocal, datable evidence about the relationship between rulers and religious communities comes from the inscriptions of the third century BCE Maurya emperor Ashoka. Although an ardent

Buddhist, the dhamma he discusses obsessively in his inscriptions includes respect for shramanas and Brahmanas. The king declares his respect for all sects (pasandas) and orders his dhamma officers to look after the welfare of them all. Ashoka extended his patronage to Buddhist establishments, but also to the Ajivikas. Most important of all, in Rock Edict 12, he expresses his desire for the growth of the essentials of all sects and for the prevalence of an atmosphere of concord (samavaya). Such a plea only makes sense in a situation of religious discord and conflict. Further, Ashoka's schism edict suggests internal bickering within the Buddhist sangha, which he tried to firmly quell. Ashoka's plea for mutual dialogue, respect, and concord amounts to much more than what is conveyed by the word 'tolerance'. In some respects—for instance his anti-war policy—Ashoka can be seen as an aberration in ancient Indian politics. But his religious policy, which emerged in the context of a large, multi-religious, multi-cultural empire, was part of a longer-term pattern.

Kharavela, the first century CE king of Kalinga, announced his devout faith in Jainism in his Hathigumpha inscription, but also his benevolent attitude towards Brahmanas, Jainas, and all sects. The Satavahanas made grants to Brahmanas and Buddhist monks. This inclusive policy continued in later centuries too. The Pala kings of Bengal are described in their inscriptions as followers of the Buddha, but the vast majority of their grants were to Brahmanas (with some patronage of Buddhist and Shaiva establishments). Rather than seeing all this as part of Ashoka's legacy, or as an intrinsic attitude of 'tolerance', it can be understood as a pragmatic response of rulers to the existence of an extremely diverse religious landscape and the desire of political elites to make alliances with different religious communities.

And yet, along with this narrative of pluralistic benevolence, ancient Indian history contains episodes of religious violence and persecution. These include the looting of religious images as trophies of war.[46] The Hathigumpha inscription talks of Kharavela retrieving and reinstalling a Jina image that had been carried off by the Nanda king of Magadha. The

---

[46]For a larger discussion, see Richard H. Davis, *Lives of Indian Images*, Delhi: Motilal Banarsidass, [1997], 1999, Chap. 2.

Chulavamsa refers to the invading Pandya army carrying off a golden Buddha image from Anuradhapura (in Sri Lanka) in the ninth century, and the subsequent recovery of the image by the Sinhala king Sena II. An eleventh century inscription on a stone dvarapala (door guardian) displayed in the Rajaraja Museum at Thanjavur triumphantly proclaims that it was wrested from the Chalukyas by the Chola king Rajadhiraja after he had burnt down the Chalukya capital Kalyanapuram. Such acts can be seen as symbolic of a king establishing his political paramountcy over another, or of encompassing him in his own power orbit. The images in question were relocated but still given respect, another political layer added to their significance and life story.

Such acts of appropriation can be distinguished from the destruction of religious images or structures. A Buddhist text, the *Ashokavadana* (second century CE), states that the Shunga king Pushyamitra destroyed the 84,000 stupas built by Ashoka, that he devastated the Kukkutarama monastery at Pataliputra and killed all its monks. Pushyamitra is also said to have announced a reward of a hundred gold coins to anyone who brought him the head of a Buddhist monk. According to the archaeologist John Marshall, the Ashokan brick core of the great stupa at Sanchi revealed evidence of wantonly inflicted damage. He connected this with Pushyamitra Shunga.[47] On the other hand, it is clear that Sanchi and other Buddhist monasteries in central India continued to exist and grow during the Shunga period, indicating that Buddhism continued to flourish on the basis of non-royal patronage despite Pushyamitra's persecution.

Buddhist texts also accuse the Huna rulers Toramana and Mihirakula (fifth/sixth centuries CE) of persecuting Buddhists. Xuanzang states that Mihirakula (whose coins and inscriptions suggest that he was inclined towards Shaivism) destroyed 1,600 monasteries in Gandhara and had 9,000 men killed or sold into slavery on the banks of the Indus. At the Dharmarajika Stupa at Taxila, archaeologists found evidence of burnt structures, a burnt birch bark manuscript, many arrowheads, severed heads, dismembered bodies and skulls (belonging to six individuals)

---

[47]John Marshall, Alfred Foucher, and N. G. Majumdar, *The Monuments of Sāñchī*, vol. 1, Calcutta: Superintendent Government Printing, 1940, p. 23.

with marks of blows. Marshall interpreted this as evidence of a Huna attack.[48] On the other hand, an inscription found at Kura in the Salt Range records the building of a Buddhist monastery by a person named Rotta Siddhavriddhi during the reign of the Huna ruler Toramana; the religious merit gained by this gift was to be shared by the donor with the king and his family members. This suggests that Buddhism was not wiped out in the Gandhara area due to Huna persecution. Interestingly, Jaina texts of the ninth and tenth centuries describe Mihirakula as a wicked, oppressive tyrant who was anti-Jaina. Shashanka, who ruled eastern India in the early seventh century, also acquired a reputation for persecuting Buddhists. Xuanzang states that he destroyed monasteries, cut down the Bodhi tree, and unsuccessfully tried to replace the image of the Buddha at Bodh Gaya with one of Shiva.

Narratives of religious persecution also come from South India. The Pallava king Mahendravarman I (c. 610–630), initially a Jaina, is said to have been converted to Shaivism by the saint Appar, and thereafter persecuted the Jainas. A Pandya king of Madurai who converted from Jainism to Shaivism is described as having impaled 8,000 Jainas in revenge for the latter's attempt to kill his Shaiva guru Sambandar. Not only is this gruesome scene depicted in a relief sculpture in the Meenakshi temple at Madurai, but the event is still celebrated in the temple's festivals today. According to Shrivaishnava hagiography, Ramanuja had to flee from the persecution of the Shaiva Chola king. According to the Divyasuricharita, a Chola king had an image of Vishnu in front of the shrine of Shiva Nataraja in Chidambaram removed and thrown into the sea. The narratives of Chola religious persecution extended to Sri Lanka. The Chulavamsa states that when Rajendra Chola's army invaded Sri Lanka in the eleventh century, it seized a great deal of treasure, the chief queen, and the king; it broke into the relic chambers and monasteries and looted images made of gold and other precious materials. These accounts of the destruction of religious structures and the looting of religious images were part of narratives of war.

---

[48]John Marshall, *Taxila: An Illustrated Account of Archaeological Excavations Carried Out at Taxila Under the Orders of the Government of India Between the Years 1913 and 1934*, vol. 2, Delhi: Motilal Banarsidass, [1951], 1975, pp. 284–85.

Kalhana's *Rajatarangini* narrates several episodes of religious persecution in the history of Kashmir. A successor of Ashoka named Jalauka (not known from any other source) is described as a Shaiva who destroyed a Buddhist monastery because he did not like the music coming from it; he later rebuilt it. Kalhana also refers to later rulers belonging to the eighth to eleventh centuries who engaged in persecution, often due to greed. Tarapida of the Karkota dynasty oppressed the Brahmanas and met a bad end. Jayapida of the same dynasty oppressed his subjects, including Brahmanas; in protest, ninety-nine Brahmanas committed suicide by drowning themselves in the Tulamulya River, a dramatic event that brought the king to his senses, but only temporarily. The Utpala dynasty ruler Shankaravarman became greedy and plundered sixty-four temples, rescinded tax-free grants, and imposed taxes on temples. King Kshemagupta destroyed the Jayendravihara monastery in Srinagara and used the material to build a temple. The conflict with the Brahmanas continued during the reign of Queen Didda. Kalhana states that King Harsha of the Lohara dynasty (during whose reign the *Rajatarangini* was written) plundered the wealth of temples and appointed an official for overthrowing the images of deities, defiling them, and melting them down for the royal treasury.

Historians have usually interpreted such narratives as indicative of a vague antipathy or hostility, not actual persecution. While the accounts no doubt use hyperbole for the sake of dramatic emphasis, there is no reason to assume that they did not actually represent episodes of persecution, sometimes driven by economic and/or political motives. They indicate that the pragmatic multi-directional patronage of rulers of ancient India was sometimes punctured by violent persecution.

Making fun of religion

These days, one dare not crack jokes about religion. In ancient times, although religion was a serious business, there was also a tradition of making fun of it. [Fig. 5.8] The *Mattavilasa-prahasana*, *Agamadambara*, and the satires of Kshemendra are some of the noteworthy examples of texts that do this.

Fig. 5.8: Detail of Mahabalipuram 'Descent of the Ganga' relief. Note that the ascetic on the top and the cat on the bottom right are both performing austerities, the latter probably an allusion to a humorous story

The genre of Sanskrit farce called prahasana especially deals with religious themes. Two farces, the *Mattavilasa-prahasana* (The Farce of Drunken Sport) and *Bhagavadajjukam-prahasana* (The Farce of the Saint-courtesan) are attributed to the seventh century Pallava king Mahendravarman. The *Mattavilasa-prahasana* opens with a drunk Kapalika monk Satyasoma and his equally drunk girlfriend Devasoma, both lurching around the streets of Kanchi.[49] The Kapalika has lost the skull that he was using as a drinking cup at a tavern. He discovers the loss just as he and his girlfriend are about to receive alms in the form of liquor at a second tavern. Satyasoma tells Devasoma to receive the liquor in a cow's horn, since that which has been offered must not be refused. They return to the first tavern and on the way, encounter a Buddhist monk who is coming from a feast thrown by a rich merchant; the monk is furtively hiding some leftover fish and meat in his bowl under his robe. The Kapalika and his woman accost the monk and demand that he show them what he is hiding. The monk leers surreptitiously at Devasoma and refuses a drink offered to him by the Kapalika only because he does not want to be seen drinking in public. A passing Pashupata is asked to adjudicate; he does so, hoping to settle scores with the Kapalika. (Devasoma was his girlfriend before Satyasoma enticed her with the lure of some cowrie shells.) The monk is finally forced to show his bowl, which is of a different size and colour than Satyasoma's, but the latter insists that it is the one he had lost. The Pashupata suggests that they take the matter to court and brushes aside Devasoma's apprehension that the Buddhist monk may bribe the court officials. Just then, a madman enters, holding a skull which he has snatched from a dog—it is none other than Satyasoma's skull-bowl. After a minor scuffle, Satyasoma gets his bowl back. The characters part ways on an amicable note. The *Mattavilasa-prahasana* makes fun of the Buddhists, Kapalikas, and Pashupatas. All of them are depicted as degenerate hypocrites and rascals.[50]

---

[49]See N. P. Unni (ed. and trans.), *Mattavilāsa Prahasana of Mahendravikramavarman*, Trivandrum: College Book House, 1974.
[50]It is interesting that at some point of time, Mahendravarman's play acquired religious

The *Agamadambara* (Much Ado About Religion) is a Sanskrit play, written in ninth/tenth century Kashmir, during the reign of Shankaravarman, a king criticized by Kalhana for exploiting his people and robbing the wealth of temples.[51] The author, Jayanta Bhatta, belonged to a prosperous Brahmana family. He was a respected Nyaya philosopher and wrote several works, including the *Nyayamanjari*. He was also an adviser to the king. The four-act play contains satire, serious philosophical discussion, and reflections on the political management of a pluralistic religious terrain. Shankaravarman and Jayanta are mentioned several times in the play, although they never appear on stage.

The protagonist Samkarshana is a follower of the Mimamsa school who has just completed his Vedic study and is eager to take up cudgels against all enemies of the Veda. Act 1 is set in the garden of an opulent Buddhist monastery, where Samkarshana and his companion observe and comment on the hypocritical attitudes of the monks, including their interest in meat, drink, and women. Samkarshana successfully debates on philosophical issues with a great Buddhist monk named Dharmottara. Act 2 opens with a Jaina monk trying to make out with a nun. This is followed by a debate in which Samkarshana defeats a great Digambara monk, Jinarakshita. This is where the issue of 'false ascetics' makes its appearance. It is applied to a sect called Nilambara (Blue/Black Blanket), whose members move around in male–female pairs wrapped together in blankets and have licentious ways. Samkarshana vows to report them to the king. In Act 3, Samkarshana has been elevated to the position of Superintendent of Dharma. On his advice, the king has ordered the Nilambaras to be exiled from the kingdom. This has led to various other sects (including Shaiva ascetics) feeling nervous about their own fate. Samkarshana and his companion criticize the Shaiva ascetics—they are

---

significance. A highly modified version of this play is performed in Shaiva temples in Kerala as a part of the Kuttiyatam tradition. The content has been modified to highlight Shaiva devotion. Naturally, much of the original satirical punch of the play has been lost in the process.

[51] For the text and translation, see Csaba Dezső (ed. and trans.), *Much Ado About Religion by Bhaṭṭa Jayanta* (The Clay Sanskrit Library), New York: JCC Foundation, New York University Press, 2005.

addicted to alcohol, meat, and sex, and threaten the order of varnas and ashramas; they too should be banished. Orders are given to round them up, but they have already fled. Unfortunately, fearing a general religious persecution, true ascetics too are running away. Samkarshana realizes that he needs to take corrective measures—after all, the king is a worshipper of Shiva and is merciful to all religions. He decides to appoint community leaders to prevent virtuous ascetics from leaving, and he himself goes to the hermitage of the Shaiva ascetic Dharmashiva (a follower of Shaiva Siddhanta) to reassure him. There is a very long debate between Dharmashiva and a Charvaka (materialist) which covers topics such as asceticism, sacrifice, the existence of god, karma, and transmigration. Dharmashiva wins. In the dialogue that follows between Dharmashiva and Samkarshana, the former says that their mutual differences are a personal matter; more important is the task of refuting the Veda-hating nastikas. Samkarshana in turn tells the Shaiva ascetics that Shiva is a great god and that the Shaivas, Pashupatas, Kalamukhas, and Mahavratins should live together peacefully and harmoniously in the kingdom, without any fear.

In the prelude to Act 4 of the *Agamadambara*, two Vaidikas are in conversation, ruing the fact that their hopes for throwing all non-Vaidikas out of the kingdom have been dashed to the ground and that the heterodox religions (bahyagamas) are still around. They attribute this to the king who is a worshipper of Shiva and his adviser Samkarshana, who thinks that all religions are authoritative. A debate between Samkarshana and the Vaishnavas is scheduled to take place (the queen, we are told, is sympathetic to them, as is a certain influential royal courtier) and Samkarshana is nervous about how he should handle this. However, it is replaced by a great debate between the Vaidikas and the preceptors of all other religions. The Nyaya expert Dhairyarishi enters and is declared umpire. This debate is not described; instead, Dhairyarishi delivers a long monologue that ends with him proclaiming that all gods and paths are one and that all scriptures are authoritative. He specifically mentions the worshippers/followers of Shiva, Pashupati, Kapila, Vishnu, Samkarshana, Jina, Buddha, and Manu. This position is endorsed by Samkarshana, who too asserts that all religions are valid and that all religious groups must follow their own ways according to established custom, but must weed out the wicked from their midst. His attitude has changed dramatically from his hard-line stance in Act 1. The play ends with Samkarshana and Dhairyarishi going off to report all that has transpired to the king.

The *Agamadabara* reveals the various religious and philosophical positions in Kashmir in the ninth and tenth centuries and critiques some of them. Debate plays an important part in the play. There is an episode of persecution against the Nilambaras, which leads to fears of rampant persecution among other groups. But having realized the serious problems that this policy has created, Samkarshana makes a strategic course correction. The compromise between the Mimamsakas, Naiyayikas, Shaivas, and Vaishnavas is significant. The end of the play, where all groups, including the Buddhists and Jainas (but not the Charvakas) are declared to be welcome to live happily in the kingdom represents a politically pragmatic solution. Persecution and conflict have been replaced by reconciliation and bonhomie.

Kshemendra's satires

As mentioned in Chapter 1, Kshemendra was a Sanskrit poet and writer who lived in Kashmir during the late tenth and eleventh centuries. His many works include the *Kalavilasa, Narmamala,* and *Deshopadesha*.[52] Kshemendra's caustic critique spares almost nobody, nobody except kings. Brahmanas, ascetics, and various kinds of holy men appear as part of a long list of frauds.

The protagonist of *Kalavilasa* is a man named Muladeva, a great authority on the arts of deception. He observes that hordes of swindlers roam about the world, offering hope to hundreds of people desirous of magic powers, leading them to ruin. These include yogis who claim to be able to bring a lover under one's control, and roadside gurus who read the palms of young women. The swindlers include sycophantic chanters of the Vedas who seep into one like sweet poison and take off after robbing everything. Along with other kinds of intoxication—

[52] See Haksar, *Kshemendra, The Courtesan's Keeper*; Kshemendra, *Three Satires*.

of wealth, folly, learning, power, lineage, obsession with purity, and drinking—Kshemendra discusses those of asceticism and devotion. The intoxication of asceticism makes one look to the sky without noticing the impediments on the ground. The intoxication of devotion makes one believe in marvels and lose sight of oneself.

The colourful characters in the *Narmamala* include an official who is initially a Buddhist, then pretends to be a worshipper of Vishnu and then, in order to protect the health of his wife, turns to the Tantric Kaulas. He invites to his house an arrogant, greedy Kaula guru, who misleads credulous folk with his initiations and ordinations. The guru is a fat, ignorant, unscrupulous, lascivious scoundrel, given to drinking and is an expert in cheating all kinds of people including prostitutes, lechers, and officials. When he turns up, gullible folk line up to offer him obeisance, and he holds a fake ritual ceremony to fool them.

The *Deshopadesha* paints a sordid picture of many religious specialists who practise false piety. Kshemendra mocks Shaiva ascetics whose matted hair, cleansed with herbs, fumigated with incense, and deloused with fistfuls of ash, serves as a cushion for courtesans; and who gorge themselves with food in the temple after practising meditation and penance. On priests:

> The priest has also been ordained, but talk with the Kaulas [Shaiva Tantra initiates] has destroyed his caste inhibitions. He has a mind to drink and comes to the guru's house with a plate of fish in hand. With gurgles does he drink the wine of Bhairava, and, filled up to the throat, then rolls about like a cracked pot full of water streaming out. Having spent the whole night drunk and puking wine, his face licked by dogs, he is restored to purity the next morning by the greetings of other priests.[53]

Kshemendra writes that he composed the *Narmamala* for the entertainment of good people, to make them laugh, and to advise them on how to avoid falling into the hands of tricksters and scoundrels. We do not know whether he faced any backlash in response to his acerbic

---

[53]*Deshopadesha*, Haksar, *Kshemendra, Three Satires*, pp. 136–37.

humour. If Kshemendra had lived in the twenty-first century rather than the eleventh, his books would have been banned. He would have been forced to give up writing and would have spent the rest of his life dragging himself from one law court to another, reduced to penury by his lawyers' fees.

◆

Ancient India had a long and lively tradition of philosophical dialogue and debate on issues such as dharma, the nature of reality and existence, ethics, and the path to liberation from samsara. Debates were usually games of one-upmanship to demonstrate mastery and superiority over other ideas or systems of thought, but they nevertheless show the existence of a spirit of vigorous thinking and questioning among intellectuals. The growth of knowledge—of any kind—is impossible without such thinking and questioning.

The crystallization, consolidation, and evolution of religious identities involved give and take, competition, critique, and polemic. Conflict and violence were part of the historical context of the incorporation of certain elements of tribal religion into Hinduism. The existence of many multi-religious sites across India reflects religious plurality but does not necessarily reflect religious harmony or peaceful coexistence. While texts—especially hagiographies of saints—give a picture of sharply defined boundaries and conflicts, actual religious practice reveals many shared elements and a picture that is much more syncretic, hybrid, and fluid. At the political level, although there were some episodes of violent religious persecution by kings, the more usual policy was one of multi-directional religious patronage, with the patronage of Brahmanas forming a constant. This pragmatic response to a variegated religious landscape led to a certain level of hybridity that became part of the culture of royal courts, and must have permeated into the large social sphere.

In more recent times, with increasingly monolithic and antagonistic understandings of religious identity, tensions between religious communities exist in a heightened state, ever ready to explode. Communal riots have become all too frequent. Shrill diatribe prevails over genuine dialogue, which does not, in fact, really seem to exist at all. The conflicts have often been most intense in the context of control of religious sites—for instance, Shaivas versus Buddhists at Bodh Gaya; Digambaras versus Shvetamabaras at Sammed Shikharji; and Hindus versus Muslims in the decades-long Ram Janmabhoomi–Babri Masjid dispute at Ayodhya. The last of these reached a legal conclusion after many decades of litigation and a great deal of tragic violence. In ancient India, there were multiple religious communities, but no state religion. Perhaps there is a lesson here for our own times.

EPILOGUE

I hope this book has convinced you that the incredible diversity and complexity of ancient Indian culture is impossible to fully describe or grasp. The sources give tantalizing glimpses into some of its aspects, but a great deal remains elusive and unknown. The past has always been as complicated and disaggregated as the present. Historians select and weave together the minutiae of details to create historical narratives. All narratives are partial and provisional and subject to revision, but all narratives are not equally reliable or acceptable. They have to be supported by evidence from the sources and must stand up to scrutiny when subjected to rigorous analysis.

Many distorted views of the past emerge from presentism—that is, judging and using the past to serve the agendas of the present. The image of ancient India as a utopia of social and religious harmony and non-violence is a false one. So is its image as a dystopia marked only by inequity, conflict, and violence. Beyond glorification and denigration, there is the possibility of trying to understand how the multiple threads of the past are intertwined with each other, not only in terms of facticity, but also of ambiguity, contrast, tension, and contradiction. While discussing the different aspects of ancient Indian cultural traditions, the conjunction 'or' is best replaced by 'and'. As shown in this book, there is evidence of both inequality as well as promises of universal salvation, a valorization of desire and detachment, goddess worship and misogyny, violence and non-violence, debate and conflict. Just as extraordinary as the range of contradictions is the fact that they seem rather familiar to Indian readers. The reason is that in spite of the passage of centuries, and the enormous changes and upheavals of history, somehow, these contradictions still live on.

Many of the texts, ideas, and symbols discussed in this book too live on in the form of appropriations, recastings, even reversals. In their various oral, written, and performative tellings, the Ramayana and Mahabharata are well known, loved, and influential across India and Southeast Asia. While the Ramayana tradition presents Rama as an exemplar of virtues, in Periyar's writings, he is a symbol of northern Aryan tyranny. Duryodhana is a villain in the Sanskrit Mahabharata, but there are temples dedicated to him in Jakhol village in Himachal Pradesh and Malanada village in Kerala. Kautilya lives on under the more popular name of Chanakya in corporate self-help books, and on a recently issued five-rupee coin commemorating 150 years of the Indian Income Tax Department. In sharp contrast to the Puranic stories of Durga Mahishasuramardini, in Dalit counternarratives, the demon Mahishasura is a heroic figure representing oppressed indigenous people and lower castes. The hard-headed and kill-rather-than-be-killed stories of the *Panchatantra* have been transformed into humorous comic books for children. Such reversals seem less surprising when we consider that they are part of very long-standing traditions of interpretation, reinterpretation, and counternarratives.

On the other hand, some ancient symbols have become routine, even banal. The adoption of the Sarnath capital of Ashoka as an emblem of the Indian nation at the time of Independence reflected the Nehruvian understanding of Ashoka as a representative of the positive values of peace, harmony, and cosmopolitanism. [Fig. 6.1] But its use has now become repetitive, monotonous, and emptied of any real meaning. A replica of the Sarnath pillar and lion capital is part of the war memorial constructed near India Gate in New Delhi. Here (perhaps due to lack of imagination or of application of mind), the symbol of a pacifist king who abhorred and renounced war has been made the central element of a memorial that commemorates the bravery of soldiers who died fighting heroically in various battles.

The ancient past and its traditions have inspired innumerable modern Indian writers, playwrights, film-makers, and artists. Among the artists, mention may be made of Nandalal Bose, Raja Ravi Varma, Ganesh Pyne, and M. F. Husain. Husain not only engaged with ancient traditions, popular culture, and Indian and global history, he was a remarkable chronicler of the everyday and extraordinary that he witnessed during

Fig 6.1: Ashoka's Sarnath capital, sandstone, Sarnath Museum

his lifetime. But let us look carefully at four paintings, one from the early twentieth century, the others from the work of some of India's greatest contemporary artists.

Abanindranath Tagore (1871–1951) was a leading figure of the Bengal school that emerged in Calcutta against the background of the Swadeshi movement.[1] The rediscovery of India's rich aesthetic traditions was central to the creation of a new Indian nationalist artistic idiom. Tagore's sources of inspiration included Mughal miniatures, Japanese landscape painting, and European Art Nouveau. His vast range of work includes themes drawn from the Ramayana and Krishna-lila, and

---

[1] See Tapati Guha-Thakurta, *The Making of a New 'Indian' Art: Artists, aesthetics and nationalism in Bengal, c. 1850-1920*, Cambridge: Cambridge University Press, 1992, Chap. 7.

historical figures such as the Buddha, Ashoka, and Shah Jahan. His iconic image of Bharat Mata, representing the nation as goddess gave powerful visual expression to nationalist aspirations. In his watercolour, 'The banished yaksha of Kalidasa's *Meghaduta*' (water colour on paper, c. 1904), a delicate yaksha sits forlorn but hopeful against a background of green forest and grey clouds, a veena by his side. [Fig. 6.2] Tagore's painting captures the melancholy romantic mood of Kalidasa's poem.

The themes of Nilima Sheikh's work include home and family, woman's body and world, love and labour, rivers and mountainscapes, journeys and travellers.[2] Sheikh has drawn inspiration from folk songs; ancient texts such as the Jatakas and Ramayana; Mughal and Pahari painting; the Dunhuang cave murals; and the poetry of Lal Ded, Mirabai, and Agha Shahid Ali. The paintings based on Partition, the conflict zone of Kashmir, and communal riots express and evoke the tragic violence unleashed by historical events and the intense personal pain caused by homelessness and displacement. 'Akka Mahadevi 3' (mixed tempera on vasli paper, 78.5 cm x 56 cm, 1995), is one of a series on the ancient bhakti saint. [Fig. 6.3] Here, Sheikh paints her naked and alone against a landscape of mountains and rivers, her head tilting slightly, her eyes closed in a meditative trance. The painting reminds us of the centrality of the body (even when it is sought to be transcended) not only in Akka's life, but in the experience of all spiritual women.

Arpita Singh's figural paintings have a playful, dream-like quality.[3] Some of them focus on the body (especially woman's) and familial relationships, weaving in ordinary objects such as furniture, cars, and planes, interspersed with words and numbers. Beneath the seemingly composed, child-like veneer are disturbing reminders of ever-present violence, loss, displacement, and death, including those connected with specific events such as the communal violence in India and the torture regime at Guantanamo Bay. 'Whatever is here...' (oil on

---

[2]For the paintings, see Kumkum Sangari (ed.), *Trace Retrace: Paintings, Nilima Sheikh,* New Delhi: Tulika Books with Gallery Espace and Chemould Prescott Road, 2013.

[3]See Ella Datta, 'Arpita Singh', essay in portfolio of Arpita Singh's paintings, New Delhi: Lalit Kala Akademi, n.d.; Deepak Ananth, *Arpita Singh,* New Delhi: Penguin Books and Vadehra Art Gallery, 2015.

canvas, 84" x 107.5", 2006), is a large map-like painting which is in fact superimposed on a map of western India. [Fig. 6.4] Dhritarashtra sits still and resigned in the centre, as Sanjaya uses a pair of binoculars to give him live time reportage. All around them is vigorous action—marching warriors, planes, horses, a tank, and men brandishing guns. The mourning women represent the lamenting widows and mothers of the Stri Parva of the Mahabharata, but also the grief that war—any war—inevitably brings in its wake.

A great deal of A. Ramachandran's work engages directly with history and mythology. The paintings that deal with the problem of violence have a dark, nightmarish quality and bring out the human propensity for self-destruction.[4] Ramachandran's sculptures of Ashoka and Gandhi reflect his preoccupation with violence, but hint at the possibility of redemption through repentence and forgiveness. His imposing 'Vision of War' mural (oil on board, 12' x 6', 1977), has on the right three receding images of the well-known ancient headless sculpture of the Kushana king Kanishka, the one in front with a modern military coat thrown over its shoulders. [Fig. 6.5] These combine with several other motifs, including a rider on a rearing stallion, a fluttering fragment of a newspaper with an image from the Vietnam war, a figure on a balloon with a Nazi flag, and an army of helmets to make a powerful, universal statement about the inexorable horror and futility of war. In works such as these, the artistic imagination collapses, distils, and reflects on many centuries of history and memory and connects them to the present in powerful visual form.

If we choose to seek inspiration from the ancient past, there is a large menu from which to choose. However, it is somewhat ironical that people living in a modern democracy should make appeals (often of diametrically opposed kinds) to traditions rooted in hierarchical and unequal societies governed by autocratic kings. These appeals are usually based on selective reading and decontextualizing of the

---

[4] See R. Siva Kumar, *A. Ramachandran: A Retrospective*, 2 vols., New Delhi: National Gallery of Modern Art and Vadehra Art Gallery, 2003; and https://www.artoframachandran.com.

Fig. 6.2: Abanindranath Tagore, 'The banished yaksha of Kalidasa's Meghaduta', water colour on paper, c. 1904

Fig. 6.3: Nilima Sheikh, 'Mahadevi Akka 3', mixed tempera on vasli paper, 78.5 cm x 56 cm, 1995

Fig. 6.4: Arpita Singh, 'Whatever is here...', oil on canvas, 7' x 8' 11" 5 1/2", 2006

Fig. 6.5: A. Ramachandran, 'Vision of War,' oil on board, 6' x 12', 1977

evidence. As mentioned at the beginning of this book, ancient societies accepted the idea of the natural inequality of social groups; this is the antithesis of the principle of natural equality, the fundamental premise of modern democracy. In ancient India, inequality was challenged from time to time, largely at the religious and soteriological levels, and this had social impact. But the principles of liberty and equality as the basis of a political community were first promulgated in the Constitution of the Indian republic. Surely the inspiration for a better future should come not from a past that is long gone, but from aspirations for a future that is yet to come, one which will hopefully be better than the past or the present.

I am saying this because in the present context of an increasingly authoritarian and intolerant state, it has become fashionable to talk about the ancient Indian tradition of debate and dissent and to present this as an inherent aspect of Indian culture and civilization. We have seen in this book that in ancient India, vigorous questioning, debate, and disagreement existed in plenty within and across disciplines and traditions. But we should not forget that participation in these was circumscribed by the unequal, hierarchical nature of social structures. If we would like to extract some political takeaways for our times from ancient India, it is more appropriate to choose some elements of the model of an ideal ruler—that such a ruler must be utterly impartial in the administration of justice, must not be motivated by considerations of personal favour or profit, and should not be swayed by a lust for power. This ideal is as valid in discussions of ancient monarchies as it is in modern democracies. So are the ideas that a ruler should be self-controlled and receptive to good advice; should recognize the line between necessary force and illegitimate violence; and should know that using excessive or unjust force against subjects is not only morally wrong but will invite dire retribution. In fact, Kautilya's warning of cruel and unjust rulers meeting their nemesis due to prakriti-kopa, 'anger of the people', suits modern democracies better than ancient monarchies. Ashoka's desire to promote genuine religious dialogue and concord is exceptional but even lesser kings did not try to create a theocratic state. Dharma was understood as greater than religion. This idea is very relevant for a modern multi-religious, multi-cultural nation.

India has never been a hermetically sealed unit. Over the centuries, there was continuous interaction with the lands and people of various parts of Asia, Europe, and Africa. Genetics proves that the present inhabitants of the Indian subcontinent represent the result of thousands of years of migrations and mingling that ultimately go back to the continent of Africa. For Indian readers, the discussion of the complexities and contradictions in early Indian history in this book has hopefully given some answers to the question: 'Who are we?' The existential question 'Who am I?' is more difficult. Its answers are better sought in philosophy than history.

ACKNOWLEDGEMENTS

I would like to thank:

My students at Ashoka University, on whom I first bounced some of these ideas;

Vijay Tankha, with whom I have had many lively conversations about this book, especially during our evening walks, and who has always been an interested listener, interlocutor, and reader;

Ella Datta, who has, over the years, awakened me to the beauty and profundity of modern Indian art, which I would like to share with readers of this book;

Madhav Tankha, for introducing me to the wonderful resource of open access images provided by some of the world's greatest museums;

The Metropolitan Museum of Art, Los Angeles County Museum of Art, Art Institute of Chicago, Cleveland Museum of Art, and the Freer and Sackler Galleries of the Smithsonian Institution, whose open access images have been used in this book (if only all museums were as generous!);

Patricia Uberoi, Kavita Singh, Erwin Neumayer, and Jayanta Sengupta, who helped me locate images;

A. Ramachandran, Nilima Sheikh, and Arpita Singh—great artists whose work I admire—for readily allowing me to use images of their paintings;

And Aleph Book Company—especially Aienla Ozukum—who made the production of this book an enjoyable experience and guided it so efficiently to publication.

PHOTO CREDITS

Chapter 1

Fig. 1.1: Terracotta tile with impressed figures of ascetics and couples on balconies, Harwan, Kashmir, fifth–sixth century; Metropolitan Museum of Art (Gift of Cynthia Hazen Polsky, 1987; 1987.424.26). Open Access.

Fig. 1.2: Jinas, sandstone, Uttar Pradesh, c. sixth century CE; Los Angeles County Museum of Art (Gift of Anna Bing Arnold, M.85.55). Open Access.

Fig. 1.3: Meditating Tirthankara, marble, Gujarat or Rajasthan, eleventh century; Metropolitan Museum of Art (Purchase, Florence and Herbert Irving Gift, 1992; 1992.131). Open Access.

Fig. 1.4: Buddha in protection-granting abhaya mudra, sandstone, Mathura, c. second century CE. Photograph: Author.

Fig. 1.5: Meditating Siddhartha in dhyana mudra, schist, Gandhara, c. third century CE; The Norton Simon Foundation (F. 1975.17.29.S). Photograph: Author.

Chapter 2

Fig. 2.1: Raja Ravi Varma, 'Shakuntala writing love letter to Dushyanta', late nineteenth century oleograph printed by Ravi Varma Press, Lonavala, from original painting by Raja Ravi Varma, c. 1894 (VMH R6689). By kind permission of the Trustees of the Victoria Memorial Hall, Kolkata.

Fig. 2.2: Shiva enraged by Parvati's interruption of his meditation, Guler, Himachal Pradesh, early nineteenth century, opaque pigments and gold on paper; Metropolitan Museum of Art (Purchase, Nancy Fessender Gift, 2019; 2019.146). Open Access.

Fig. 2.3: Mara attacks Siddhartha as the latter calls on the earth as witness, schist, Gandhara. Freer and Sackler Gallery (F 1949.9c; purchase), Smithsonian Museums. Photograph: Author.

Fig. 2.4: Tirthankara Parshvanatha, sandstone, Uttar Pradesh, c. sixth century CE; Art Institute of Chicago (Gift of Marilynn B. Alsdorf; 2012.687). Open Access.

Fig. 2.5: Jaina monk walking along a riverbank, ink and colour on paper by Basavana, c. 1600; Cleveland Museum of Art (Severance and Greta Millikin Collection 1967.244). Open Access.

Fig. 2.6: Mithuna couple, terracotta, Uttar Pradesh, first–second century CE; Metropolitan Museum of Art (Gift of Cynthia Hazen Polsky, 1986; 1986.506.11). Open Access.

Fig. 2.7: Chanda yakshi, sandstone, Bharhut; Indian Museum, Kolkata. Photograph: Author.

Fig. 2.8: Lovers, sandstone with limestone wash, Rajasthan, tenth century; Cleveland Museum of Art (Purchase from the J. H. Wade Fund 1962.165). Open Access.

Fig. 2.9: Celestial dancer, sandstone, Madhya Pradesh, eleventh century; Metropolitan Museum of Art (Gift of Florence and Herbert Irving, 2015; 2015.5000.4.14). Open Access.

Fig. 2.10: Goddess Ganga, Kailasanatha temple, Ellora, eighth century. Photograph: Author.

Fig. 2.11: Queen Sembiyan Mahadevi/Parvati, bronze, Tamil Nadu, tenth century; Freer Gallery (Purchase, Charles Lang Freer Endowment, F 1929.84). Open Access.

Fig. 2.12: Ravana lifting Mount Kailasa with Shiva and Parvati seated on it, Kailasanatha temple, Ellora. Photograph: Author.

Fig. 2.13: Krishna and Radha strolling in the rain; opaque water colour, gold, and ink on paper, Jaipur, c. 1775; Los Angeles County Museum of Art (Gift of Paul F. Walter; M.87.278.15). Open Access.

Fig. 2.14: Kamadeva, stone, Kashmir, eighth century; Metropolitan Museum of Art (Purchase, Lita Annenberg Hazen Charitable Trust Gift, 1993; 1993.175). Photograph: Author.

Fig. 2.15: Andal, copper alloy, Tamil Nadu, fourteenth century; Los Angeles Museum of Art (Purchased with funds provided by Mr and Mrs Edgar G. Richards, M. 86.94.2). Open Access.

Fig. 2.16: Kali and Bhairava in union, watercolour on paper, Nepal, eighteenth century; Los Angeles County Museum of Art (Gift of Dr and Mrs Robert S. Coles; M.81.206.7). Open Access.

Chapter 3

Fig. 3.1: Terracotta goddess, third/second century BCE; Metropolitan Museum of Art (Anonymous Gift, 1978; 1978.539). Open Access.

Fig. 3.2: Goddess with weapons in her hair, Chandraketugarh terracotta, first century BCE–first century CE; Metropolitan Museum of Art (Purchase, Florence and Herbert Irving Gift, 1990; 1990.281). Open Access.

Fig. 3.3: Chulakoka yakshi, Bharhut; Indian Museum, Kolkata. Photograph: Author.

Fig. 3.4: Sanchi nagi. Photograph: Author.

Fig. 3.5: Lakshmi, Kailasanatha temple, Ellora. Photograph: Author.

Fig. 3.6: Gaja-Lakshmi, Sanchi. Photograph: Author.

Fig. 3.7: Lakshmi, Raja Ravi Varma, lithograph print, 1894; Metropolitan Museum of Art (Purchase, Gift of Mrs William J. Calhoun and Bequest of Nina Bunshaft, by exchange, 2013; 2013.10). Open Access.

Fig. 3.8: Durga Mahishasuramardini, Mahabalipuram. Photograph: Author.

Fig. 3.9: Durga Mahishasuramardini, stone, Badra, Central Northeastern style, ninth century; Cleveland Museum of Art (Gift of Dr Norman Zaworski, 2006.204). Open Access.

Fig. 3.10: Yogini, stone, Musée Guimet. Photograph: Author.

Fig. 3.11: Yogini Hayagriva, stone, eleventh century; Art Institute of Chicago (Gift of Marilynn B. Alsdorf, 1997.708). Open Access.

Fig. 3.12: Yogini Chamunda, marble, Rajasthan, ninth century; Norton Simon Museum (F.1978.07.S). Photograph: Author.

Fig. 3.13: Kali, Kalighat watercolour, graphite, and ink on paper, 1800s; Cleveland Museum of Art (Gift of William E. Ward in memory of his wife, Evelyn Svec Ward, 2003.116). Open Access.

Fig. 3.14: Radha pining for Krishna, opaque watercolour and gold on paper, folio from *Gita Govinda*, c. 1775–80, attributed to Kangra or Guler, Panjab hills; Metropolitan Museum of Art (Gift of Stevan Kossack, the Kronos Collections, 2020; 2020.383). Open Access.

Fig. 3.15: White Tara, Bhutan. Photograph: Raghav Tankha.

Fig. 3.16: Digambara yakshi Kushmandini, schist, Karnataka, c. 900; Norton Simon Museum (F.1975.17.08.S). Photograph: Author.

Fig. 3.17: Ambika, Ellora. Photograph: Author.

Fig. 3.18: Shiva Ardhanarishvara, copper inlaid with garnets and emerald, with traces of paint, Nepal c. 1000; Los Angeles County Museum of Art (From the Nasli and Alice Heeramaneck Collection, Museum Associates Purchase, M82.6.1). Open Access.

Fig. 3.19: Sati stone, Bhojpur, Madhya Pradesh. Photograph: Author.

Fig. 3.20: Sati stone, Government Museum, Chennai. Photograph: Author.

Fig. 3.21: Karaikkal Ammaiyar, copper alloy, late thirteenth century; Metropolitan Museum of Art (Purchase, Edward J. Gallagher Jr. Bequest, in memory of his father, Edward Joseph Gallagher, his mother, Ann Hay Galagher, and his son, Edward Joseph Gallagher III, 1982; 1982.220.11). Open Access.

Fig. 3.22: Bharat Mata poster. Courtesy: Erwin Neumayer and Christine Schelberger.

Chapter 4

Fig. 4.1: Hero stone outside Vidisha Museum. Photograph: Author.

Fig. 4.2: Ekasar hero stone, Mumbai. Photograph: Author.

Fig. 4.3: Mahabharata panels, Kailasanatha temple, Ellora. Photograph: Author.

Fig. 4.4: Mahabharata battle, Paithan school, ink and colour on paper;

Cleveland Museum of Art (Gift of Professor Walter and Nesta Spink in honour of Stanislaw Czuma, 2005.68). Open Access.

Fig. 4.5: Bhima defeats Duryodhana, Folio from *Razmnama* (a Mahabharata translation commissioned by Akbar); ink, watercolour, and gold on paper, early seventeenth century; Metropolitan Museum of Art (Rogers Fund, 55.121.32). Open Access.

Fig. 4.6: Allahabad pillar. Photograph: Author.

Fig. 4.7: Jaimini Roy, 'Jatayu, Sita and Ravana', tempera on paper, c. 1940; Victoria Memorial hall Collection (VMH R5081). By kind permission of the Trustees of the Victoria Memorial Hall, Kolkata.

Fig 4.8: Jaina saint Bahubali performing austerities in perfect stillness; Ellora. Photograph: Author.

Fig 4.9: Jaina hero stone panel, Cave 32, tenth/eleventh century. Photograph: Author.

Fig 4.10: Meditating Buddha, sandstone, Sarnath Museum, fourth/fifth century CE. Photograph: Author.

Fig 4.11: Ashoka and his consort, limestone, Kanaganahalli. Photograph: Author.

Chapter 5

Fig. 5.1: Swami Vivekananda poster. Courtesy: Erwin Neumayer and Christine Schelberger.

Fig. 5.2: Sages deep in discussion, Kailasanatha temple, Kanchipuram. Photograph: Author.

Fig. 5.3: Ascetics conversing; Mukteshwar temple, Bhubaneshwar, c. 950–75. Courtesy: Jinah Kim.

Fig. 5.4: Monks and laity listening attentively to the Buddha preaching, schist, Gandhara, late second–early third century; Freer and Sackler galleries, Smithsonian Museums (F1949.9b). Photograph: Author.

Fig. 5.5: Fierce Buddhist deities, Bhutan monastery. Photograph: Raghav Tankha.

Fig. 5.6: Bhairava, Nepal, twelfth century; Los Angeles County Museum of Art (Gift of Ramesh and Urmil Kapoor, M.91.293.1). Photograph: Author.

Fig. 5.7: Aparajita trampling Ganesha, Bihar Museum. Photograph: Author.

Fig. 5.8: Detail of Mahabalipuram 'Descent of the Ganga' relief. Photograph: Author.

Epilogue

Fig. 6.1: Ashoka's Sarnath capital, sandstone, Sarnath museum. Photograph: Aditya Arya.

Fig. 6.2: Abanindranath Tagore, 'The banished yaksha of Kalidasa's *Meghaduta*', water colour on paper, c. 1904. The Rabindra Bharati Society collection in the Victoria Memorial Hall (RBS 26 / VMH 26). By kind permission of the Trustees of the Victoria Memorial Hall, Kolkata.

Fig. 6.3: Nilima Sheikh, 'Mahadevi Akka 3', mixed tempera on vasli paper, 78.5 cm x 56 cm, 1995. Courtesy: Nilima Sheikh.

Fig. 6.4: Arpita Singh, 'Whatever is here...', oil on canvas, 7' x 8' 11' 5 1/2", 2006. Courtesy: Arpita Singh.

Fig. 6.5: A. Ramachandran, 'Vision of War,' oil on board, 6' x 12', 1977. Courtesy: A. Ramachandran.

BIBLIOGRAPHY

Ali, Daud, *Courtly Culture and Political Life in Early Medieval India*, Cambridge: Cambridge University Press, 2004.

Amar, Abhishek S., 'Buddhist Responses to Brāhmaṇa Challenges in Medieval India: Bodhgayā and Gayā', *Journal of the Royal Asiatic Society*, third series, vol. 22, no. 1, January 2012.

Ambedkar, B. R., 'The Annihilation of Caste', Valerian Rodrigues (ed.), *The Essential Writings of B. R. Ambedkar*, pp. 263–305, New Delhi: Oxford University Press, [2002], 2004.

———, 'Waiting for a Visa', *Dr. Babasaheb Ambedkar: Writings and Speeches*, vol. 12, pp. 661–69, compiled by Vasant Moon, New Delhi: Dr. Ambedkar Foundation, 2004.

Ananth, Deepak, *Arpita Singh*, New Delhi: Penguin Books and Vadehra Art Gallery, 2015.

Bader, Jonathan, *Conquest of the Four Quarters: Traditional Accounts of the Life of Śaṅkara*, New Delhi: Aditya Prakashan, 2000.

Bailey, Greg (trans.), *Love Lyrics by Amaru & Bhartihari* (Clay Sanskrit Library), New York: New York University Press, 2005.

Banerjee-Dube, Ishita (ed.), *Caste in History* (Themes in Indian History series), New Delhi: Oxford University Press, 2010.

Basak, Radhagovinda (trans.), *The Prākrit Gāthā-Saptaśatī Compiled by Sātavāhana King Hāla*, Calcutta: Asiatic Society, 1971.

Béteille, André, 'The idea of natural inequality', André Béteille, *The Idea of Natural Inequality and Other Essays*, pp. 7–34, New Delhi: Oxford University Press, [1983], 2003.

Black, Brian, *Priests, Kings, and Women in the Early Upaniṣads: The Character of Self in Ancient India*, Delhi: Motilal Banarsidass, 2014.

Bodewitz, Henk W., 'Hindu ahiṁsā and its roots', Jan E. M. Houben and Karel R. van Kooij (eds.), *Violence Denied: Violence, Non-Violence and the Rationalization of Violence in South Asian Cultural History*, pp. 17–44, Boston: Brill, 1999.

Bodhi, Bhikkhu (trans.), *The Connected Discourses: A translation of the Saṁyutta Nikāya*, Boston: Wisdom Publications, 2000.

Brough, J., *Poems from the Sanskrit*, Harmondsworth: Penguin Classics L 198, 1968.

Buitenen, J. A. B. van (trans. and ed.), *The Mahabharata, Book 2: The Book of the Assembly Hall and Book 3: The Book of the Forest*, Chicago: University of Chicago Press, 1975.

———, *The Bhagavadgītā in the Mahābhārata: Text and Translation*, Chicago and London: University of Chicago Press, 1981.

Chakrabarti, Kunal, 'A History of Intolerance: The Representation of Buddhists in the Bengal Purāṇas', *Social Scientist*, vol. 44, nos. 5/6 May–June 2016, pp. 11-27.

―――, *Religious Process: The Purāṇas and the Making of a Regional Tradition*, New Delhi: Oxford University Press, 2001.

Chakravarti, Uma, *The Social Dimensions of Early Buddhism*, New Delhi: Oxford University Press, 1987.

―――, 'The world of the bhaktin in South Indian traditions—the body and beyond', Uma Chakravarti, *Everyday Lives, Everyday Histories: Beyond the Kings and Brahmanas of 'Ancient' India*, pp. 275-92. New Delhi: Tulika, [2006], 2020.

―――, *Everyday Lives, Everyday Histories: Beyond the Kings and Brahmanas of 'Ancient' India*, New Delhi: Tulika, [2006], 2020.

Chanana, Dev Raj, *Slavery in Ancient India*, New Delhi: People's Publishing House, [1960], 1990.

Chatterjee, Indrani and Richard M. Eaton (eds.), *Slavery and South Asian History*, Bloomington: Indiana University Press, 2006.

Chaudhari, J. B., *Sanskrit Poetesses: Contributions of Women to Sanskrit Literature*, vol. 2., Calcutta: self-published, 1941.

Chhabra, B. and G. S. Gai, *Corpus Inscriptionum Indicarum*, vol. 3, revised by D. R. Bhandarkar, New Delhi: Archaeological Survey of India, 1981.

Clark, Mathew, *The Daśanāmī Saṁnyāsīs: The Integration of Ascetic Lineages into an Order*, Leiden, Boston: Brill, 2006.

Collins, Steven, *Aggañña Sutta: The Discourse on What is Primary (An Annotated Translation from Pali)*, Delhi: Sahitya Akademi, 2001.

Coomaraswamy, Ananda K., *Yakshas*, New Delhi: Munshiram Manoharlal, [1928], 1980.

Cort, John E., 'Medieval Jaina Goddess Traditions', *Numen*, vol. 34, fasc. 2, December 1987, pp. 235-55.

―――, 'Intellectual Ahimsa' Revisited: Jaina tolerance and the intolerance of others', *Philosophy East and West*, vol. 50, no. 3, July 2000, pp. 325-47.

Datta, Ella, 'Arpita Singh', essay in portfolio of Arpita Singh's paintings, New Delhi: Lalit Kala Akademi, n.d.

Davidson, Ronald M., *Indian Esoteric Buddhism: A Social History of the Tantric Movement*, New York: Columbia University Press, 2002.

Davenport, Guy (trans.), *Archilochus, Sappho, Alkman: Three Lyric Poets of the Late Greek Bronze Age*, Berkeley: University of California Press, 1980.

Davis, Richard H., 'The story of the disappearing Jainas: Retelling the Śaiva-Jaina encounter in medieval South India', John E. Cort (ed.), *Open Boundaries: Jaina Communities and Cultures in Indian History*, pp. 213-24, Delhi: Sri Satguru Publications, [1998], 1999.

Davis, Richard H., *Lives of Indian Images*, Delhi: Motilal Banarsidass, [1997], 1999.

Dayal, Naina, 'Sūtas, Nāstikas and Retelling the Mahābhārata', Naina Dayal and Kumkum Roy (eds.), *Questioning Paradigms, Constructing Histories: A Festschrift for Romila*

Thapar, pp. 196–201, New Delhi: Aleph Book Company, 2019.

Dehejia, Vidya, *Slaves of the Lord: The Path of the Tamil Saints*, New Delhi: Munshiram Manoharlal, 1988.

_____, *The Body Adorned: Dissolving Boundaries Between Sacred and Profane in India's Art*, Ahmedabad: Mapin, 2009.

Derrett, J. Duncan M., 'Monastic Masturbation in Pāli Buddhist Texts', *Journal of the History of Sexuality*, vol. 15, no. 1, January 2006, pp. 1–13.

Desai, Devangana, *Erotic Sculpture of India: A Socio-Cultural Study*, New Delhi: Tata McGraw Hill, 1975.

Devadhar, C. R. (ed. and trans.), *Works of Kālidāsa*, vol. 1, Delhi: Motilal Banarsidass, [1966], 2005.

_____, *Raghuvaṁśa of Kālidāsa*, Edited with Critical Introduction, Delhi: Motilal Banarsidass, 1985.

Dezső, Csaba (ed. and trans.), *Much Ado About Religion by Bhaṭṭa Jayanta*, The Clay Sanskrit Library, New York: JCC Foundation, New York University Press, 2005.

Dube, Leela, 'Kinship and Gender in South and Southeast Asia: Patterns and Contrasts', 9th J. P. Naik Memorial Lecture, 1994; available at http://www.cwds.ac.in/wp-content/uploads/2016/09/Kinship-and-Gender.pdf.

Dundas, Paul, *The Jainas*, London and New York: Routledge, 1992.

Esposito, Anna Aurelia, 'Didactic Dialogues: Communication of Doctrine and Strategies of Narrative in Jaina Literature', Brian Black and Laurie Patton (eds.), *Dialogues in Early South Asian Religions: Hindu, Buddhist and Jaina Traditions*, pp. 79–98, London and New York: Routledge, 2015.

Fitzgerald, James L. (ed. and annotated), *Mahābhārata*, vol. 7: *11: The Book of Women and 12: The Book of Peace, Vols. I and. II*, Chicago: University of Chicago Press, 2004.

Finley, M. I., *Economy and Society in Ancient Greece*, Brent Shaw and Richard Saller (eds.), New York: Viking, 1982.

Ganeri, Jonardan, *Philosophy in Classical India: An Introduction and Analysis*, London: Routledge, 2001.

_____, (ed.) *Indian Philosophy: A Reader*, London: Routledge, 2019.

Gethin, Rupert, *The Foundations of Buddhism*, Oxford and New York: Oxford University Press, 1998.

_____, 'Can killing a living being ever be an act of compassion? The analysis of the act of killing in the Abhidhamma and Pali Commentaries', *Journal of Buddhist Ethics*, vol. 11, 2004, pp. 71–174.

_____, 'Buddhist monks, Buddhist kings, Buddhist violence: On the early Buddhist attitudes to violence', John R. Hinnells and Richard King, (eds.), *Religion and Violence in South Asia: Theory and Practice*, pp. 62–82, London and New York: Routledge, 2007.

Goldin, Paul Rakita, *The Culture of Sex in Ancient China*, Honolulu: University of Hawai'i Press, 2002.

Goldman, Robert P., 'Transsexualism, Gender and Anxiety in Traditional India', *Journal of the American Oriental Society*, vol. 113, no. 3, July–September 1993, pp. 374–401.

Goldman, Robert P. (gen. ed.), *The Rāmāyaṇa of Vālmīki: An Epic of Ancient India*, 6 volumes, Delhi: Motilal Banarsidass, [1984], 2007.

Goldman, Robert P. and Sally J. Goldman (trans.), *The Rāmāyaṇa of Vālmīki: An Epic of Ancient India*, vol. 7, Uttarakāṇḍa, Princeton: Princeton University Press, 2017.

Guha-Thakurta, Tapati, *The Making of a New 'Indian' Art: Artists, aesthetics and nationalism in Bengal*, c. 1850–1920, Cambridge: Cambridge University Press, 1992.

Gupta, Dipankar, *Interrogating Caste: Understanding Hierarchy and Difference in Indian Society*, New Delhi: Penguin Books, 2000.

Haksar, A. N. D. (trans.), *Kshemendra, Three Satires from Ancient Kashmir*, Gurgaon: Penguin Random House, 2011.

———, *Kshemendra, The Courtesan's Keeper: Samaya Mātrikā*, Gurgaon: Penguin Random House, 2014.

Hallisey, Charles (trans.), *Therigatha: Poems of the First Buddhist Women* (Murty Classical Library of India), Cambridge MA: Harvard University Press, 2015.

Hanumanthan, K. R., 'Evolution of Untouchability in Tamil Nadu up to AD 1600', Aloka Parasher Sen (ed.), *Subordinate and Marginalized Groups in Early India*, pp. 125–56, New Delhi: Oxford University Press, 2004.

Hara, Minoru, 'The Holding of the Hair (Keśa-grahaṇa)', *Acta Orientalia*, vol. 47, 1986.

———, 'Words for Love in Sanskrit', *Rivista degli studi orientali*, Nuova Serie, vol. 80, fasc. 1/4, Atti Del Convegno: 'Passioni ed Emozioni in India e in Tibet', Sapienza—Universita di Roma, 2007, pp. 81–106.

Hart, George L. and Hank Heifetz, *The Puranāṉūṟu: Four Hundred Songs of War and Wisdom: An Anthology of Poems from Classical Tamil*, New Delhi: Penguin Books, [1999], 2002.

Hart, George L., *Poets of the Tamil Anthologies: Ancient Poems of Love and War*, Princeton: Princeton University Press, 1979.

Harvey, Peter, *An Introduction to Buddhist Ethics*, Cambridge: Cambridge University Press, 2000.

———, *An Introduction to Buddhism: Teachings,* Hultzsch entry should come after the 2 Hawley entries *History and Practices*, Cambridge: Cambridge University Press, [1990], 2012.

Hawley, John Stratton and Donna Marie Wulff (eds.), *The Divine Consort: Rādhā and the Goddesses of India*, Delhi: Motilal Banarsidass, [1982], 1984.

———, *Devī: Goddesses of India*, Delhi: Motilal Banarsidass, [1996], 1998.

Hiltebeitel, Alf, *Rethinking the Mahābhārata: A Reader's Guide to the Education of the Dharma King*, New Delhi: Oxford University Press, [2001], 2002.

Houben, Jan E. M., 'To kill or not to kill: the sacrificial animal (yajña-paśu)? Arguments and perspectives in Brahmanical ethical philosophy', Jan E. M. Houben and Karel R. van Kooij (eds.), *Violence denied Violence: Non-Violence and the Rationalization of Violence in South Asian Cultural History*, pp. 105–83, Boston: Brill, 1999.

Hultzsch, E., *Corpus Inscriptionum Indicarum: Inscriptions of Aśoka*, New Delhi, vol. 1: Archaeological Survey of India, [1924], 1991.

Jaini, Padmanabh S., *The Jaina Path of Purification*, Delhi: Motilal Banarsidass, 1979.

———, *Gender and Salvation: Jaina Debates on the Spiritual Liberation of Women*, New Delhi: Munshiram Manoharlal, [1979], 2001.

———, 'Ahiṁsā: A Jaina Way of Spiritual Discipline', Padmanabh S. Jaini (ed.), *Collected Papers on Jaina Studies*, pp. 3–19, Delhi: Motilal Banarsidass, 2000.

———, 'Jaina Debates on the Spiritual Liberation of Women', Padmanabh S. Jaini, *Collected Papers on Jaina Studies*, pp. 163–97, Delhi, Motilal Banarsidass, 2000.

———, 'Fear of Food: Jaina Attitudes on Eating', Padmanabh S. Jaini, *Collected Papers on Jaina Studies*, pp. 281–96, Delhi: Motilal Banarsidass, 2000.

Jaiswal, Suvira, *The Origin and Development of Vaiṣṇavism*, New Delhi: Munshiram Manoharlal, [1967], 1981.

Jamison, Stephanie W., and Joel P. Brereton (trans.), *The Rigveda: The Earliest Religious Poetry of India*, 3 vols., New York: Oxford University Press, 2014 (South Asia Research series); available at https://www.academia.edu.

Jha, Vivekanand, 'Caṇḍāla and the Origin of Untouchability', *Indian Historical Review*, vol. 13, 1986-87, reprinted in Aloka Parasher-Sen (ed.), *Subordinate and Marginal Groups in Early India* (Themes in Indian History series), pp. 157–209, New Delhi: Oxford University Press, 2004.

Joseph, Tony, *Early Indians: The Story of Our Ancestors and Where We Came From*, New Delhi: Juggernaut Books, 2018.

Kakar, Sudhir and Wendy Doniger, *Kamasutra: A New Complete Translation of the Sanskrit Text with Excerpts from the Sanskrit Jayamangala Commentary of Yashodhara Indrapada, the Hindi Jaya Commentary of Devadatta Shastri, and Explanatory Notes*, Oxford: Oxford University Press, 2002.

Kale, M. R., *The Mrichchhakatika of Śūdraka*, Bombay: Booksellers' Publishing Co., [1924], 1962.

Kane, P. V., *History of Dharmaśāstra*, (*Ancient and Mediaeval Religious and Civil Law*), vol. 2, part 1, 3rd edn., Pune: Bhandarkar Oriental Research Institute, [1941], 1997.

Kinsley, David, *Hindu Goddesses: Vision of the Divine Feminine in the Hindu Religious Tradition*, Delhi: Motilal Banarsidass, [1986], 1987.

Kishore Saxena, Kanika, *Before Kṛṣṇa: Religious Diversity in Ancient Mathura*, New Delhi: Oxford University Press, 2021.

Krishna, Daya, 'Vedanta in the first millennium AD: The case study of a retrospective illusion imposed by the historiography of Indian philosophy', *Journal of the Indian Council of Philosophical Research*, 1996, pp. 201–07.

———, 'Comparative Philosophy: What it is and what it ought to be', Nalini Bhushan, Jay L. Garfield, Daniel Raveh (eds.), *Contrary Thinking: Selected Essays of Daya Krishna*, pp. 59–77, Oxford, New York: Oxford University Press, 2007.

Lahiri, Nayanjot, *Ashoka in Ancient India*, Ranikhet: Permanent Black, in association with Ashoka University, 2015.

Lath, Mukund, 'The concept of Ānṛśaṁsya in the Mahābhārata', R. N. Dandekar (ed.), *The Mahābhārata Revisited*, Papers presented at the International Seminar on the Mahābhārata organized by the Sahitya Akademi at New Delhi on 17-20 February 1987, pp. 113-19, New Delhi: Sahitya Akademi, 1990.

Lienhard, Siegfried, *A History of Classical Poetry: Sanskrit-Pali-Prakrit*, Jan Gonda (gen. ed.), *A History of Indian Literature*, vol. 3, fasc. 1, Wiesbaden: Otto Harrassowitz, 1984.

Lorenzen, David N., 'The Life of Shankaracharya', Fred W. Clothey and J. Bruce Long (eds.), *Experiencing Siva: Encounters with a Hindu Deity*, pp. 155-75, New Delhi: Manohar, 1983.

_____, 'Who invented Hinduism?', David N. Lorenzen, *Who Invented Hinduism: Essays on Religion in History*, pp. 1-36, New Delhi: Yoda Press, 2006.

Lüders, H., 'A List of Brāhmī Inscriptions from the Earliest Times to About A. D. 400', *Epigraphia Indica*, vol. 10, 1909-10, Appendix.

Marshall, John, *Taxila: An Illustrated Account of Archaeological Excavations Carried Out at Taxila under the Orders of the Government of India Between the years 1913 and 1934*, vol. 2, Delhi: Motilal Banarsidass [1951], 1975.

Marshall, John, Alfred Foucher, and N. G. Majumdar, *The Monuments of Sāñchī*, vol. 1, Calcutta: Superintendent Government Printing, 1940.

Matilal, Bimal K., 'Toward defining religion in the Indian context', Jonardan Ganeri (ed.), *Philosophy, Culture and Religion: The Collected Essays of Bimal Krishna Matilal*, pp. 166-74, New Delhi: Oxford University Press, 2002.

_____, 'Religion and value', Jonardan Ganeri (ed.), *Philosophy, Culture and Religion: The Collected Essays of Bimal Krishna Matilal*, pp. 175-95, New Delhi: Oxford University Press, 2002.

Mehrotra, Arvind Krishna, *The Absent Traveller: Prākrit Love Poetry from the Gāthāsaptaśatī of Sātavāhana Hāla*, Delhi: Ravi Dayal, 1991.

Miller, Barbara Stoller (trans.), *The Hermit and the Love-thief: Bhartrihari and Bilhana*, New Delhi: Penguin Books, [1978], 1990.

_____, *Theatre of Memory: Plays of Kālidāsa*, Delhi: Motilal Banarsidass, [1984], 1999.

Misra, R. N., *Yaksha Cult and Iconography*, New Delhi: Munshiram Manoharlal, [1979], 1981.

Mitra, Rajendralala (ed.), *The Nītisāra, or The Elements of Polity by Kāmandaki*, revised with English translation by Sisir Kumar Mitra, Calcutta: Asiatic Society, [1861] 1982 (Bibliotheca Indica series, no. 179).

Monius, Anne, 'Love, Violence, and the Aesthetics of Disgust: Śaivas and Jainas in Medieval South India', *Journal of Indian Philosophy*, vol. 32, nos. 2/3, June 2004, pp. 113-72.

Mukhopadhyaya, Sujit Kumar, *The Vajrasuchi of Asvaghosa*, Santiniketan: Visva-Bharati, [1950], 1960.

Murcott, Susan, *The First Buddhist Women: Translations and Commentaries on the*

Therigatha, Berkeley: Parallax Press, 1991.

Nandi, R. N., *State Formation, Agrarian Growth and Social Change in Feudal South India (c. AD 600–1200)*, New Delhi: Manohar, 2000.

Nichols, Michael, 'Bowing to the Buddha: The Relationship between Literary and Social Dialogue in the Nikāyas', Brian Black and Laurie Patton (eds.), *Dialogues in Early South Asian Religions: Hindu, Buddhist and Jaina Traditions*, pp. 173–90, London and New York: Routledge, 2015.

Nicholson, Andrew J., *Unifying Hinduism: Philosophy and Identity in Indian Intellectual History*, Ranikhet: Permanent Black, [2010], 2011.

Nikhilananda, Swami, *The Upanishads: A New Translation*, New York: Ramakrishna Vivekananda Centre, [1949–59], 1959.

Olivelle, Patrick, *The Āśrama System: The History and Hermeneutics of a Religious Institution*, New York, Oxford: Oxford University Press, 1993.

_____ (trans.), *The Early Upaniṣads: Annotated Text and Translation*, New Delhi: Munshiram Manoharlal, 1998.

_____ (trans.), *Manu's Code of Law: A Critical Edition and Translation of the Mānava-Dharmaśāstra*, New Delhi: Oxford University Press, [2005], 2006.

_____ *Kingship, Governance, and Law in Ancient India: Kauṭilya's Arthaśāstra*, New Delhi: Oxford University Press, 2013.

_____ (ed.), *Dharma: Studies in its Semantic, Cultural and Religious History*, Delhi: Motilal Banarsidass, 2009.

_____ (ed.), *Gṛhastha: The Householder in Ancient Indian Religious Culture*, New Delhi: Oxford University Press, 2019.

Orr, Leslie, 'Women's Wealth and Worship: Female Patronage of Hinduism, Jainism, and Buddhism in Medieval Tamil Nadu', Mandakranta Bose (ed.), *Faces of the Feminine in Ancient, Medieval, and Modern India*, pp. 124–47, New Delhi: Oxford University Press, 2000.

_____, 'Identity and Divinity: Boundary-Crossing Goddesses in Medieval South India', *Journal of the American Academy of Religion*, vol. 73, no. 1, March 2005, pp. 9–43.

Padoux, André, *The Hindu Tantric World: An Overview*, Chicago and London: University of Chicago Press, 2017.

Pande, G. C., *Life and Thought of Śaṅkarācārya*, Delhi: Motilal Banarsidass, [1994], 1998.

Pandit, R. S. (trans.), *Kalhaṇa's Rājataraṅgiṇī: The saga of the kings of Kaśmīr*, New Delhi: Sahitya Akademi, [1935], 1968.

Pappu, Shanti, Yanni Gunnell, Akhilesh Kumar, Régis Braucher, Maurice Taieb, François Demory, and Nicholas Thouveny, 'Early Pleistocene presence of Acheulian hominins in South India', *Science*, vol. 331, issue 6024, 25 March 2011, pp. 1,596–99.

Paul, Diana Y., *Women in Buddhism: Images of the Feminine in the Mahayana Tradition*, Berkeley: Asian Humanities Press, 1979.

Potter, Karl (gen. ed.), *Encyclopaedia of Indian Philosophies*, 25 vols., Delhi: Motilal Banarsidass, 1955–2019.

Quigley, Declan, *Interpretation of Caste*, New Delhi: Oxford University Press, [1993], 1999.

Rajagopalachari, C., *Auvaiyar: A Great Tamil Poetess*, Bombay: Bharatiya Vidya Bhavan, 1971.

Ramanujan, A. K. (trans.), *Speaking of Śiva*, Harmondsworth: Penguin Books, 1973.

_____, *The Interior Landscape: Love Poems from a Classical Tamil Anthology*, Bloomingdale and London: Indian University Press, 1975.

Ramaswamy, Vijaya, *Walking Naked: Women, Society, Spirituality in South India*, Simla: Institute of Advanced Studies, 1997.

_____, 'Aspects of women and work in early South India', Kumkum Roy (ed.), *Women in Early Indian Societies*, pp. 150–71, New Delhi: Manohar, [1989], 1999.

Rangachari, Devika, *Invisible Women, Visible Histories: Gender, Society and Polity in North India (Seventh to Twelfth Century AD)*, New Delhi: Manohar, 2009.

Reich, David, *Who We Are and How We Got Here*, Oxford: Oxford University Press, 2018.

Roy, Anamika, *Sixty-four Yoginis: Cult, Icons and Goddesses*, New Delhi: Primus, 2015.

Roy, Kumkum, *The Power of Gender and the Gender of Power: Explorations in Early Indian History*, New Delhi: Oxford University Press, 2010.

Sanderson, Alexis, 'Śaivism and Brahmanism in the Early Medieval Period', Gonda lecture 2006, available at https://www.academia.edu.

_____, 'How Public was Śaivism', Keynote Lecture at the Symposium [on] Tantric Communities in Context: Sacred Secrets and Public Rituals, Vienna, February 2015; available at https://www.academia.edu.

_____, 'Tolerance, Exclusivity, Inclusivity, and Persecution in Indian Religion During the Early Mediaeval Period', John Makinson (ed.), *Honoris Causa: Essays in Honour of Aveek Sarkar*, pp. 155–224, London: Allen Lane, 2015; available at https://www.academia.edu.

Sangari, Kumkum (ed.), *Trace Retrace: Paintings, Nilima Sheikh*, New Delhi: Tulika Books with Gallery Espace and Chemould Prescott Road, 2013.

Sargeant, Winthrop (trans.), *The Bhagavad Gītā*, New Delhi: Aleph Book Company, 2016.

Sattar, Arshia, *The Rāmāyaṇa: Vālmīki*, New Delhi: Penguin/Viking, 1996.

Schelling, Andrew (trans. and selected), *The Cane Groves of Narmada River: Erotic Poems from Old India*, New Delhi: Aleph Book Company, 2017.

Schmithausen, Lambert L., 'Aspects of the Buddhist attitude towards war', Jan E. M. Houben and Karel R. van Kooij (eds.), *Violence Denied: Violence, Non-Violence and the Rationalization of Violence in South Asian Cultural History*, pp. 45–68, Boston: Brill, 1999.

Selby, Martha Ann, 'Desire for Meaning: Providing Contexts for Prākrit Gāthās', *Journal of Asian Studies*, vol. 55, issue 1, February 1996, pp. 81–93.

_____, *Grow Long, Blessed Night: Love Poems from Classical India*, New York: Oxford University Press, 2000.

Settar, S. and Gunther D., Sontheimer (eds.), *Memorial Stones: A Study of Their Origin,*

Significance and Variety, Dharwar: Institute of Indian Art History, Karnatak University, and South Asia Institute, University of Heidelberg, n.d.

Shah, A. M., *The Family in India: Critical Essays*, New Delhi: Orient Longman, 1998.

Shah, Shalini, *Love, Eroticism and Female Sexuality in Classical Sanskrit Literature: Seventh-Thirteenth Century*, New Delhi: Manohar, 2009.

Shaw, Miranda, *Buddhist Goddesses of India*, Princeton: Princeton University Press, 2006.

Shepherd, Kancha Ilaiah, *Why I am Not a Hindu: A Sudra Critique of Hindutva Philosophy, Culture and Political Economy*, New Delhi: SAGE, [1996], 2019.

Singh, Upinder, *A History of Ancient and Early Medieval India: From the Stone Age to the 12th Century*, New Delhi: Pearson, 2008.

_____, 'Sanchi: The History of the Patronage of an Ancient Buddhist Establishment', Upinder Singh, *The Idea of Ancient India: Essays on Religion, Politics, and Archaeology*, pp. 3–42, New Delhi: SAGE: 2016.

_____, 'Portraits of power: Aśoka and Kauṭilya', 31st K. P. Jayaswal Memorial lectures, 27 November 2016; published as Upinder Singh, *Portraits of Power*, Patna: K. P. Jayaswal Research Institute.

_____, 'Nagarjunakonda: Buddhism in the "City of Victory"', Upinder Singh, *The Idea of Ancient India: Essays on Religion, Politics, and Archaeology*, pp. 43–72, New Delhi: SAGE: 2016.

_____, *Political Violence in Ancient India*, Cambridge MA: Harvard University Press, 2017.

Siva Kumar, R., *A. Ramachandran: A Retrospective*, 2 vols., New Delhi: National Gallery of Modern Art and Vadehra Art Gallery, 2003.

Smith, Brian K., *Classifying the Universe: The Ancient Indian Varṇa System and the Origins of Caste*, New York and Oxford: Oxford University Press, 1994.

Smith, David (trans.), *The Birth of Kumāra by Kālidāsa* (Clay Sanskrit Library), New York: New York University Press, 2005.

Smith, John D., *The Mahābhārata: An Abridged Translation*, New Delhi: Penguin Books, 2009.

Solomon, Esther A., *Indian Dialectics: Methods of Philosophical Discussion*, 2 vols., Ahmedabad: B. J. Institute of Learning and Research, 1978.

Subbarayalu, R., 'State and Society during the Chola period', R. Champakalakshmi, Kesavan Veluthat, and T. R. Venugopalan (eds.), *State and Society in Pre-Modern South India*, pp. 84–95, Thrissur: Cosmobooks, 2002.

Suryanarayan, Akshyeta, Miriam Cubas, Oliver E. Craig, Carl P. Heron, Vasant S. Shinde, Ravindra N. Singh, Tamsin C. O'Connell, and Cameron A. Petrie, 'Lipid residues in pottery from the Indus Civilisation in northwest India', *Journal of Archaeological Science*, vol. 125, 2021, pp. 1–16.

Thapar, Romila, *Aśoka and the Decline of the Mauryas*, 3rd edn., New Delhi, Oxford University Press, 2012.

Teltumbde, Anand, *Dalits: Past, Present and Future*, London and New York: Routledge,

[2017], 2020.

Trautmann, Thomas R., *Elephants and Kings: An Environmental History*, Ranikhet: Permanent Black, 2015.

Tripathi, Gaya Charan, Anncharlott Eschman, and Hermann Kulke, *The Cult of Jagannath and the Regional Tradition of Orissa*, New Delhi: Manohar, 2014.

Uberoi, Patricia (ed.), *Family, Kinship and Marriage in India*, T. N. Madan (gen. ed.), Oxford in India Readings in Sociology and Social Anthropology, New Delhi: Oxford University Press, 1993.

Ulrich, Katherine E., 'Food Fights: Buddhist, Hindu, and Jaina Dietary Polemics in South India', *History of Religions*, vol. 46, no. 3, February 2007, pp. 228–61.

Unni, N. P. (ed and trans.), *Mattavilāsa Prahasana of Mahendravikramavarman*, Trivandraum: College Book House, 1974.

Verardi, Giovanni, *The Gods and the Heretics: Crisis and Ruin of Indian Buddhism*, New Delhi: Aditya Prakashan, 2018.

Wagle, Narendra, *Society at the Time of the Buddha*, Bombay: Popular Prakashan, [1966], 1995.

Walshe, Maurice, *Long Discourses of the Buddha: A Translation of the Dīgha Nikāya*, Boston: Wisdom Publications, 1995.

Warder, A. K., *Indian Kāvya Literature*, vol. 3, Delhi: Motilal Banarsidass, [1977], 1990.

White, David Gordon, *Kiss of the Yoginī: 'Tantric Sex' in its South Asian Contexts*, Chicago and London: University of Chicago Press, 2003.

INDEX

Abhijnanashakuntala, 52–54
Abhinavagupta, 38, 78, 203
Advaita Vedanta, 198, 200, 212–14
Agamadambara, 219, 222, 223
Agganna Sutta, 30, 134
ahimsa, 14, 65, 159, 161, 166–67, 170–72, 195, 205
Ajatashatru 133
Ajivika/s, 191, 216
akam, 43
Akka Mahadevi, 122, 231
Al-Biruni, 183
Alchi, 103
Allahabad pillar/inscription, 148–49
Altekar, A. S., 83
Alvar/s, 33, 34, 74, 120–21, 204
Amaravati, 69, 209
Amaru-shataka, 46
Ambedkar, B. R., 3n2, 8, 25, 180
Ambika, 104, 105, 106
Amoghasiddhi, 103
Analects, 188
Anangaranga, 62
ananku, 118
anekantavada, 194
anirshamsya, 14, 171
antahpura (harem), 126
anuvratas, 65, 161
Apabhramsha, xi
apad-dharma, 12, 21, 196
Apastamba Dharmasutra, 19
Appar, 34, 35, 204–05, 206, 218
arambhaja himsa, 161
aramikas, 30

Ardhanarishvara, 106
Arjuna, 33, 49, 50, 68, 140, 142, 155, 198
army/armies, 63, 101, 133, 138, 142, 143, 146, 152, 153, 217, 218, 232
arsha (marriage), 109, 110
artha, 150
Arthashastra, xi, 9, 13–14, 20, 112, 125–26, 136, 145–47, 151–52, 155, 158, 173, 174
arya, 5, 6, 9, 21, 83, 133
Aryan/Indo-Aryan/s, 5, 6, 87n4, 229
Aryavarta, 133
ascetic/s, 24, 36, 38, 55, 76, 77, 81, 118, 121, 156, 172, 187, 197, 220, 222–25
asceticism, 50, 55, 72–74, 123, 172, 191, 206, 223, 225
Ashoka, 29, 132, 134, 148, 172–76, 177, 215–17, 219, 229, 230–33
Ashoka's edicts/inscriptions, 29n26, 148, 172–76, 216
Ashokavadana, 217
ashrama (hermitage), 52, 72,
ashrama/s (stage of life), 10, 11, 12, 14, 22, 67, 153, 196, 203, 223,
Ashvaghosha, 36
ashvamedha, 133
Ashvatthama, 144
assault, 61, 146, 156–57
astika/s, 185, 198–201
astrologers, 14, 38
asura (marriage), 109, 110
Atharva Veda, 5, 73, 109
Atimarga, 77

252

atman, 5, 13, 22, 64, 68, 142, 191, 197, 212
Atranjikhera, 90
Attirampakkam, xiii
Avalokiteshvara, 102
avatara/s, 207–08
Avvaiyar, 35
Ayurveda, 57
Bactro-Indo-Greek, 186
Baghor, 85
Bahubali, 162, 164
Basavanna/Basava, 35, 205
bestiality, 76
Bhagavad Gita, 13, 32, 33, 68, 140, 142, 183, 197–98, 213
Bhagavata Purana, 99, 100
Bhairava, 77, 79, 97, 99, 208, 211, 225
bhakti, 13, 22, 32–36, 39, 74, 84, 87, 100, 120–23, 142, 154, 183, 198, 204–05, 231
Bharata (king), 54, 125
Bharatavarsha, 54
Bharhut, 71, 82, 88, 90
Bhartrihari, 80–81
bhava/s, 51
Bhavaviveka, 199
Bhedabheda/Bhedabhedin, 183n7, 199, 213
bhikkhu sangha, 115
bhikkhuni sangha, 113, 115, 117
Bhima, 49, 144, 145
Bhishma, 7, 49, 62, 156, 171
Bhojajaniya Jataka, 168
Bimbisara, 133
Bodh Gaya, 90, 218, 227
Bodhi tree, 63, 101, 218
bodhisattva/s, 31, 70, 101, 102, 115, 167, 168, 169, 208
Bodhisattvabhumi, 201
Bose, Nandalal, 229
Brahma (god), 11n13, 55, 97, 150

brahma (marriage), 109, 110
brahmacharya/brahmachari, 10, 12, 65, 67, 170
brahmadeya, 153
brahman, 5, 68, 181n3, 190, 212
Brahmana/s, 5, 8, 10–15, 17–25, 28–31, 33–37, 55, 67, 77, 109, 112, 113, 125, 143, 152–53, 154, 156, 170, 182, 188–90, 192–93, 194, 196, 200, 202–05, 212, 215, 216, 219, 222, 224, 226
Brahmanical, 8, 12, 14, 17, 18, 30, 32, 37, 67, 68, 77, 111–12, 166, 169, 170, 195, 200, 202, 204, 205
Brahmanism, 184n8, 192, 208
Brahmasutras, 213
Brahmavaivarta Purana, 100
brahmodya, 190
Brihadaranyaka Upanishad, 109, 190
Buddha avatara (of Vishnu), 207–08
Buddha/Buddha's teaching, xii, 11, 23, 25, 27, 29–31, 38, 63, 64, 67, 70, 90, 101–03, 113, 115, 131–33, 166, 167, 175, 177, 191–93, 204, 207–08, 216, 217, 218, 223, 231
Buddha's date, death, 23n22
Buddhism, 11, 12, 23, 25, 30–32, 35, 39, 64, 65, 67, 69, 79, 87, 101–03, 105, 113, 115, 134, 154, 159, 165–69, 180, 182, 185, 192, 199, 200, 202, 208, 209, 214, 217
Buddhism and Shaivism, 208
Buddhism and Vaishnavism, 207–08
Buddhist goddesses, 101–03, 105
Buddhist monastery/monasteries, 30, 209, 217–19, 222
Buddhist monk/s, 30, 31, 81, 187, 192, 199, 214, 216, 217, 221, 222
Buddhist sangha/Order, 67, 113–15, 117, 124, 159, 165, 192, 216
Buddhist sites/establishments, 43, 63, 69, 88, 90, 101, 105, 124, 125

253

Buddhist, fierce deities, 210
Buddhist/s, 11, 17, 21–23, 28, 38, 39, 67, 81, 87, 106, 112–115, 134, 159, 165–69, 180, 184, 186–87, 191, 192, 193, 194, 195, 197, 199, 200, 201, 203, 206–10, 213, 214–215, 216, 217, 218, 219, 221, 222, 224, 225, 227
capital punishment, 136 (also see death penalty)
caste, 1, 3, 8, 15–19, 21, 22, 31, 32, 35, 39, 84, 87, 107, 128, 129, 132, 153, 180, 205, 225, 229
celibacy, 49, 65, 67, 72, 113, 115, 128, 191
Chalukya/s, 50, 127, 217
Chammak copper plate, 152
Chamunda, 95, 96, 105
Chamundaraya, 164
Chanakya, 229
Chanda yakshi, 71, 82
Chandala/s, 19–21, 24, 25, 30, 31, 36, 37, 196
Chandragupta II (Gupta king), 127
Chandragupta Maurya, 3, 134
Chandraketugarh, 70, 86
Charvaka/s, 200, 223
chastity, 62, 65, 107, 109–12, 117, 118, 156
child, 9, 49, 80, 84, 102, 107, 109, 110, 112, 153, 231
childbirth, 104, 118, 129
childhood, 100, 111
children, 6, 14, 89, 99, 109, 110, 113, 126, 229
China, 39
Chinese, 4, 61, 183
Chintamani, 206
Chola/s, 15, 33, 95, 125, 134, 138, 154, 206, 217, 218
Chulavamsa, 217, 218
Chunda, 31, 167

coercion, 39, 134, 135, 153
cognatic/bilateral kinship systems, 107
compassion/compassionate, 29, 36, 51n24, 101, 102, 114, 143, 153, 165n24, 167–69, 171, 173, 175, 207
Confucius, 188
critique, 1, 25, 32, 35–37, 166, 180, 204, 205, 214, 224, 226
daiva (marriage), 109
Dakini/s, 103
Daksha, 97
Dakshina, 109
Dalit/s, 1, 3n2, 39, 180, 229
Damara rebellion, 153
dana, 109, 146, 201
Dandimahadevi, 127
dasa/s, 3–9, 28, 133
dasi/s, 3, 6, 7, 9, 28, 29
dasyu/s, 6n5, 133
death penalty, 152, 176n35 (also see capital punishment)
debate/s, x, xiv, 1, 21, 23n22, 35, 49n19, 57, 58, 62, 63, 69, 105, 116, 125, 140, 163, 168, 170, 178, 183, 185–198, 207, 208, 213–15, 222–24, 226, 228, 233
Dehejia, Vidya, 35n31, 69, 70
Deshopadesha, 38, 224, 225
desire/s, xiv, 34, 36, 40–43, 45, 46, 49, 50, 61–69, 72, 77, 80–82, 100, 105, 109, 116, 121, 142, 155, 156, 163, 166, 167, 198, 216, 228, 233
detachment, xiv, 13, 40, 68, 69, 80, 196, 228
devadasi, 40
Devi, 33, 93, 95, 97, 202
Devi-Mahatmya, 93, 97
dhamma, 29, 30, 113, 172–74, 175–76, 192, 216
dhamma-vijaya, 176
dharma, 8, 11–14, 20, 29, 36, 49n, 57–60, 68, 81, 110, 140, 142, 145, 150,

155, 170, 171, 181, 196, 197, 199, 200, 203, 204, 222, 226, 233
Dharmakirti, 215
Dharmamahadevi, 127
Dharmarajika stupa, 217
Dharmashastra, 8, 11, 12, 17, 20, 36, 60, 67, 109, 110, 118, 155, 170, 183, 188
dharma-vijaya/vijayi, 146, 147, 176
dharma-yuddha, 140, 142
Dholavira, 5
Dhritarashtra, 7, 8, 49, 72, 232
dhvani, 46
Didda, 127-28, 219
Digambara/s, 104, 105, 116, 117, 162, 163, 222, 227
Digha Nikaya, 134
digvijaya, 149, 212, 214
Dilwara temples, 104
Diodorus Siculus, 119
Dirghatamas, 6
Divabbarasi, 127
dohada, 70
Draupadi, 7, 8, 50, 125, 156
Dronacharya/Drona, 14, 144
Duhshasana, 7, 8, 156
dukkha, 64
Durga, 89, 93-99, 106, 229
Duryodhana, 7, 114, 145, 151, 229
Dushyanta, 52-54
Dvaita (Vedanta), 199, 214
Elephanta, 73
Ellora, 72-74, 91, 105, 141, 162, 165, 184
equality, 1, 2, 25, 32, 38, 39, 107, 130, 233
erotic, 42, 47, 69, 81, 123
eroticism, 45, 74, 100
ethics, 32, 159, 173, 226
Ettutokai, 43
food, 8, 15, 17, 20, 25, 31, 113, 125, 131, 132, 163, 167, 168, 169, 170, 174, 196, 203, 206, 225
force/forced, 61, 97, 118, 132, 133-36, 146, 147, 155-59, 177, 221, 226, 233
forest/s, 18, 19, 21, 44, 49, 52, 55, 67, 72, 87, 93, 97, 102, 122, 135, 146, 152, 157, 168, 174, 180, 204, 231
forest animals, 167
forest people/dwellers, 18, 135, 152, 176, 196
forest tribes, 19, 97, 135, 151
forest troops, 146
Four Noble Truths, 64
Gaja Lakshmi, 90, 91, 101
Gandhara, 27, 64, 70, 193, 217, 218
gandharva (marriage), 53, 54, 60, 109-10, 155
gandharva (demigod), 143
Gandhi, M. K., 177, 180, 232
ganika/s, 37, 59
Gatha Sattasai, 45-48, 84
gendered violence, 155-59
Ghosha (woman sage), 108
Gita Govinda, 73, 100
goddess/goddesses, xiv, 63, 70, 72, 78, 83-107
Gonanda (dynasty), 127
'Great Goddess', 85, 87, 93, 202
Greece, 4n4, 42
Greek, 4n4, 29n26, 63, 119, 183, 186, 188
grihastha, 10, 12, 170
guna/s, 145, 194
Gupta kings/dynasty, 52, 90, 126, 127, 148-49
hagiography/hagiographies, 34, 101, 121-23, 160, 185, 206, 208, 212-15, 218, 226
Hala, 46
Harappa/Harappan civilization, xii, xiii, 5, 85-86, 131-33
harem/s, 53, 60, 126, 155

Haribhadra, 195, 200
Harikeshiya, 25
Hariti, 102
Harivamsha, 93, 99
Haryanka (dynasty), 133
hatha yoga, 78
Hathigumpha inscription, 216
hero stone/s, 119, 137–40, 154, 165
heterosexual, 42, 61
himsa, 161, 164, 170
Hinayana, 101n12, 199
Hindu god/s, 73, 208
Hindu goddess/es, 89–101, 105, 106
Hindu/s, 36, 87, 89, 105, 106, 125, 132, 178, 180, 182–84, 208, 212, 227
Hinduism, 33, 39, 87, 101, 104, 169, 178–80, 182–85, 207, 208, 226
Hinduization, 181
Hindu Tantra, 77n42
homosexual, 42
homosexuality, 61
Huna/s, 217-18
Ikshvaku (dynasty), 124, 126, 138, 149
Indica, 4
Indo-Aryan/s, 5, 6
Indra, 10, 24, 62, 63, 109, 128, 168
inequality, xiv, 1–5, 25, 35, 36, 38–40, 108, 117, 133, 153, 159, 228, 233
intellectual non-violence, 195
intolerance, 185
Isainaniyar, 121
Islam, xv$n$8, 39, 181, 183
Islamicate, xv &n8
Jaina/s, xi, 11, 22–25, 29, 64, 66, 70, 76, 81, 87, 104–06, 115, 116, 124, 125, 159–65, 184, 192–95, 199, 200, 203, 206–07, 208–09, 213, 215, 216, 218, 222, 224
Jaina goddess/es, 87, 104–06
Jaina monk/s, 24, 66, 105, 124, 164, 206, 207, 222

Jaina nuns, 124
Jaina sangha, 25, 65, 115, 116
Jainism, 12, 23, 25, 30–32, 35, 65, 67, 79, 87, 101, 104, 105, 115, 124, 154, 159–64, 182, 185, 193–95, 200, 202, 205, 214, 216, 218
Jalauka, 219
Janguli, 102
Jataka/s, 14, 31, 167, 168, 231
jati/s, 15–18, 28, 30, 182, 202
Jayadeva, 73, 100
Jayanta Bhatta, 222
Jina/s, 23, 26, 116, 194, 195, 204, 216, 223
Jogimara cave inscription, 40, 41
Jvalamalini, 104
Kadamba (dynasty), 14, 127, 164
Kakshivan, 6
Kalavilasa, 38, 224
Kalhana, 127-28, 219, 222
Kali (dasi), 29
Kali (goddess), 79, 97–99
Kali age, 196, 202, 207
Kalidasa, 52–57, 73, 148, 149–50, 231
Kalika Purana, 95, 201
Kalinga, 164, 175, 216
Kalki, 207
kama, 42, 46, 50, 57–60, 78, 81
Kamadeva, 55, 63, 73, 76
Kamakhya temple, 97
Kamandaka, 147
Kamashastra, 60, 188
Kamasutra, 57–62, 155, 158
Kanishka, 232
Kanva (sage), 52, 53
Kanva (dynasty), 14
Karaikkal Ammaiyar, 120–22
karma, 64, 65, 160, 161, 182, 191, 204, 206, 223
karma-yoga, 197
Karna, 7, 49, 144

Kaula, 204, 225
Kaumudimahotsava, 50
Kaurava/s, 7, 145
Kaushambi, 70
Kautilya, 9, 13, 20, 125–26, 136, 145–47, 151–52, 158, 172–76, 229, 233
Kavasha Ailusha, 6
kavya, 38, 49, 50, 52, 59, 112, 155
kevalin, 163
Khajuraho, 76
Kharavela, 164, 216
king/s, 3, 6, 9, 10, 15, 18, 20–22, 24, 37, 38, 46, 50–54, 59, 60, 62, 68, 70, 76, 80, 87, 90, 101, 104, 112, 117n25, 118, 124, 125, 126, 133–36, 138, 142, 145–47, 149–56, 158–59, 164, 167, 168, 172–76, 186–87, 189, 190, 196, 197, 200, 204, 206, 214, 215–19, 221–24, 226, 229, 232, 233
kingdom/s, 3, 7, 15, 16, 18, 87, 125, 126, 127, 133, 134, 142, 149, 152–54, 209, 215, 222–24
kingship ,16, 18, 19, 69, 125, 134, 135, 149–51, 172, 215
kinship system/s, 84, 107–08, 129
Kitab al-Hind, 183
Kopperuncholan, 138
Korravai, 95
Krishna, 8, 33, 50, 73, 75, 99–101, 118, 140, 142, 145, 198, 230
Kshatriya/s, 10, 12–14, 17, 22–24, 30, 31, 140, 155, 189
Kshatriya dharma, 155
Kshemagupta, 127, 219
Kshemendra, 37, 38, 219, 224–25
Kumarasambhava, 52, 55–57, 73
Kumarila Bhatta, 199, 203, 208, 213
Kunti, 49, 118
kuti/s, 15, 18
laity, 159, 161, 165, 167, 192, 193
Lakshmi, 89–92, 93, 102, 104, 105

laymen, 115
laywomen, 112, 115–16, 124
Linga Purana, 99, 201
Lingayat, 35
Lokayata, 199, 201
Lorenzen, David, 183
love, 10, 33, 35, 37, 39, 40–57, 60, 61, 63, 73, 74, 80–82, 99, 100, 102, 108, 110, 112, 118, 123, 155, 156, 158, 176, 204, 214, 229, 231
lovemaking, 47, 57, 58, 60, 61, 73, 158
lover/s, 33, 37, 40, 41, 44, 46, 47, 53, 55, 70, 71, 126, 157, 224
Madhvacharya, 214
Madhyamaka-hridayakarika, 60, 61, 199
Mahabalipuram, 94, 220
Mahabharata, xi, xii, 7, 8, 12, 13, 19, 21, 36, 38, 42, 49, 50, 62, 68, 72, 90, 93, 118–19, 125, 134, 135, 137, 140–45, 150–51, 155–57, 171, 172, 196–98, 200, 229, 232
mahajanapadas, 133
Mahapajapati Gotami, 113
Mahasilava Jataka, 168
mahavratas, 65, 161
Mahayana, 101, 102, 114, 115, 169
Mahishasuramardini (Durga), 93–95, 106, 229
maithuna, 70, 76, 78
Makkhali Gosala, 23, 191
Malavikagnimitra, 52
Manava Dharmashastra, 8
Mandanamishra, 213–14
Mangaiyarkarasiyar, 120
Manimekalai, 199
Mannargudi inscription, 154
Mantramarga, 77
mantra-shakti, 147
Manu Smriti, 8, 9, 20, 36, 59, 111, 155, 170, 200, 203
Mara, 63, 64, 101

Marichi, 102
Markandeya Purana, 93
marriage/s, 13, 15–17, 22, 49n18, 55, 56, 60, 61, 82, 84, 108–11, 113, 122, 123, 127, 147, 155
Marshall, John, 217, 218
materialist/s, 191, 200, 201, 223
Mathura, 27, 70, 88–90, 95, 105, 124, 184
matriarchy/matriarchal, 107
Matrika/s, 95
matriliny/matrilineal, 107
matsya-nyaya, 135
Mattavilasa-prahasana, 219, 221
Maurya/s, 3, 9, 29, 134, 148, 172, 215,
meat/meat-eating, 21, 78, 93, 95, 131, 163, 166, 167, 169, 170, 196, 206, 221–23
Megasthenes, 3, 4
Meghaduta, 52, 54, 55, 231
Menander, 186
menstruation, 109, 110, 116, 118
Middle Indic, 45n9
Mihirakula, 217–18
Milinda, 186-87
Milindapanha, 186
Mimamsa, 185, 199–200, 222
Mimamsaka, 199, 203, 208, 213, 224
misogyny, xiv, 83, 228
mithuna figures/couples, 69, 70, 76
mlechchha/s, 18, 93n8, 133, 135, 151, 196
moksha, 13, 22, 23, 57, 68, 81, 116–17, 140, 182, 189, 195, 197
moksha-dharma, 13–14, 68, 196
monism, 181n3, 198
monolatry, 181n3, 197, 201
monotheism/monotheistic, 181n3, 182, 185
'Mother Goddess', 85
Mrichchhakatika, 9, 37

Muslim/s, 36, 83, 132, 178, 180, 181, 183n6, 227
mutilation, 136, 152
Myanmar, 180
naga/s, 104
nagaraka, 59, 60
Nagarjunakonda, 69, 119, 124, 138, 184
Nagasena, 187
nagi, 87–89
Naiyayikas, 224
Nanda/s (dynasty), 133–34, 216
Nandanar, 34
Nandika, 67
Narada Smriti, 9, 20
Narmamala, 38, 224–25
Nasadiya-sukta, 42, 188
nastika/s, 185, 198–201, 223
natukal, 138
Natyashastra, 51
Nayanar/Nayanmar/s, 33, 34, 120, 121, 204, 206
Neminatha, 160
Neolithic, 85
nibbana, 25, 28, 101, 113
Nigrodhamiga Jataka, 167
Nilakechi, 105, 106
Nirgranthas, 192
nirvana, 64
Nishada, 19, 135, 150
Nishumbhamardini, 95
Nitisara, 147
Niti-shataka, 80
niyoga, 49n19
non-vegetarian, 131
non-violence, 29, 65, 131, 132, 159–65, 169–77, 180, 191, 192, 195, 196, 207, 228
nudity, 70, 116, 122, 191
Nyaya (school), 185, 199, 200, 222–23
Nyayamanjari, 222
outcaste/s, 20, 34, 38

258

Padmavati, 87, 104, 106
paishacha (marriage), 109-10, 155
Pakudha Kachchayana, 23, 191
Pala/s (dynasty), 209, 216
Palaeolithic, 84
Pancharatra, 172, 199, 202, 213
Panchatantra, 36, 37, 229
Parnashavari, 102
Parshvanatha, 65, 76, 104
Parvati, 55-57, 73, 74, 98, 99,106,
Pashupata/s, 199, 203, 221, 223
Patachara, 113, 114
Patanjali, 183, 192
patriarchy/patriarchal, 43, 107-09, 111, 112, 118, 129, 153
patrilineal/patrilineal, 107-08, 111, 128
patronage of writers, 50, 52
patrons of debate, 185, 192
Pattupattu, 43
Periyapuranam, 206
persecution, 180, 203n 29, 209, 216-19, 223, 224, 226
pitha/s, 97
plunder, 146, 219
polygamy, 49n18
polygyny, 49n18, 109
polytheism, 181 &n3
Prabhavatigupta, 127
prabhu-shakti, 125, 147
prajapatya (marriage), 109, 110
Prajnaparamita, 102
Prakrit, xi, 18, 29n26, 40, 42, 45n9, 50, 81, 112
prakriti-kopa, 152, 233
Pravarasena (II), 127, 152
Prithivimahadevi, 127
Prithu, 150
Prithvi (goddess), 89, 101
punishment/s, 9, 13, 20, 67, 112, 135-36, 151-52, 158, 174, 176, 187
Punitavati, 121

Purab aur Pashchim, 83
puram, 137
Purana Kassapa, 23, 191, 192
Purana/s, xii, 12, 32, 73, 89, 90, 93, 95, 97, 99, 100, 172, 183, 184, 201, 207
Purananuru, 118
Puranic Hinduism, 184
purusharthas, 57
Purusha-sukta, 10, 188
Pushyamitra Shunga, 217
race, 1, 2, 15
Radha, 73, 75, 99-101
Raghuvamsha, 52, 148, 149-50
raja-mandala, 145
rajasuya, 133
Rajatarangini, 127-28, 219
Rakhigarhi, 5
rakshasa (marriage), 109, 110, 155
Raktabija, 98
Rama, 42, 49, 142-43, 149, 153, 157, 229
Ramachandran, A., 232, **Fig. 6.5**
Ramanuja, 122, 214, 218
Ramayana, 12, 21, 38, 42, 49, 90, 118, 125, 137, 140, 142, 153, 156-57, 164, 229-31
rape, 155-58
rasa, 51n24
rasa-lila, 101
Ratirahasya, 62
Ravana, 74, 142-43, 151, 156-58, 164
rebellion/s, 39, 152-53
rebirth, 13, 64, 115, 117, 161, 191, 196
religion/s, 23, 25, 32, 39, 69, 74, 77, 79, 85, 87, 108, 159, 177-84, 188, 192, 195, 206, 215, 219, 223, 226-27
religious patrons/patronage, 22, 25, 76, 123-25, 134, 153, 164, 202, 203, 206, 207, 209, 210, 215-17, 219, 226
renunciation, 10, 12, 13, 43, 67, 68, 70, 80, 82, 116, 150, 151, 159, 171, 172,

197, 198
Rock edict 13 (of Ashoka), 175–76
Rotta Siddhavriddhi, 218
Roy, Jaimini, 157
Roy, Rammohan, 183
sadharana dharma, 14, 170, 196
Sakka (Indra), 168
sallekhana, 164
salvation, xiv, 1, 3n3, 25, 32, 113, 115, 116, 117, 123, 161, 212, 228
samanya dharma, 196
Samayamatrika, 38
Sambandar, 206, 218
same-sex love, 42
Samkhya, 13, 183, 197, 199, 200, 203
Sammed Shikharji, 227
samsara, 13, 22, 82, 159, 171, 182, 191, 226
Samudragupta, 148–49
Sanchi, 69, 88, 90, 91, 102, 124, 209, 217
Sanderson, Alexis, 202
Sangam poems/texts, 15, 18, 21, 22, 43, 45, 46, 84, 92, 118, 119, 137, 138
Sangam poets, 44
Sangam society, 18
sangha/s (oligarchies), 133
sankalpaja himsa, 161
sannyasa, 10, 12, 67 68
sannyasi, 67, 82, 171, 212–14
Sanskrit xi, 6, 9, 15, 17, 18, 29, 32, 37, 38, 42, 43, 46, 49, 50, 52, 54, 57, 59, 61, 62, 73, 80, 81, 108, 112, 118, 126, 137, 155, 181, 202, 221–22, 224, 229
Sanskritization, 16
Sarasvati (goddess), 89, 93, 102, 104–05, 214
Saraswati, Dayanand, 178
Sarvadarshana-samgraha, 200
Satavahana/s, 14, 46, 126, 216
Sati (goddess), 55, 97– 98

sati, 118–20
satire/s, 36, 37, 38, 185, 219, 222, 224
Scheduled Castes, 25
Sekkilar, 206
Selby, Martha Ann, 46
Seleucus Nicator, 3
Sembiyan Mahadevi, 73, 125
semen, 57, 67, 72, 78
sensual, 57, 58, 62, 69, 82, 111, 114
sensuality, 81
sensuous, 43, 69, 70, 73, 88, 104
Setaketu Jataka, 31
sex, 41– 43, 45–46, 49, 57–62, 70, 72, 76, 78, 81–82, 110, 116, 158–59, 170, 214, 223
sex change, 42, 115
sexual, 4, 20, 41, 42, 46, 49, 51, 57–63, 65, 67, 69, 70, 72, 73, 76–79, 81, 85, 95, 99, 116, 155–57, 167
sexual abstinence, 50, 72
sexual assault, 156, 157
sexual rites/rituals in Tantra, 76–79, 95, 99
sexual violence, 157, 159
sexuality, 16, 43, 84, 107, 112, 115, 128, 157
Seyya Jataka, 168
Shaddarshana-samuchchaya, 200
Shaishunaga (dynasty), 133
Shaiva/s, 33, 34, 77, 99, 120, 122, 199, 201–04, 206, 207, 213, 216, 218, 219, 222–24, 225, 227
Shaivism, 77, 97, 181n3, 182, 185, 202, 203, 208, 217, 218
Shakuntala, 52–54
shalabhanjika/s, 69, 88
Shambuka, 153–54
Shankara/Shankaracharya, 198, 212–14
Shankara-digvijaya, 212
Shantara (dynasty), 87, 104
Shataka-trayi, 80

Shatapatha Brahmana, 108, 109
Sheikh, Nilima, 231, **Fig. 6.3**
Shilappadikaram, 101
Shiva, 33–35, 46, 55–57, 73, 74, 76, 77, 89, 97–99, 106, 121–23, 202-05, 207, 208, 212, 218, 223
shramana/s, 23, 29, 191–92, 216
shramanic, 191–92
Shravana Belgola, 104, 164
Shri (goddess), 89, 90, 105
shringara rasa, 51n24, 80
Shringara-shataka, 80
Shringeri matha, 200, 212n42
Shrivaishnava/s, 122, 218
shruti, 12, 200
Shudra/s, 10–14, 17– 18, 20, 32– 33, 36, 112, 153
Shudraka, 9, 37
Shurpanakha, 157–58
Shvetamabara/s, 163
Siddhartha, 27, 63, 64, 101
Singh, Arpita, 231, **Fig. 6.4**
Sinivali, 89
Sita, 42, 49, 98, 142, 156–58
slave, 4–9
slavery, 3–10
smriti, 12, 200, 203
soteriological, 3n2, 39, 233
Sri Lanka, xii, 17, 30, 107, 117, 217–18
Stambheshvari, 87
Stone Age, 85, 131
stridhana, 110
stri-dharma, 14
Sugandha, 127
Sulabha, 197
Sutanuka, 40, 41
sva-dharma, 142
syadavada, 194
Tagore, Abanindranath, 230, 231, **Fig. 6.2**
Taittiriya Samhita, 109

Tamil xi, xiii, 15, 33, 42–44, 50, 73, 76, 81, 101, 104, 117, 118, 124, 125, 137, 199
Tamilakam, 15, 43n
Tanishq, 178
Tantra, 78, 79, 99, 201, 202, 225
Tantra in Jainism, 103, 202
Tantra, sex and ritual in, 76–79, 81
Tantraloka, 78, 203
Tantravarttika, 199, 203
Tantric, 79, 79, 99, 201–03, 208, 213, 225
Tantric Buddhism, 101–03, 202, 209
Tantric Buddhist goddesses, 102, 103
Tantric deities, 99, 202, 208, 201, 210
Tantric goddesses, 70, 78, 99, 104
Tantric goddesses in Jainism, 104
Tantric sects, 99, 202–03
Tantric vidyadevis, (in Jainism) 104
tapas, 72, 204
Tara, 102, 103
taxes/taxation, 134, 135, 137, 151, 154, 219
tax-free grants, 219
Taxila, 217, 218
Therigatha, 28, 84, 113–14
Tipitaka, xi, 17, 112, 113, 192
Tiresias, 63
Tirthankara/s, 23–26, 65, 70, 104, 105, 117, 160
Tiruppan Alvar, 34
Tiruttontarpuranam, 206
tolerance, 178, 179, 180, 185, 195, 216
Toramana, 217–18
torture/tortured, 136, 158, 231
transgender/transgenderism 61, 84
tribal/s, 21, 23, 85, 87, 107, 133, 135, 180
tribal religion, 87, 180, 181, 226
tribe/s, 133, 135, 151
Tribhuvanamahadevi, 127

Triratna, 161
Trishanku, 21
tritiya prakriti (third nature), 42, 61, 62, 61, 62
'untouchable/s', 19–22, 34, 35, 180, 203
untouchability, 1, 3, 8, 19, 22, 39, 153, 180
Upapuranas, 207
upayas, 145
Ushas, 89
Utpala (dynasty), 127, 219
utsaha-shakti, 125, 147
Vaidika/s, 201, 203, 204, 210, 215, 223
Vaidika Brahmana/s, 33, 202–04, 215
Vaikhanasa, 172
Vairagya-shataka, 80–81
Vaishnava/s, 33, 34, 38, 90, 100, 120, 122, 172, 201–04, 207, 208, 213, 223, 224
Vaishnavism, 90, 93, 172, 181n3, 182, 202, 208
Vaishya/s, 10, 12–14, 17, 33
vajapeya, 133
Vajrasuchi, 36
Vajrayana (Buddhism), 169, 202
Vajrayogini, 103
Vakataka/s, 14, 127, 152
Valkulamahadevi, 127
Valmiki, 42
vanaprastha, 10, 12, 68, 171
vanara/s, 143
Varma, Raja Ravi, 53, 92, 229
varna, 3, 10–18, 22, 24, 28, 30, 36, 109, 142, 153, 170, 182, 196, 202, 203, 223
varna-dharma, 13, 68, 142, 170, 197
varna-sankara, 17
Vasudhara, 102
Vatsyayana, 57–62, 158
Vedavati, 118, 156
Vedic Hinduism, 184

vegetarian, 106, 131, 167, 168
vegetarianism, 16, 132, 167, 168, 177
Vemula, Rohith, 1
Vena, 150–51
veshya, 9, 59
Vidagdha, 190
vidushaka, 37
vidyadevi/s, 104
Vijayamahadevi, 127
vijigishu, 145, 147
Vijjika, 50
Vijnanabhikshu, 183n7, 199
Vikramorvashiya, 52
vinaya, 136
Vinaya Pitaka, 28, 65, 168
violence, xiv, 19, 39, 61, 108, 131–77, 178, 180, 181, 197, 208–10, 215, 216, 226–27, 228, 231, 232, 233
virakal, 138
Virashaiva/s, 35, 122, 205
virodhi himsa, 164
Vishishtadvaita, 199, 214
Vishnu, 33, 34, 38, 76, 89, 90, 97, 99, 143, 150, 172, 184, 199, 202, 204, 207, 208, 218, 223, 225
Vishnu Purana, 172
Vishvamitra, 21, 52, 72, 196
vita, 37
Vivekananda, Swami, 178, 179
Vyasa, 49, 72
vyasana/s, 51, 155
war/warfare, 6, 4n, 6, 8, 119, 120, 125, 133–34, 136–47, 149, 150, 153, 159, 163, 164, 168–69, 172, 174–77, 197, 216, 218, 229, 232
warrior/s, 10, 102, 119, 133, 137–45, 155, 159, 190, 232
weapon/s, 86, 95, 133, 138, 142, 147, 149, 210
widow/s, 38, 111, 118–19, 214, 232
Xuanzang, 217–18

Yajnavalkya, 190–91
yaksha/s, 25, 54, 87–89, 143, 231
yakshi/s, 43, 54, 69, 71, 82, 87–89, 102, 104, 105, 207
Yashaskara (dynasty), 127
Yashovati, 127

Yoga (school), 13, 68, 197, 199, 200, 203
yoga, 68, 78, 150
Yogasutra, 183
Yogini/s, 78, 87, 95–97
Yudhishthira, 7, 8, 49, 62, 68, 140, 171, 196